A Love Supreme

Pauline Hopkins

Published by

THE X PRESS, 55 BROADWAY MARKET, LONDON E8 4PH.

TEL: 0171 729 1199

(c) The X Press 1995.

Distributed by Turnaround, 27 Horsell Road, London N5 1XL
Tel: 0171 609 7836

Printed by BPC Paperbacks Ltd, Aylesbury, Bucks.

ISBN 1-874509-27-1

Introduction

'Love conquers all', the central theme of *A Love Supreme* (Contending Forces), is Hopkins' enduring legacy as a novelist. For Sappho Clark and Will Smith, the star-crossed African-American lovers at the centre of her story, this means, no amount of chains binding people of their colour can restrain their affection for one another. *A Love Supreme* is, however, not just the story of romantic love, but also a thought provoking novel for the "upliftment" of the race.

"No one will uplift the race for us," Pauline Hopkins wrote in1900, "we must ourselves develop the men and women who will faithfully portray the innermost thoughts and feelings of the Negro with all the fire and romance which lie dormant in our history.

"In giving this little romance expression in print, I am not actuated by desire for notoriety or for profit, but to do all that I can in an humble way to raise the stigma of degradation from my race."

It is against this 'conscious' backdrop that *A Love Supreme* (Contending Forces) can be seen as the 'greatest romantic story ever told', a love story especially written to effect social change for African-Americans subjugated to racial, political, social and sexual oppressions. In particular, the novel is an attack on the white popular media of the time which regularly depicted black people as governed by 'uncontrollable passions'. This contention led directly to the widespread stereotype of the black male as rapist and the black female as sexually promiscuous, themes which are central to *A Love Supreme*. Against these negative images, *A Love Supreme's* main characters are upwardly mobile and eloquent black people who are positive and forward thinking and the novel is a compelling depiction of African-American bourgeois life at the time. For example, the American Coloured League, an organisation made up of aspiring black men, and a forum for *A Love Supreme's* central male character to engage in political debates and to confront violent racial oppression. Then there's the Sewing Circle, the female equivalent, where black women meet weekly to review events of interest pertaining to their race and through which Sappho Clark is able to come to terms with the dark secrets of her tormented and guilt, shame and hurt riddled life.

As a romance, the story really is 'a love supreme' and as an answer to that age-old question 'How we gonna make the Black nation rise?' *A Love Supreme* is the perfect mouthpiece for what Hopkins has to say about the way forward.

Hopkins always argued that fiction is an increasingly effective mechanism in shaping attitudes and awareness within the black community. She was right, and though it will entertain you, *A Love Supreme* will leave you wanting to shout it loud: BLACK AND PROUD.

LINDA KAYE, December 1995

About The Author

Pauline Elizabeth Hopkins was born in Portland, Maine, in 1859 to a talented family (her granduncle was the poet James M Whitfield).

At the age of fifteen she encounted her first literary success by winning the ten dollar prize contest sponsored by the well known black writer William Wells Brown (author of *The President's Daughter, Clotel*) and the Congregational Publishing Society of Boston. Early in her life she also showed promise as both a playwright and an actress. In 1880 she wrote and starred in her play *Slaves' Escape* or *the Underground Railroad*, which she performed at concerts in Boston. Her interest in both stage and black history continued into the 1890's, however like most aspiring African-American authors at the time she found out that in order to write, she first had to make a living. As a result she studied stenography and worked for the Bureau of Statistics for four years.

In 1900, Hopkins opened a new chapter in her literary career. Her short story, *The Mystery Within Us*, appeared in the Boston-based Coloured American Magazine where she later became literary editor. Similarly between 1900-1905 she published four novels (three of them serially), seven short stories, one historical booklet, over twenty biographical sketches, many essays and feature articles. Furthermore, *A Love Supreme* (Contending Forces) was Pauline Hopkins' best known novel and her only fiction published in book form during her lifetime. After its publication she spent several years writing for the Coloured American. When the magazine moved to New York she left to set up her own publishing company.

In 1916, she and Walter Wallace founded a magazine known as New Era. Unfortunately, it lasted for only two issues and then ceased publication. She resumed working as a stenographer at the Massachusetts Institute of Technology until her death in 1930.

CHAPTER 1

*T*o go back a little way in the romantic history of the emancipation of the slaves in the Caribbean islands will not take much time, and will, I hope, be as instructive as interesting:

In the early part of the year 1800, the agitation of the inhabitants of Great Britain over the increasing horrors of the slave trade carried on in the West Indian possessions of the Empire, was about reaching a climax. Every day the terrible things done to slaves were becoming public talk, until the best English humanitarians, searching for light upon the subject, became sick at heart over the discoveries that they made and were led to declare the principle: "The air of England is too pure for any slave to breathe.'

However, the slave trade was still carried on in ships sailing under the protection of false flags. Tales of the cruelties practiced upon the helpless chattels were continually reaching the ears of the British public, some of them such as to sicken the most cold-hearted and indifferent. For instance: causing a child to whip his mother until the blood ran; if a slave looked his master in the face, his limbs were broken; women in the first stages of their pregnancy, upon refusing to work, were placed in the treadmill, where terrible things happened, too dreadful to relate.

Through the efforts of Granville Sharpe, the chairman of the London committee, Lord Stanley, minister of the colonies, introduced into the House of Commons his bill for emancipation.

Lord Stanley's bill proposed gradual emancipation, and was the best thing those men of wisdom could devise. Earnestly devoted to their task, they sought to wipe from the fair reputation of the Empire the awful blot which was upon it. By the adoption of the bill Great Britain not only liberated a people from the cruelties of their masters, but at the same time took an important step forward in the onward march of progress, which the most enlightened nations are unconsciously forced to make by the great law of advancement; "for the civility of no race can be perfect whilst another race is degraded."

In this bill of gradual emancipation certain conditions were proposed. All slaves were entitled to be known as apprenticed laborers, and to acquire thereby all the rights and privileges of freemen. "These conditions were that praedials should owe three-fourths of the profits of their labors to their masters for six years, and the non-praedials for four years. The other fourth of the apprentice's time was to be his own, which he might sell to his master or to other persons, and at the end of the term of years fixed, he should be free."

In the winter of 1790, when these important changes in the life of the Negro

1

in the West Indies were pending, many planters were following the course of events with great anxiety. Many feared that in the end their slaves would be taken from them without recompense, and thereby render them and their families destitute. Among these planters was the family of Charles Montfort, of the island of Bermuda.

Bermuda's fifteen square miles of area lies six hundred miles from the nearest American coast. Delightful is this land, formed from coral reefs, flat and fertile, which to the eye appears as but a pin point upon the ocean's broad bosom, one of "a thousand islands in a tropic sea".

Once Bermuda was second only to Virginia in its importance as a British colony; once it held the carrying trade of the New World; once it was known as the "Gibraltar of the Atlantic," although its history has been that of a simple and peaceful people. Its importance to the mother country as a military and naval station has drawn the paternal bonds of interest closer as the years have flown by. Indeed, Great Britain has been kind to the colonists of this favored island from its infancy, sheltering and shielding them so carefully that the iron hand of the master has never shown beneath the velvet glove. So Bermuda has always been intensely British—intensely loyal. Today, at the beginning of the new century, Bermuda presents itself, outside of its importance as a military station for a great power, as a vast sanatorium for the benefit of invalids. A temperate climate, limpid rivers, the balmy fragrance and freshness of the air, no winter—nature changing only in the tints of its foliage—have contributed to its renown as a health-giving region; and thus Shakespeare's magic island of Prospero and Miranda has become, indeed, to the traveller:

The spot of earth uncursed
To show how all things were created first.

Mr Montfort was the owner of about seven hundred slaves. He was well known as an exporter of tobacco, sugar, coffee, onions and other products so easily grown in that sultry climate, from which he received large returns. He was neither a cruel man, nor an avaricious one, but like all men in commercial life, or traders doing business in their own productions, he lost sight of the individual right or wrong of the matter, or we might say with more truth, that he perverted right to be what was conducive to his own interests, and felt that by owning slaves he did no man a wrong, since it was the common practice of those all about him, and he had been accustomed to this peculiar institution all his life.

Indeed, slavery never reached its lowest depths in this beautiful island; but a desire for England's honor and greatness had become a pas-

2

sion with the inhabitants, and restrained the planters from committing the ferocious acts of brutality so commonly practiced by the Spaniards. In many cases African blood had become diluted from amalgamation with the 'higher' race, and many of these 'colored people became rich planters or business men (themselves owning slaves) through the favors heaped upon them by their white parents. This being the case, there might even have been a strain of African blood polluting the fair stream of Montfort's vitality, or even his wife's, which in fact would not have caused him one instant's uneasiness. Moreover, he was a good master, and felt that while he housed his slaves well, fed them with the best of food suited to their occupations and the climate, and did not cruelly beat them, they fared better with him than they would have with another, perhaps, or even if they held property themselves.

The general trend of public sentiment as expressed through the medium of the British press, had now begun to make an impression upon some of the more humane of the planters on this island, and among them was Mr Montfort. Unease now took the place of his former security; thought would obtrude itself upon him, and in the quiet hours of the night this man fought out the battle which conscience waged within him, and right prevailed to the extent of his deciding that he would free his slaves, but in his own way. He determined to leave Bermuda, and after settling in some other land, he would gradually free his slaves without impoverishing himself; bestow on each one a piece of land, and finally, with easy conscience, he would retire to England, and there lead the happy life of an English gentleman of fortune.

With this end in view, he turned his eyes towards the United States, where the institution flourished, and the people had not yet actually awakened to the folly and wickedness exemplified in the enslavement of their fellow beings. For reasons which were never known, he finally made choice of Newbern, North Carolina, for a home.

Sunday was and is the high holiday in all tropical climes. On that day the slave forgot his bonds. It was noon; the early service of the Church of England was ended. The clergyman of the parish had accompanied Charles Montfort home. Mrs. Montfort was visiting friends, so the two gentlemen dined alone. The clergyman was rather glad that he had the opportunity of seeing Mr Montfort alone, and had used all his powers of persuasion to turn him from his proposed exodus. It was of no avails as the good man soon found; and with a sigh, he finally took his hat and prepared to leave. Both stood outside the house upon the broad walk beneath the shade of the fragrant cedars and the fruitful tamarind trees. The silence of deep feeling was between these two men. The clergyman could only remember the reverence he had always received, and the loving service given him by this family. Montfort thought with pain of the

3

holy ministrations of this silver-haired man, who had pronounced the solemn words that bound him to his gentle wife, had baptised his children, and had buried the little daughter whose grave was yonder, beneath the flowering trees in the churchyard. Yes, it was sad to part and leave all these tender ties of friendship behind.

"The bishop will come himself, Charles, to persuade you that this is a dangerous step you are about to take," finally the good man said, breaking the silence.

"Why dangerous? Is it any more so for me than for those who left England to build a home here in the wilderness?"

"Different, very different. The mother hand was still over them, even in these wilds. "Out there," and he pointed in the direction of the bay, "they tell me that for all their boasted freedom, the liberty of England is not found and human life is held cheaply in the eyes of men who are mere outlaws. Ah! but the bishop," he continued with a sigh, "he can tell you; he has seen; he is not a weak old man like me. He will talk you out of this plan of separation from all your friends."

Again silence fell upon them. In the direction of the square a crowd of slaves were enjoying the time of idleness. Men were dancing with men, and women with women, to the strange monotonous music of drums without tune, relics of the tom-tom in the wild African life which haunted them in dreamland. Still, there was pleasure for even a cultivated musical ear in the peculiar variation of the rhythm. The scanty raiment of gay-colored cotton stuffs set off the varied complexions—yellow, bronze, white—the flashing eyes, the gleaming teeth, and gave infinite variety to the scene. Over there, waterfalls fell in the sunlight in silvery waves; party-colored butterflies of vivid coloring, and hummingbirds flashed through the air with electrical radiance; gay parakeets swung and chattered from the branches of the trees.

"Where, my son," said the clergyman, indicating the landscape with a wave of his hand, "will you find a scene more beautiful than this? How can you leave it and those who love you and yours?"

"Beautiful, indeed. And I will confess that it grows dearer as the time for my departure draws near," answered Montfort. "I will walk with you," he continued, as the clergyman turned in the direction of the road. As they passed through the wide entrance gates a Negro woman was weeding her little garden; her pickaninny was astride her back, spurring his mother as a rider his horse. The woman and the child looked up and smiled at the master and his guest, and the woman put the child on the ground and stood upright to bob a queer little courtesy. They walked along in silence until they reached the plaza.

"My son, will you not be persuaded?"

"Father, I have made up my mind firmly, after due consideration. I

4

believe it is for the best."

They paused a moment at the square; then the holy man said solemnly, as he raised his hand in benediction: "If it then be for the best, which God grant it may be, I pray the good Father of us all to keep you in safety and in perfect peace." He turned and disappeared in the crowd.

Charles Montfort was immediately surrounded by his friends, who greeted him joyously, for he was a genial man and had endeared himself greatly to his neighbors.

"Still determined to leave us, Charles?" inquired one.

"Yes, for the good of myself and family. How can we submit tamely to the loss of our patrimonies without an effort to reimburse ourselves when a friendly land invites us to share its hospitality?"

"There is truth in your argument for all who, like you, Charles, have a large venture in slaves. Thank heaven I am so poor that a change of laws will not affect me," said one.

"Where a man's treasure is, there also is his heart. It is nature. Almost you persuade me, Charles, to do likewise," remarked another.

"As I have told you, I will retain my patrimony and free my slaves, in the United States under a more liberal government than ours."

"Ah, Charles," remarked another listener, "you forget the real difference between our government and that of the United States. And then the social laws are so different. You will never be able to accustom yourself to the habits of a republic. Do you not remember the planters from Georgia and Carolina who fought for good King George, and were stanch Royalists? They retired to the Bahamas when our cause was lost in the American colonies. My brother has just returned from a trip there. He tells strange tales of their surprise at many things we do here. I fear it is but a cold welcome you will receive from men of their class."

"Certainly," replied Montfort, "I shall try to be a good subject of whatever country I may be compelled to reside in for a long or short time."

"But surely you will not expose your wife to the inconveniences of life in that country," said another.

"She has had her choice, but prefers hardships with me to life without me," proudly returned Montfort.

"A willful man must have his way," murmured one who had not yet spoken, "and I will give you three months to stay in the land of savages before you will be returning to us bag and baggage."

"Well," laughed Montfort, "we shall see."

Twilight had fallen now, and Montfort bared his head to the refreshing sea breeze which fluttered every leaf. When he bade his friends good night, finally, and started on his homeward walk, the arguments of the good clergyman and of his friends were present in his harassed mind, and he wondered if he were doing wrong not to be prevailed upon to yield to the opinions of others. Once he almost determined that he would give it all up and remain in this land of love and beauty. To collect his scattered thoughts and calm his mind he turned toward the bay, and stood upon the beach, still allowing the breeze to play about his heated temples. Never before had he appreciated his home so much as now, when he contrasted it with the comparative barrenness of the new spot he had chosen. The water was alive with marine creatures; the sea aflame. The air was full of light-giving insects, incessantly moving, which illumined the darkness and gave life to every inanimate object. Over all the moon and stars were set in the cloudless deep blue sky of coming night. Alas, his good angel fled with the darkness, and morning found him more determined than ever to go on with his project.

When it became known that Charles Montfort had decided to leave the place of his birth and establish himself in a foreign land, many friends gathered about him and advised him to reconsider his determination. Montfort laughingly invited them to join him in his new venture, and pointed out the dangers which threatened their fortunes. He painted his plans in glowing colors, and ended by promising them that in less than twenty-five years he would land in England, a retired planter, his former slaves free and happy, and he himself rich and honored.

Having an immense amount of property to transport, Montfort was compelled to make two trips to Newbern before he removed his family to their new home; but after much energetic work and many difficulties, the little family looked through blinding tears at the receding shores of what had been a happy home. A week later a noble ship stood off the shores of North Carolina. On the deck was Charles Montfort; his wife hung upon his arm; beside the devoted couple were Charles Jr., named for his father, and Jesse, the young darling of his mother's heart. Silently they gazed upon the fair scene before them, each longing for the land so recently left behind them, though no word of regret was spoken.

CHAPTER 2

The shores of Pamlico Sound presented a motley crowd of slaves, overseers, owners of vessels, and a phantasmagoric landscape very charming to eyes unaccustomed to such scenes. It was near the noon siesta. In the harbor lay three or four vessels ready to be loaded with their freight of rice, tobacco or cotton. The sun poured its level rays straight down upon the heads of all. A band of slaves sang in a musical monotone, and kept time to the music of their song as they unloaded a barge that had just arrived:

> Turn dat han' spike roun' an' roun',
> Hol' hard, honey; hol' hard, honey.
> Black man tote the buckra's load,
> Hol' hard, honey; hol' hard, honey
>
> Never before seed a nigger like you,
> Hol' hard, honey; hol' hard, honey.
> Always thinkin' 'bout your ol' black Sue,
> Hol' hard, honey; hol' hard, honey.
>
> If I was an alligator what'd I do?
> Hol' hard, honey; hol' hard, honey.
> Run 'way wid ol' black Sue,
> Hol' hard, honey; hol' hard, honey.
>
> Massa ketch you, what'd he do?
> Hi, hi, honey; hi, hi, honey.
> Cut your back an' ol' black Sue's,
> He, he, honey; he, he, honey.
>
> I cuss massa behind the fence,
> Hol' hard, honey; hol' hard, honey.
> Massa don't hear make no difference,
> Hol' hard, honey; hol' hard, honey.
>
> Turn that hand spike roun' and roun',
> Hold hard, honey; hold hard, honey.
> Black man tote the buckra's load,

7

Hol' hard, honey; hol' hard honey.

As the refrain died away, the bell for the noon rest sounded faintly in the distance, gradually drawing nearer, and again their rich and plaintive voices blended together in sweet cadences as they finished placing the heavy load to the satisfaction of their drivers:

Hark, dat merry, pretty bell go
Jing-a-lingle, jing-a-lingle, jingle bell,
Jinga-lingle, jing-a-lingle, jing-a-lingle bell,
Jingle bell, jingle bell,

Even so sang the children of Israel in their captivity, as they sat by the rivers of Babylon awaiting deliverance.

Just now a ship, which had some time since appeared as a dark spot on the horizon, turned her majestic prow and steered for the entrance to the sound. Immediately the pilot boat in the harbor put out to her. Everyone on the shore became eagerly intent upon the strange ship, and they watched the pilot climb aboard with all the interest which usually attends the slightest cause for excitement in a small community.

The ship came on very slowly, for there was little wind, under topsail, jib and foresail, the British flag at the peak and the American flag at the fore. The people on shore could see the captain standing by the pilot, the anchor ready to be dropped, and the bowsprit shrouds loose. But now their interest was divided with a new arrival. A man on horseback rode down to the shaky wooden platform which served as a landing place for passengers; behind him, at a respectful distance, rode a white-haired Mulatto. The man leaped from his horse and threw his reins to the slave, signaled a couple of Negroes in a boat, jumped into it as they, obedient to his sign, pulled alongside the wharf, and was rowed swiftly out to the advancing ship, which was now making considerable headway toward the shore.

Among the idlers on the wharf was one whom everyone addressed as Bill. He was large, or rather burly, carried a rawhide in his hand, and from his air of authority toward them, was evidently the overseer of the gang of slaves who were loading the tobacco barge. From out the crowd, a man who had been sitting idly on a bale of cotton moved toward him.

"Hello, Bill," he said, addressing the owner of the rawhide.

"Howdy, Hank," returned Bill, surveying the other curiously, "what in time did you drop from?"

Hank did not reply directly. He shifted the chewing tobacco in his mouth from one cheek to the other, then with a nod of the head toward the approaching vessel, asked: "Where she from?"

8

"Ain't been in town lately, I reckon, or you'd know all about the 'Island Queen' from Bermuda. Planter named Montfort on her. He's moving his niggers here to Carolina; getting too hot for him back there," replied Bill, with a backward jerk of his thumb in the supposed direction of Bermuda. "How's things up your way?"

"Fair, fair to middling, Bill; there's been some talk 'bout a rising among the niggers, and so we just took a few of them and strung them up for a example to the rest. I tell you, Bill, we just don't expect to have no fooling 'bout this your question of who's on top as regards a gentleman's owning his niggers, and whom so ever goes to fooling with that particular point of discussion is going to be made a example of, even if it's a white man. Didn't here nothing 'bout a circus up our way, did you?"

Bill scratched his chin and shook his head in the negative.

"Well, it was this way: Jed Powers, you remember Dan Powers' Jed, don't you? Dan that was tarred and feathered for selling good whiskey to niggers?" Bill nodded in the affirmative. "Jed Powers was seen walking with Jimison's wench Violy. Be blowed if he wasn't getting ready to cut and run to Canada with her!"

"Don't believe you, darned if I do," said Bill.

"Fact! Be darned if it ain't just so."

"Well, of all the unnatural causes!"

"But his worst offence, in general, was that he was meaning for to marry her!" Hank paused in his narrative to allow a full appreciation of his statement to be impressed upon Bill's mind.

"Was and was!" groaned the latter. "What is we coming to, by thunder! I always took Jed to be a decent sort of course, too. What's the committee doing 'bout it?"

"Well, we sort out to stop that fun, anyhow. We got him after a hot chase, and we put him in jail; and last week we gave him his trial. Judge sentenced him to fifty lashes and hanging by the neck until he was dead. But somehow or another folks is getting squeamish. Judge don't trust to hang him; he'll just give him the fifty lashes and a talking to on the immorality of his acts and ways. Judge told him he was young and had a chance to repent from the desolate ways of his youth, of which his worst failing was a-wanting to marry niggers, leastwise he'd end in he sure. Judge told him everything according to law and justice. We was calculating to have a celebration to which all the leading citizens of county woulda been invited, but, of course, not having the hanging of took the ginger out of the whole business."

"I am in no doubt of your hospitality in case of the event, Hank; always got along mighty comfortable together," replied Bill, nodding emphatic approval of all that Hank had said. The whole speech had

9

liberally punctuated with copious floods of tobacco juice, which formed a small river between the two men.

"Best thing I know of down our way," said Bill, after they had taken another good look at the ship, "the best thing I know of was a raffle over to Jellison's auction rooms. A raffle's a great thing for picking up bargains in niggers and horses. This particular one was for a bay horse, a new light buggy and harness, and a mulatto gal Sal. The whole thing was worth fifteen hundred dollars, and we had fifteen hundred chances at a dollar a head. Highest throw took first choice; lowest, the remainder. Winners to pay twenty dollars each for refreshments."

"Little bit selfish of you, Bill, to keep all that to yourself," said Hank, giving Bill a reproachful glance.

"Maybe so, maybe so. But you won't lose nothing, Hank, if I can help you in the future. 'Pears like someone was telling me," he continued reflectively, "that you was working for the county 'bout that time for board and clothes."

"Be darned if I wasn't," replied Hank with great candor. "Shot at a free nigger and killed Brady's dog Pete. If it had been the nigger I'd happened to kill, it woulda been all right; but being it was a blood hound that had tracked hundreds of runaways, it was another question; and not having the money to pay a fine, and Brady being pretty mad, why in I went for a month."

"Well, as I was saying, to proceed, by a lucky chance it was my first choice, and I choose the gal. I knowed she was a first class breeder and my money was sure for a hundred per cent on her."

"I swear to gosh, but you are right, Bill; mate her with the right sort and you's got your own money."

Both men now turned their attention to the advancing ship.

"see old Pollock's got them in tow," remarked Hank reflectively, moment's silence. "Ans Pollock's as crafty as can be. No offence you know; seems he's your boss still; mean because if he's rich as he continued, "suppose they've got a heap of money, too."

"say as to that," replied Bill, "but they bought Pollock's old t looks as though money might be plenty the way everything ed up for the missus."

hours were now over, and a great deal of confusion reigned, arrival of a ship in port with so rich a man as Mr Montfort o friends became separated in the ensuing bustle which ding of the party. During the preceding conversation a s for transporting the baggage and slaves had drawn ore; and as Mr Montfort stepped on the rickety wharf e to do the same, a murmur of involuntary admira-e motley crowd of rough white men and ignorant

10

slaves.

Grace Montfort was a dream of beauty even among beautiful women. Tall and slender; her form was willowy, although perfectly moulded. Her complexion was creamy in its whiteness, of the tint of the camellia; her hair, a rich golden brown, fell in rippling masses far below the waist line; brown eyes, large and soft as those seen in the fawn; heavy black eyebrows marking a high white forehead, and features as clearly cut as a cameo, completed a most lovely type of Southern beauty.

The two children followed their mother closely. They were sturdy boys, who resembled her in the beauty of their features; and in Jesse, the baby, a still greater resemblance could be traced, because the hair had been allowed to remain in long, soft curls. So they came ashore to their new home, obsequiously waited upon by Mr Pollock, and lovingly attended by their numerous slaves. In an instant the family was seated in the waiting vehicle; and before the spectators could fully realise the beauty and elegance of the newcomers, they were whirled away, and the carriage was lost in a cloud of dust. Hank Davis and Bill Sampson met once more before they left the wharf. "If they ain't got an overseer, I'm going to apply for the job," said Hank, "never seen such a beauty in my life."

Bill Sampson scratched his head meditatively: "Strikes me, Hank, that that female has got a black streak in her somewhere."

Hank stared at Bill a moment, as though he thought he had suddenly lost his senses; then he burst into a loud guffaw.

"You get out, Bill Sampson."

"Well, maybe," said Bill, "maybe so." That's too much cream color in the face and too little blood seen under the skin for a genuine white woman. You can't tell nothing 'bout these Britishers; they are always squeamish 'bout their nigger brats. Yes sir, very squeamish. I've heard tell that they think nothing of ejecting their black brats, and freeing him, and making him rich."

"You go to the devil," returned Hank, as he moved away, "you are worse than an ol' nigger, always seeing a possum up a tree, when it ain't no possum but a skunk."

CHAPTER 3

The old Pollock homestead was an exquisite spot. The house was a long, low, rambling structure, consisting of many large, airy rooms inside, and ornamented throughout by piazzas supported by huge pillars. Immense trees shaded the driveway and embowered the stately white mansion. Gay flowers ornamented the rolling lawn, which divided the great house from the Negro quarters which were picturesquely visible at a convenient distance from it.

Within the house Mr Montfort had gathered all the treasures which could possibly add to the comfort and pleasure of his lovely wife. Beautiful rugs covered the floors, fine paintings adorned the walls, gleaming statuary flashed upon one from odd nooks and corners. In the library music had found a home in the most comfortable corner of the room. On a table one might find a volume of Goethe in the original; on the grand piano the score of a popular opera; while a magnificent harp, standing near, hinted of musical talents highly cultivated.

Business had prospered with Montfort; his crops flourished; but a nameless trouble seemed to be halting upon the threshold of the home he loved, and to threaten those whom he cherished so fondly.

The first year of residence in Newbern had been very pleasant for the Montforts. Society, such as it was, opened its arms to the family and voted the highly cultured wife and cherub children great additions. The house was a favorite resort for all the young people of the neighborhood. Mrs. Montfort had been educated in England, and had brought with her to the provincial families with whom she now associated all the refinements of the Old World. Having great wealth for the times she had always been indulged in every whim by the doting bachelor uncle who had made her his heiress, but who had died soon after her marriage to Charles Montfort. As Grace Montfort, she found again the love her uncle had delighted to lavish upon his adopted child. Possessed of a bright, joyous nature, she liked nothing better than to gather about her the young men and women of the neighborhood and make life pleasant for them; and they in turn learned from her customs and refinements which otherwise might never have come their way. Everyone voted her the dearest and most beautiful woman they had ever known, and all would have gone merry as a marriage bell, but into this paradise of good feelings and admiration came Anson Pollock with his bitter envy and his unlawful love, and finally with his determination to possess the lovely Grace Montfort at all hazards.

Gradually the friendly relations of the neighbors turned to coldness and reserve. It was whispered about that Montfort was about to free his slaves. This in itself was a dangerous doctrine at that time in that part of the world, and a man suspected of entertaining ideas of freedom for slaves must either change his tactics or his residence, or else forfeit life and property. Then again, Bill Sampson's words to Hank Davis had somehow found a voice, and the suspicion of Negro blood in the veins of Mrs. Montfort was a deathblow to a proud spirit and social aspirations. These two serious charges had spread abroad like wildfire. It was a hot morning, a very hot morning in early summer. There had been no rain for some time. Mrs. Montfort lay in a hammock outside the breakfast room windows. Lucy, her maid, was mending lace and children's garments a short distance away.

Lucy was Mrs. Montfort's foster sister; both were born on the same day. Their relations had always been those of inseparable friends rather than of mistress and slave.

"No rain today, Lucy. I never used to mind the heat at home," she sighed. "How fair it must be over the blue waters of the bay; I can almost smell the cedars outside the entrance gates."

"Yes, Miss Grace." To Lucy her mistress was always 'Miss Grace'. "I do feel sort of squeamish myself sometimes when I think of the gals all dancing Sundays in the square, but reckon we'll get used to these people here after a while; leastwise, I hope so."

Mrs Montfort did not reply, and her maid noticed, as she glanced anxiously at her mistress, that a frown was on her face. Lucy sighed. 'Miss Grace' had been noted once for her sunny, cheerful temper. Now all was changed.

Beyond the rolling lawn fields of cotton could be seen, the leaves twisting in the heat and the steady glare of the sun. Zigzag fences separated the cotton from fields of corn, away in the distance dim aisles of pine trees stretched their dark arms towards the heavens, their dark foliage suggestive of cool shadows and quiet glades. The road wound in and out among the pines, through a woodland, and terminated in the highway just visible from the piazza. Inside the long, open windows little Jesse played at building houses with the bags of golden eagles that his father kept in a drawer of his escritoire.

"Grace, Grace, Lucy," called the child, "my houses won't stay up; come in and help me."

Just then a group appeared coming around a corner of an outbuild-

13

ing. Two men walked beside a pony, astride whose back sat Master Charles. As they approached the house the gentlemen swept off their wide-brimmed hats in a gallant salute to Mrs Montfort, which she returned by rising from her recumbent position and dropping a low courtesy. The gentlemen were Mr Montfort and Mr Pollock. Jesse, hearing the pony's feet, came out the window and ran down the piazza steps to his father, who, as Charles sprang to the ground, lifted the excited child to the pony's back. Mrs Montfort watched the approach of the little procession with a pleased smile. She made a fair picture in her elaborately embroidered white morning robe, her beautiful hair arranged in drooping curls at the sides of her head, as was the fashion of the time.

"See me, Mama Grace," cried Jesse, as he clapped his little hands, and dug the heels of his tiny-slippered feet into the pony's side, in imitation of his father on horseback. As Montfort watched him, the picture of his last Sunday in Bermuda arose before him: the little Negro child astride his mother's back, spurring her like a rider his horse, and in his ears rang the pleasant voice of his silver-haired pastor. At the piazza steps he called a servant to take away the pony, and turned to enter the house, followed by Mr Pollock, with Jesse in his arms and Charles by his side. Jesse kept up an incessant chatter. They passed through the breakfast room, where Montfort placed the child upon the floor.

"Charles, help me build my houses!" he cried, attracted to his late employment at the sight of the golden eagles. "See, papa, all my houses tumble down. Charles' houses don't fall down, but mine always do. Come and help me, Charles."

"You are not patient enough, my son," replied the father, smiling down upon his petulance. "You must be patient and persevere, and after awhile you will be able to make your houses stand. Isn't that right, Mr Pollock."

Pollock stood a little apart, gazing in amazement at the scene before him. Golden eagles given to a child to play with was a little beyond him. He made no direct reply to Mr Montfort's remark, and if the latter had been an observant man, he might have been a bit puzzled at the expression on his face. But Charles Montfort was ingenuousness itself, seeing in no man an enemy. Anson Pollock was his opposite; his ruling passion was covetousness. His eyes were fairly dazzled by the sight of the gold so carelessly strewing the floor. It positively took away his breath.

"Come, Pollock, we will talk over those matters in my study," said Montfort presently. "My son," he added, as he paused at the doorway, "be careful not to lose your ducats. They are your portion to pay your college bills when you cross the ocean to finish your education."

"Going to send him abroad to study?" inquired Pollock.

"Oh, yes; America's all right for me, but bonny England for my boys."

Anson Pollock, whom Charles Montfort had chosen for his friend, was a man of dashing appearance. He carried his years jauntily, and had a good opinion of himself where women were concerned. He was made much of by the ladies in the vicinity because of his wealth. It mattered not that his wife had died mysteriously. Rumour said his ill treatment and infidelity had driven her to suicide; it had even been whispered that he had not hesitated to whip her by proxy through his overseer, Bill Sampson, in the same way he did his slaves; but rumor is a lying jade. Nevertheless, his fair speech, auburn curls and deep blue eyes, so falsely smiling, won his way, and Mr Pollock was the popular ladies' man of two counties.

He had showered Mrs Montfort with assiduous attention since her arrival three years before, but he soon found that he made no headway. Once he dared to tell her of his passion—that from the first moment he saw her aboard the Island Queen he had been maddened by her beauty.

"Why do you tell me this?" she cried, in angry amazement at his daring. "Am I so careless of my husband's honour that his friends feel at liberty to insult me?"

"Granted that I overstep the bounds of friendship in speaking thus to you, but it is from no lack of respect; rather the deed of one who risks all upon one throw of the dice. Have mercy, I pray you, and grant me your friendship—your love." Then Grace Montfort said, while her eyes blazed with wrath: "Mr Pollock, we are strangers here, my husband and I. He trusts you, and I have no wish to disturb that trust; but if you ever address such words to me again, I shall let Mr Montfort know the kind of man you are. I promise you that he will know how to deal with you. "This conversation had taken place one night at a grand fete, where Grace had been the belle of the assembly; they were in the conservatory at the time. Anson Pollock was not accustomed to having his advances received in this way by any woman whom he elected to honour with his admiration. As the indignant woman swept back to the ballroom, he stood and watched her with an evil look, which meant no good. After that they met as usual, but Pollock had never ventured to speak to her again of love. Outwardly he was the same suave, genial gentleman, but within his breast was a living fire of hatred. The two men became faster friends than ever. Mrs Montfort was pleased to have it so; they had so few friends in this alien land; she felt so lonely, so helpless. She dreaded making enemies. It was but the lull before the storm.

When the study door had closed behind the two men, Mr Montfort dropped his pleasant, careless manner and faced Mr Pollock with an anxious face.

"Pollock," he began abruptly, "I'm worried."

15

"What about?" asked Pollock, turning from the window, where he seemed to be viewing the landscape.

"Have you heard the rumors about my wife being of African descent?" Montfort asked, coming very close to Pollock, as though afraid the very air would hear him. "There are threats, too, against my life because of my desire to free my slaves."

"Nonsense!" exclaimed Pollock. "I have heard the rumors about Mrs Montfort, but that is nothing—nothing but the malice of some malicious, jealous woman. As for the threats against your life, how can you think of such things a second time. You are among the most chivalrous people on the face of the earth, who will protect you in your home."

Montfort stood a moment before his friend, gazing at him earnestly; then he said: "Pollock, if anything happens to me, I want you to promise me to help my wife and babies to get back to Bermuda."

"Why, what can happen, man; you are nervous without a cause."

"In that safe," continued Montfort, not heeding the interruption, "you will find money and deeds; promise me that you will save them for my family."

"I promise; but it is all nonsense."

"I shall hold you to your promise," replied Montfort solemnly.

The committee on public safety generally met once a month. They had a chairman, but no one knew his identity save a chosen few of the committee. Indeed very little was known positively as to the identity of any of the members; certainly no one would ever have suspected the elegant Anson Pollock of being connected with such an organisation.

On this particular evening Bill Sampson lounged by the Jefferson house on the lookout for some of his friends. Anson Pollock sat on the broad steps, evidently on the watch for someone, too. "Hi Bill!" he called, as the latter came in sight.

"Hello!" returned Bill; and at a nod from his employer, he followed him through the entrance to a small back room, generally used for the meetings of the committee.

"Anything new for the committee tonight?" asked Pollock, as he lounged over the back of a chair. Bill took a seat on the edge of the table and began cutting circles in the air with his rawhide. Bill Sampson was a character in his way. One could not imagine Newbern without Bill, and no one could possibly imagine Bill without his rawhide.

"Well, maybe, maybe; depends on what you call work. Somebody," with a sly glance at Pollock from beneath his bushy eyebrows, "somebody's been circulating a report about a friend of yours."

"Well," replied Pollock sharply.

"Somebody says how Montfort's slaves is working for part pay; leastways, every mother's son of them'll be free inside of five years."

"Anything else?"

"We kind of thought that would do for a spell. He's done enough in that year to convict him and buy his halter. That'll do for one pint."

"But that don't cover the case. What luck have you had in spreading the other report?"

"Well," said Bill, as he shot a copious draught of tobacco juice over the sanded floor, "most the fellas think it a pity 'bout Miss Montfort. Blamed nice woman. She's been mighty good to Jeff Peterson's family, and Jeff he feels mighty uncomfortable 'bout hurting on her, darned if he don't."

"You and Jeff want to do your duty," replied Pollock. "No matter about sentiment. Influence is great with certain people, and if niggers are tolerated in any way, it will end in weakening the law, and then goodbye to our institutions."

"Course, course; we intend to do our duty; yes, sir, our whole duty. But all this 'bout Miss Montfort...I knowed she was mixed the minute I seed her, but ain't enough to attract attention. "He paused a moment, and then said with a sigh: "Well, Captain, what's your orders?"

Pollock saw that the man's sympathy was more than half enlisted on the woman's side, and with arch diplomacy changed his tactics. He handed Bill a cigar, saying, "We may as well make ourselves comfortable," and before the latter had fairly begun to enjoy the fragrant weed, had called for whiskey and was pressing him to help himself. Under its stimulating influence Bill soon lost what slight scruples he had felt, and was as eager for the downfall of the unfortunate family as his patron.

"Well, Bill," continued Pollock, "the first thing to be done is to put Montfort out of the way; then it will be plain sailing. The next question is: Who will do that job?"

"Reckon I know just the man—a man of the tight spirit, who'll be glad to serve his country for a reasonable consideration. And that reminds me, how much of the property is to be reserved for you?"

"The boys may have what they can get of it; I don't care for any part of the spoils; all I want is the mother and the children."

"Just so; well, now, seeing as I understand the case just as you want it, I'll lay low, set the boys on; you keep shady and stand ready the minute the man is fired. I ain't got a cuss against Montfort myself, but the institution must be respected. Sure there's plenty of whiskey and stuff in the cellar? It would look kind of mean in Montfort not to have a full cellar. It's a big job, and the boys'll be thirsty." With this, the two worthier arose from their seats and sauntered through the door and up to the bar.

A day or two after the foregoing, Hank Davis, true to his word, formally applied to Mr Montfort for the position of overseer on his plantation.

"What made you think that I wanted an overseer?" asked Montfort, as he pushed his hat off his face a little further and eyed the petitioner critically, mentally vowing that he would never place even a horse in the power of such an ill-favored, beastly looking fellow.

"Well, most Southern gentlemen don't care to have a nigger overseer. It spoils them; they gives themselves airs, and get ideas above their place. Thought maybe you, being a stranger, might know our ways. You see, it's just here, we have certain rules in this community that we all must abide by if we want to avoid trouble." As Hank ventured this last remark in a cautious manner, he scraped the gravel of the walk with one foot while he slyly noted the reception of his venture by an upward cast of his eye.

Charles Montfort looked at him a moment with a slumbering wrath before he asked with dangerous coolness: "What do I understand by what you have just said, Mr Davis? Do you mean to insinuate that a man cannot do as he will with his own property?"

"Well, no; not exactly; but it's just here, to speak plainly as between friends," replied Hank, as he shifted his tobacco to the other side of his mouth. "The plain fact is: I want the job of driving your niggers, and you'll want me to keep the community friendly to you now it's got out that you are going to set the gang free by an' by."

Charles Montfort possessed one characteristic of the West Indian to a marked degree, and that was a bad temper under just provocation. Without more ado he seized the offending Hank by the collar, and with his riding whip, which he carried in his hand, he administered a sound flogging to the offender. As he released him, he said: "When you leave my grounds, don't you ever set your foot inside the gates again, or it will be the worse for you."

Hank said nothing as he raised himself from the ground where the irate man had thrown him, but as he turned to leave the place he looked at Mr Montfort; and even in his wrath at the insolence of such a mongrel cur, as he mentally styled Davis, Charles Montfort felt a shudder of real physical fear pass over him for a moment. Surprised at himself, he turned to enter the house, dismissing the whole incident as a piece of impudence which he had done well to chastise.

Taking it all in all, Mr Montfort was not feeling very happy on this June morning, as he sat upon the piazza thinking over the late encounter. An hour passed swiftly away; still the master of the house continued his meditations; but now he had changed his seat for a thoughtful promenade up and down the broad piazza. Finally he said softly to himself: "Yes, that is just what I will do; I'll send Gracie and the little fellows home for a while on a visit, and there they shall stay until I know just what the trouble is here about the slaves, and certain insinuations con-

18

cerning my family are cleared up. "When a man makes up his mind that he has solved a difficult problem that has worried him, he generally has an air of relief which is the more pathetic, that in nine cases out of ten he does not believe that his remedy will prove effective, although he fancies that he so believes.

When Hank Davis left Mr Montfort, he moved slowly down the sun-baked road, nursing his wrath and swearing vengeance. Nothing but the life of the man who had inflicted such an insult upon him could wipe it out. He had received the same treatment that he had given hundreds of his associates, until his name and presence had become a terror in the county where he resided. Hitherto he had given his orders and they had been obeyed; but here was a man, a comparative stranger, for whom he considered that he had been willing to do a great kindness, for a consideration, and not only had he met with a refusal of his request but at the same time had received personal violence of a character that was most galling to the spirit of any free born Southern man—an ordinary cowhiding, such as he would hand out to his slave. As he thought more and more about the matter he grew more and more filled with a desire for vengeance—not the ordinary kind, but something extraordinary. As he gradually turned over in his mind schemes for the undoing of the Montforts, he was accosted by the voice of Bill Sampson, calling to him from across the fields. Bill was overseeing the harvesting of a great field of cotton, and the voices of the slaves could be heard droning out their weird and plaintive notes, as they sought by song movement to lighten the monotony of their heavy tasks and bring solace to their sad hearts. Some, in their simple ignorance, may not have known why they were sad, but, like the captive bird, their hearts longed for that which was ever the birthright of man—property in himself. Crushed out of sight for many years, the seed of desire for all those things which make a man, and sweeten toil, was struggling ever toward the light of civilisation denied to these poor, ignorant, enslaved souls.

Hank sat down on a log by the wayside and beckoned Bill over to him. The latter came slowly across the field and seated himself astride one end of the log.

Greetings passed between the two cronies.

"Appears like to me, Hank, you are looking pale," remarked Bill, as he trailed his whip backward and forward in the dust. Hank could stand it no longer; and with a terrible imprecation, he unfolded to his friend his tale of woe and insult. Bill listened with eager curiosity, and a satisfied, knowing look might have been seen to settle about the corners of his eyes and mouth.

"Well, well," said he, "these are great times when a West angry half-white nigger can raise his hand against a white man. Be you hurt much,

Hank?"

"Some in my body, but more in my feelings."

"What are we coming to? I tell you, Hank, it is 'bout time something was done."

"That's all well enough to talk," replied Hank, "but what can a man do against the money that that fella's got to back him up? I can't see a handle on him."

"Well," replied Bill, "I can."

"You can!" exclaimed Hank, while a slow smile of derision covered his face;"well, I'd just like to know how."

"You can laugh, Hank Davis, but it's a fact. That is not going to be no hard job to get all that money, all them pretty trinkets and fine furniture, and the seven hundred niggers in our pockets if..." And here he paused as though to give emphasis to his words. "...If we work the thing right."

"Damn it all, man, why don't you let out?" demanded Hank, as he rose excitedly from his seat on the log. "I'm the man to help on anything against that man, and you knows it. No need of you being so infernal aggravating 'bout telling me."

Bill laughed at his companion's excitement. "Easy Hank. This is a mighty delicate job, but we can work it—we can work it. First place, you see Montfort's brought them slaves of his here and don't tend to keep them only 'bout ten years, and then every one of them will have bought himself, according to the laws that are governing them over to the West Indies. Now, you know there is a bad example to set before the niggers around this town. Anyway, we are going to think so," drawled Bill, with an expressive wink at his friend. "It's a law of the United States that if any man is caught creating dissatisfaction among the slaves he deserves death, and death he gets. Now, this Montfort has been causing trouble for us by his example. Every nigger round here knows all 'bout his arrangements for giving his slaves that freedom, and I tell you, Hank, it's causing dissatisfaction among all our slaves. And then the money, honey, the money! All done up in little shammy skin bags, and that boy Jesse sitting on the floor amusing himself building houses with them gold eagles!"

Hank listened to his companion's words with open mouth. As the latter finished he said, with a look of admiration: "Well, I'll be damned! Now, look here, Bill Sampson, you needn't tell me that it's all your own ideas, because you could no more have got them thoughts through your thick head than I could. Someone's been fixing you up. Out with it now, and tell me the whole thing. If we's going into this business, we's got to be square on the deal with our friends. Who's the bottom of this thing?"

Bill produced a plug of tobacco, offered his friend a chew and took one himself. "What I'm telling you, Hank, is between friends," said he, chewing and crossing his legs.

"Yes' so," replied Hank.

"I was telling you the originator of this plan, or I was about to."Bill paused to spit out some of his tobacco juice on the ground, so that it would not overflow the tank, so to speak, and run out of each corner of his mouth. "Beats all reason, Hank, how a man'll get dead set unto a piece of calico."

"Meaning by that, Bill, that Ans Pollock's got set on some gal."

"Fact!" said Bill, with a wink.

"Who's?" asked Hank.

"It most be Miss Montfort herself, Hank."

"You don't say," said Hank, with a wicked look. "Don't blame him, blamed if I do. But that's all the good it'll do him."

Bill cut the air into imaginary circles with his whip, and without taking any notice of his friend, continued: "As I was saying, Ans Pollock, he says to me, 'Bill, that's a real pretty woman of Montfort's', and I told him what I thought 'bout her having black blood in her somewhere. 'Maybe,' says he, 'maybe.' And then he says, kind of generous like, 'I'd take the woman and the two brats, and the boys might have the slaves, and the money, and the fixing in the house.' I told him I knew the boys' stand by him in anything he might do to rid a peaceful neighborhood of such a disturbing critter as Montfort. I told him I thought you would be 'bout the very match to light on Montfort, so he wouldn't give us any more trouble. And so we've been waiting for the business to develop itself good and ripe, and I just think this attack of Montfort's on you will 'bout do the business for the whole of them.

"Bill," said Hank Davis, as he held out his hand to his friend, "we always been partners, and I reckon we always will be."

CHAPTER 4

K ismet," says the Oriental, when unaccountable evils beset his path; "It is fate," says the Anglo-Saxon, under like circumstances: but fate is the will of Providence after all. Nature avenges herself upon us for every law violated in the mad rush for wealth or position or personal comfort where the rights of others of the human family are not respected. If Charles Montfort had been contented to accept the rulings of the English Parliament, and had allowed his human property to come under the new laws just made for its government, although poorer in the end, he would have spared himself and family all the horrors which were to follow his selfish flight to save that property.

The sun rose clear and resplendent a few mornings later. On this particular morning Nature outdid herself. There was a blending together of all the sweet forces—odorous air, golden sunshine, musical sounds from bird and from bush; it was pure happiness to feel the lifeblood leaping in one's veins; to feel the marvellous joy of living.

Eight o'clock was the usual breakfast hour for the Montforts. The family had just assembled at the table; Aunt Cindy had brought in the great silver coffee urn and placed it beside Mrs Montfort. Mr Montfort had settled himself in his chair with a weekly paper, for in this rural neighborhood a newspaper once in a week was a great luxury, when his attention was caught by the sound of hoofbeats of several horses on the road. Mrs Montfort, with usual Southern hospitality, looked over her well-appointed board to make sure that all was in order for dispensing those creature comforts so dear to the entertainer and the entertained.

The hoofbeats drew nearer and paused on the graveled walk. Montfort hastened to the door, while Mrs Montfort turned toward the entrance of the breakfast room with a pleasant smile of welcome on her lips. She heard a number of voices speaking together in an excited jumble, then a shot, followed by a heavy fall. Little Jesse ran from his station by his mother's side through one of the long windows opening upon the piazza. She heard his scream of "papa, papa!" and then again the jumble of excited voices. With little Charles clinging to her skirts she stumbled blindly to the entrance and faced the crowd of angry men, headed by Anson Pollock. Hank Davis had done his work well, and Charles Montfort lay dead with a bullet in his brain, sped by an unseen hand. Mrs Montfort's arms were grasped by rude hands, and she was forcibly

22

drawn out upon the veranda, where in the sunlight of the beautiful morning she saw the body of her husband lying face downward. She was dimly conscious of hearing the cries of frightened slaves mingled with the screams of her children. Through it all she realised but two things—that the lifeless object lying there so still was the body of her husband, and that the sensual face of Anson Pollock, whom she had grown to loathe and fear, was gloating over her agony, devilish in its triumph. Then she lost consciousness.

As she lay upon the green sward, oblivious to thought and feeling, supported by her weeping maid, who had been ordered to care for her mistress by Mr Pollock, Hank Davis came and stood for a moment looking down upon the unconscious woman. Suddenly an evil smile lighted up his countenance. He looked around, but saw nothing of Anson Pollock, who had disappeared within the house, searching for money and papers in the safe. Now was his time. This woman's husband had flogged him—he would have a sweet revenge. Those lily-like limbs, the tender flesh that had never known aught but the touch of love, should feel the lash as he had.

He called to Bill Sampson to help lift her; and despite the prayers and tears of the poor slave girl who followed her beloved mistress until Sampson knocked her senseless with the butt end of his rawhide, they bore the hapless lady to the whipping post. She revived as they reached the spot, and when she realised the fate in store for her, the sweet woman's strong soul failed her. She uttered a wild cry of agony as the rough hand of Hank Davis was laid upon her to tear her garments from her shrinking shoulders.

"Charles, my husband, save me!" she cried, and fell fainting upon the ground. There was none to answer the heart-rending appeal. He who would have shed his heart's best blood for her, lay cold in death. She was soon restored to consciousness, for Hank's savage instinct for revenge would only be appeased by the victim's full realisation of her sufferings.

She was bound to the whipping post as the victim to the stake, and lashed with rawhides alternately by the two strong, savage men. Hank Davis drew first blood by reason of his wrongs at Mr Montfort's hands. With all his mighty strength he brought the lash down upon the frail and shrinking form. O God! was there none to rescue her! The air whistled as the snaky leather thong curled and writhed in its rapid, vengeful descent. A shriek from the victim—a spurt of blood that spattered the torturer—a long, raw gash across a tender, white back. Hank gazed at the cut with critical satisfaction, as he compared its depth with the skin and blood that encased the long, tapering lash. It was now Bill's turn.

"I'll go you one better," he said, as he sighted the distance and exact place to make his mark with mathematical precision, at the same time

23

shifting his tobacco from the right to the left cheek. Again the rawhide whistled through the air, falling across the other cut squarely in the center. Another shriek, a stifled sob, a long-drawn quivering sigh—then the deep stillness of unconsciousness. Again and again was the outrage repeated. Fainting fit followed fainting fit. The blood stood in a pool about her feet.

When Hank Davis had satiated his vengeful thirst he cut the ropes which bound her. She sank upon the ground again—unconscious, bleeding, friendless, alone. Lucy had hidden in the smokehouse with the two children, that they might not witness their mother's agony.

Meantime, the committee on public safety, instigated by Anson Pollock to put down an imaginary insurrection (having no existence but in his own mind, and supposed to have originated with the slaves of Charles Montfort) and to legalise the looting of the house, took possession of the mansion. Soon the crowd had stripped it of its furniture and all the articles of value. The house itself was fired, and Grace Montfort again became conscious of her misery in time to see the dead body of her husband flung amid the burning rafters of his dwelling. Two and two the slaves were handcuffed together to be driven to the market place. Mrs Montfort, secured to her maid, was placed in a wagon with her two children; and so the miserable woman was driven away from her outraged home.

In those old days, if accused of aiding slaves in a revolt, a white man stood no more chance than a Negro accused of the same crime. He forfeited life and property. This power of the law Anson Pollock had invoked; and to add to the devilishness of the plot, had used Bill Sampson's suggestion of black blood in Mrs Montfort to further his scheme for possessing the beautiful woman. So the two children and their mother fell to the lot of Anson Pollock as his portion of the spoils. Shortly after these events Grace Montfort disappeared and was never seen again. The waters of Pamlico Sound tell of sweet oblivion for the brokenhearted found within their soft embrace.

After the loss of their mother the two lads clung very closely to each other. So many changes had come to them, such desperate, bloody scenes had dazed their brains and terrified them, that even the loss of their mother seemed but in keeping with the rest. Bewilderment at so much sorrow, the numbness of black despair was ever with them.

Pollock's rage was terrible when he learned that Mrs Montfort had destroyed herself. He grew morose and unsociable, so that his society was no longer sought in the county. He seemed to have a superstitious fear of the children, and for a long time would not tolerate them in his presence. It was common talk among the slaves that Mrs Montfort walked, weeping and wringing her hands, night after night about the

24

plantation.

But wonder could go no further when Pollock elected to take Lucy in the place he had designed for Mrs Montfort. God's mysteries are past man's understanding; and thus the poor black girl became his instrument to temper the wind to the shorn lambs. Night after night she stole away to the little attic under the eaves laden with dainties to tempt the appetite of the children. For hours she would sit hushing Jesse's sobs upon her ample breast, and speaking words of comfort in her poor, blind way to Charles.

When a year had dragged its slow length past, a stranger in the town stopped Bill Sampson on the street one day and asked him if he knew where he could hire a likely boy to go with him into the woods for a few days and help arrange specimens of the quartz in that locality. He was looking up the minerals in that section for speculators, he said. Bill promised to get him a boy, and asked Pollock's permission for Charles to go with the man.

"I don't care what you do with him, only keep him away from me. I'll sell him south soon," said Pollock.

So it happened that Charles went every day for a month with the mineralogist. The lad's appearance, education and refinement puzzled the man for a time, until he learned the tragic story.

"Charles," said he, a few weeks later, "I am about to leave this part of the country. I don't want to leave you here. Do you think Mr Pollock could be induced to part with you?" "O sir!" cried Charles, throwing himself at the gentleman's feet, "for the love of God buy me and my little brother. If you will only take us to Bermuda, someone there will pay you back. My father had money there; we have friends there. O sir, for the love of God!"

The man looked at the weeping boy as through a mist. He had a tender heart.

"I will tell you something, Charles," said he kindly, as he raised the lad and drew him to a seat beside him on the grass, with his arm tenderly enfolding the child. "I am an Englishman, but it will not do to have that fact known here, for then I would be powerless to help you. Anson Pollock would never sell you to me if he knew that fact. I have been trying to buy you and Jesse, but Pollock wants to keep the boy for a valet. He intends to sell you south; you are too old to forget, and he fears you. Now I propose to buy you; and as soon as possible I shall take you to Bermuda, collect the proofs there concerning your family, and then go to England, invoke the power of the home government, and demand Jesse's freedom and indemnity from the United States government for all the outrages perpetrated against your family. Can you keep this secret, and will you try and be patient until I can accomplish my purpose?"

"I will do anything you say," replied the boy humbly, "but I hate to leave Jesse. O mama, mama, my beautiful mama!" and with a burst of grief he cast himself upon the velvet turf.

The mineralogist lost no time in completing the purchase of Charles, and in a few days they left the town. Then little Jesse, the petted darling of a luxurious home, found himself alone in the power of Anson Pollock. He must wait upon him obsequiously by day, and be ready to answer his call at any hour of the night. Under his enemy's eye by day and night, hopeless, utterly alone upon the wide waste of waters which represented his life. Oh, how black, boundless, trackless, was the unknown future to this unfortunate child. Once, after his brother was sold, he resisted his master. Rebelled with all his puny strength. He was severely flogged. That night he slept in the lonely cabin kept as a sort of prison for refractory slaves. Not a sigh disturbed the silence of the night as he lay in pain, gazing up at the stars which shone so peacefully through the dilapidated roof. He thought himself delirious, or was it indeed possible that God had taken compassion on his loneliness and allowed the comfort and help of communion with the dead! He saw his murdered father and mother. Hand in hand they passed over the gaping holes in the roof of the hut. His father's noble, loving face smiled upon him; his mother's curls moved in the faint breeze, while her loving glance seemed to say: "Courage, courage, we are ever near you."

"Father, mother, speak to me!" he shrieked in agony.

Then he seemed to feel their actual presence, tangible though viewless, beside him in the hut. Calmness came to him, and a change grand to see in that slight frame. Unconsciously he asked the question: "How long must I endure before I join you in heaven?"

It seemed to him that he was answered: "Many days, and even years; but fear not, we will never leave you."

After that night Jesse's childhood appeared to slip from him, and he became a man in thought. He studied his master, and matched low cunning with lofty determination. He rebelled no more, was silent, not provoking Anson Pollock's wrath. The time seemed long and dreary waiting for the freedom he had resolved to have; still he was patient. Sometimes at night, when rolled in his blanket on the hard floor, he would weep over the painful past. Then he would feel the touch of a tiny hand upon his eyelids, It was his mother's hand; he knew it to be so. Then he would lose himself in sweet dreams and awaken in the morning refreshed and comforted. So the years rolled on until he was sixteen. Meantime, nothing was heard from Charles and his supposed friend. Jesse had made up his mind that Charles was either dead or else lost to him forever.

Jesse was now a man in stature, though still slender, with the same haughty bearing and distinguished appearance that had marked his father. Anson Pollock, upon whom age and the memory of dreadful crimes were making fearful inroads, began to look up to the boy and lean upon him for aid in his various plans for making money. He had spoken to him of making him the overseer, in place of Bill Sampson, and had even hinted at his taking a mate. Then Jesse knew that his probation was nearly over. That spring Pollock, as was the common practice among planters, made out passes for Jesse and sent him to New York in charge of a vessel filled with produce, and charged to bring back necessary merchandise for use on the plantation. Pollock thought the boy still too young to venture to leave him. Indeed Jesse had no such idea when he started on his trip to the North. When the vessel reached New York, Jesse performed all the necessary duties—disposed of the produce, and reloaded the ship for its homeward voyage. The night before they were to sail he sat on the wharf watching the crews of other vessels making ready for departure. His mind was engrossed with thoughts of Charles. He feared some evil had befallen him.

"At any rate," he said to himself, "I shall never see him again. And must I remain in servitude? Can I do nothing to help myself, since all hope is gone in that direction?" Just then a group of men paused in front of him. They did not know he was a slave.

"Will you give passage to two on board your vessel? You are bound for Newbern in the morning, aren't you? We'll pay you what you charge," said one of the group respectfully.

"Speak to the captain," called out a man standing near, "that's nothing but a nigger you're talking to."

"Well," said the one who had first addressed him, "you're a likely boy, anyhow; who do you belong to?"

Jesse arose from his seat, white with passion, and said to the man: "I am no man's property; I belong to Jesus Christ!" The question had answered itself. When the vessel sailed the next morning, Jesse was far on his road to Boston.

Travelling then was done by stage, and was a slow process; but about a week later he stood beside the stone wall that enclosed the historic Boston Common, and as he watched the cows chewing their peaceful cuds and inhaled deep draughts of freedom's air, he vowed to die rather than return to Anson Pollock.

He found work in Boston. It mattered not that it was menial work; he was happy. But fate or Providence was not done with him yet.

One day he received word that Anson Pollock was on his way to Boston in search of him. Again he made a hurried journey. This time to Exeter, N. J. In his character of a fugitive slave, the lad had from the first

27

cast his lot with the colored people of the community, and when he left Boston he was directed to see Mr Whitfield, a negro in Exeter, who could and would help the fugitive.

Late one afternoon, just before tea time, a comely black woman stood in her long, low-raftered kitchen preparing supper before the open fireplace. There was every indication of plenty in the homely furnishings. As the woman passed rapidly from the cupboard to the table she would touch with her foot the rockers of the little red cradle which stood in the center of the floor. The baby in it was crying in a fretful way. "Oh, hush, Lizzie," said the mother; "don't be so cross." There came a low rap at the open door, and in answer to her "Come in," Jesse stepped into the room.

"Is Mr Whitfield in?" he asked, as he doffed his hat respectfully.

"No," was the reply, "but I expect him every minute. Sit down, won't you? He'll soon be in to his supper, I guess."

Mrs Whitfield thought him a white man, come on business with her husband. "A handsome lad," she thought. Jesse seated himself, and then as the child continued to cry, said: "Shall I rock the cradle for you, ma'am? The child seems fretful."

Fifteen years later Jesse married Elizabeth Whitfield, the baby he had rocked to sleep the first night of his arrival in Exeter. By her he had a large family.

Thus he was absorbed into that unfortunate black race, of whom it is said that a man had better be born dead than to come into the world as part and parcel of it.

CHAPTER 5

"Thank heaven that is done," said Dora, as she sat down wearily in her mother's large rocker in the cosy kitchen. She had been upstairs the best portion of the day preparing a room for an expected lodger. There had been windows to wash, paint to clean, a carpet to tack down, curtains to hang and furniture to place in position—in short, the thousand and one things to do that are essential to the comfort of the lodger and the good reputation of the house.

"Are you very tired, daughter?" queried her mother, as she glanced with loving pride at the graceful figure before her, at the smooth bands of dark brown hair, now a little ruffled and disordered, and at the delicate brown face, now somewhat puckered and out of sorts from weariness, "Well, not very tired, mummy dear; only this continual scrub and dig is not always the cheerful work we would like to think it. Still I don't care as long as the house pays."

The mother sighed as she asked: "Did you give her the front or back square?"

"Oh, I gave her the front square after all. She's too beautiful for that dreary back room. I know that it is not business to let a good-paying room go under our usual price, but she's a 'steady'; she has the best of references. Father Andrew gives her the best of characters, and so I'll chance getting my money back out of the next cross-grained old bachelor who comes along. See how mercenary I am getting to be since I undertook to direct the fortunes of a lodging house," and with a gay laugh the daughter jumped from her seat, every trace of fatigue gone, and grasping her mother about the waist, whirled her around the room to the accompaniment of a sweet, shrill whistle of the latest popular waltz. In the midst of the frolic there came a loud ring of the doorbell, and placing her panting and protesting mother in the rocker just vacated, she vanished; and soon her voice was heard above, as she directed the placing of the luggage of the expected lodger.

The Smith family consisted of the mother, daughter and son. A few years before the beginning of our story the father had died, leaving a delicate wife, a young daughter, and a son just ready to enter college, also a house in a respectable part of the South End of Boston, Mass, with a heavy mortgage upon it. Like many colored men living in large cities, his life had been a continual struggle with poverty and hard work, combined with a desire for advancement for his children, and a clean, self-

29

respecting citizenship for himself. Smith was a free born Southern Negro—a Virginian. His father had bought himself and married a free woman. After the birth of Henry his mother died; and when his father married again, his aunts brought him to the city of New Bedford, where he had imbibed, along with copious draughts of salt air, an unwavering desire for all the blessings of liberty, and strong notions that a man must depend upon himself in great measure and carve out his own fortune to the best of his ability with such tools as God had furnished him.

Henry Smith's early manhood was spent upon the sea; and when he at last settled in Boston, he could converse about foreign ports and countries with the ease and familiarity of personal knowledge. Possessed of very little education, yet he concealed the fact admirably under a naturally intelligent manner. Soon after he ceased to follow the sea he married a handsome Mulattress from New Hampshire, and with her help saved a small sum of money enough to make the first payment on a home; then began the struggle of their lives. The masses of the Negro race find for employment only the most laborious work at the scantiest remuneration. A man, though a skilled mechanic, has the door of the shop closed in his face here among the descendants of the liberty-loving Puritans. The foreign element who come to the shores of America soon learn that there is a class which is called its inferior, and will not work in this or that business if "niggers" are hired; and the master or owner, being neither able nor willing to secure enough of the despised class to fill the places of the white laborers, acquiesces in the general demand, and the poor Negro finds himself banned in almost every kind of employment. Henry Smith had his ambitions; but like all of his meek race, he would not or at least had no desire to contend with the force of prejudice, and quietly took up his little business of repairing old clothes.

Two children were born to this worthy couple—William Jesse Montfort and Dora Grace Montfort. When Willie was seventeen and Dora twelve, their father sickened and died. Thenceforth the burden of the support of the little family fell upon the mother. Willie was preparing to enter college, but he cheerfully gave up his plans and secured a place as bellboy in one of the fashionable hostelries with which Boston abounds; and soon by his attention to business, his gentlemanly manners, and intelligent understanding of all that was required of him, made himself invaluable to his employers. Twenty dollars a month with board and tips was a very respectable showing for a lad of seventeen, and Willie felt himself repaid when he saw the great help and comfort his small earnings gave to his dear mother. Dora was kept at her studies until she was graduated from the high school. Meantime Mrs Smith, or Ma Smith, as she was called by all the young people of her acquaintance, increased their income by letting furnished rooms. The mother and daughter shared the same sleeping room, and Will declared himself in favor of an attic chamber as being the least desirable for renting purposes. There he established himself in a very comfortable nest, furnished after the fashion dear to all young fellows' hearts, with everything handy. The only occasions upon which Will and Dora were known to quarrel were the weekly cleaning days, when the latter would insist on tidying up Will's room. Then shoes were moved from the mantel and the blacking brushes from the top of the dressing case; collars, cuffs and ties were placed in their proper receptacles, and garments hung in the clothes-press. Then Will would scold a good deal because he "couldn't find things", but by the next morning he would have them at hand again. Many lodgers were obtained through Will's acquaintance with young men at the hotel where he worked, and very soon the mother was able to see that the debt upon the home which she hoped to leave her children, was slowly but surely disappearing. Deep in her heart was the cherished hope that when the mortgage was paid Willie would be free to choose a profession; but they never mentioned among themselves the hope which was cherished in each breast.

As the years rolled slowly by the children saw that their mother could not do as much as formerly; and so by degrees, after Dora had finished school, the burden of the care of the house fell upon her strong young shoulders, and 1896 found her taking full charge, and proving herself to be a woman of ability and the best of managers, husbanding their small income to the best advantage. With about every avenue for business closed against them, it is surprising that so many families of color manage to live as well as they do and to educate their children and give them a few of the refinements of living—such as cultivating a musical talent, gratifying a penchant for languages, or for carving, or for any of the arts of a higher civilisation, so common among the whites, but supposed to be beyond the reach of a race just released from a degrading bondage. Whatever grace or accomplishment may be the order of the hour, it is copied or practiced among some portion of the colored population. We may well ask ourselves how this is done. Among the white Americans who perform domestic or personal service, how rare it is to meet the brilliant genius of a Frederick Douglass; but amongst colored people it is a common occurrence to find a genius in a profession, trade, or invention, evolved from the rude nurturing received at the hands of a poor father and mother engaged in the lowliest of service, who see not the nobility of their sacrifices in the delight afforded them in watching the unfolding of the bud of promise in their offspring. From the bosom of the earth we take the diamond; pearls from the depth of the sea; from the lowliest walks of life we cull the hope of a future life beyond the perplexing questions of this present existence. Why should we wonder or question, then, when we see the steady advance of a race overriding the barriers set by prejudice and injustice? Man has said that from lack of means and social caste the Negro shall remain in a position of serfdom all his days, but the mighty working of cause and effect, the mighty unexpected results of the law of evolution, seem to point to a different solution of the Negro question than any worked out by the most fertile brain of the highly cultured Caucasian. Then again, we do not allow for the infusion of white blood, which became pretty generally distributed in the inferior black race during the existence of slavery. Some of this blood, too, was the best in the country. Combinations of plants, or trees, or of any productive living thing, sometimes generate rare specimens of the plant or tree; why not, then, of the genus homo? Surely the Negro race must be productive of some valuable specimens, if only from the infusion which amalgamation with a superior race must eventually bring. This is a mighty question. Today still, the Negro question will not die down; it is the most important, the mightiest in the land, and is quietly assuming greater proportions as it forges its way to the front to take its place shortly as the gravest question in the councils of the nation.

When Dora returned to the kitchen her mother had about finished the preparations for supper. The short winter afternoon had dropped into early twilight. Every alternate night was Will Smith's early night home from the hotel, and the little family always managed to have an inviting tea and to pass a cheerful evening together. Lately another person had attached himself to the Smiths; a fellow waiter with Will had finally worked himself into the profession of law, and having established himself in business in a downtown office, had put his admiration for Dora into words, and it was understood that in due course of time they would marry.

Dora lighted the lamps, drew the curtains, and looked about the cosy kitchen with a satisfaction which might well be pardoned, for even in palatial homes a more inviting nest could not be found. The table was carefully spread with a nicely ironed cloth of spotless white, red-bordered napkins lay at each plate, a good quality of plated silverware mingled with the plain, inexpensive white ware in which the meal was to be served. Ma Smith, in her neat calico dress and long white apron, busied herself in making the tea and coffee and seeing that the delicate muffins were browned to just the right turn, while Dora busied herself in putting the finishing touches to a house dress for her mother.

"Well, Dora," said her mother, as she bustled about the room, "does the young woman seem pleased with your arrangements? I am sure she ought to after all the labour you spent on that room."

"She says she is greatly pleased with everything. Say, ma, she's got a typewriter, and she says she picks up a good living at home with it. Talk about your beauties! My, but she's the prettiest creature I ever saw! I expect all the men in this house will be crazy over her."

"Yes, dear," replied her mother with a quiet laugh; "you don't want John making eyes at her, do you?"

Dora laughed as she said: "I'd just drop John P. Langley if I thought he admired any woman more than he did me. But really, ma, you won't be able to keep from loving her; she has the sweetest and saddest face I ever saw. I have read of the woman with a story written on her face, but I never believed it anything but a fairy tale. You'll believe me when you see her and talk with her."

"There are the boys," said her mother, as the sound of voices reached their ears, together with the closing of the front door and great stamping of feet to brush away the snow. The next moment the door opened, and two young men entered the cheerful room, and with jest and laugh bade the two women good evening.

Will Smith was tall and finely formed, with features almost perfectly chiselled, and a complexion the colour of an almond shell. His hair was black and curly, with just a tinge of crispness to denote the existence of Negro blood. His eyes were dark and piercing as an eagle's. Ladies of high position followed his tall form with admiring glances as he moved about his duties at the hotel, and wondered that so much manly beauty should be wasted upon an 'inferior' race.

John Langley, his companion, was shorter in stature and very fair in complexion. His hair was dark and had no indication of Negro blood in its waves; his features were of the Caucasian cut. He possessed a gentle refinement of manner, apt to take well with the opposite sex; but to a reader of character, the strong manhood and honesty of purpose which existed in Will Smith were lacking in John Langley. He was a North Carolinian—a descendant of slaves and Southern 'crackers'. We might call this a bad mixture—the combination of the worst features of a dominant race with an enslaved race; and in some measure John Langley would bear out the unfavorable supposition upon close acquaintance. Many of his young friends did not care for him because he developed a revengeful trait of character. He liked his ease, and enjoyed indulging himself in every luxury that his modest means would allow. He had, moreover, a carefully concealed strain of sensuality in his nature, which as yet had never been aroused to an overindulgence in illegitimate and questionable pleasures; and with it all he had a mercenary streak, which made love of money his great passion. He possessed great political acumen and was strong in debate, which attracted a certain class of politicians around him. These attributes, combined with the practice of his profession, might eventually make or mar his fortunes in the untried future that stretched before him.

Seated at the pleasant tea table, the gay laugh and jolly joke went round, and even Ma Smith forgot her years and contributed her share of mirth to the general good time.

"Talking about funny things happening," said Ma Smith, "your grandfather, Will, was a comical genius. You know that I have told you there were fourteen in our family—all girls, and very near each other in age. When your aunts, Fanny and Lottie, began to receive company there was a great time to keep it from father for a while. Mother was heart and hand with the girls and wanted to see them have a pleasant time, but father did not like it. Your grandfather worked hard and at night was very tired, so the dear old man would go to bed soon after his supper and pipe. Then was the girls' time. A fire was made in the parlor, which was at the front of the house, a good distance away from father's room, and by the time the young man arrived to make his call the old gentleman was generally sound asleep. One night, however, things did not work so well. In those days we had large open fireplaces; stoves did not come in until I was about five years old. I can see that low-ceilinged parlor now with its brick hearth and brass and irons holding the glowing logs, the flames crackling and shooting upward, the firelight dancing and shining on the little cupboard doors on each side of the chimney. There was a rag carpet on the floor—your grandmother made her own carpets from rags; and our floors were covered with large handmade rag mats, for no housekeeper was counted much who did not have a large supply of such things. There were china figures on the mantel, and vases filled with golden rod gathered the summer before. The furniture was mahogany, polished until you could see your face in any part of it. There was a red cloth on the table which stood between the two windows, and in the center of it was a large astral lamp trimmed about the edges with long crystal pendants, which we children called diamonds. We thought nothing could be more elegant than that lamp. It was a wedding present to your grandmother."

"Did you have kerosene in those days, ma?" asked Dora.

"Lord bless you, no; we burned whale oil or sperm oil in that lamp. Poor people used candles. Your grandmother used to save her fat and mix it with beeswax to harden it, and we made our candles every week as regularly as we did the family cooking. Sometimes there was danger of the supply of oil running out in the stores, and then oil cost a great deal of money. But in a few weeks some New Bedford whaler would be in port with a large cargo of whale oil, and then there would be a big supply selling cheap."

"I don't see how you got along without stoves and things," observed Dora, "baking day must have been a terror."

"We had tin kitchens and Dutch ovens. We never had any trouble."

"What's a tin kitchen?" asked John.

"It's an oven made of tin, for roasting meat. It stood on four legs about a foot from the floor, and had a place for a charcoal fire at the back, and a chimney to carry off the smoke. The front fastened by a hasp to the back and could be let down to put the food on the little grate inside. It was a very convenient arrangement, and I wish I had one this minute. A Dutch oven was very much like our iron kettles which we use for boiling; there was a grate inside to hold the food."

"It must have been a great nuisance keeping house under such circumstances."

"Well, what became of the young man that particular evening, ma?" chimed in Will.

"This night father was restless and did not retire with his usual promptness, and we had only just got him out of the way when the expected caller arrived. However, everything went on very well, and you may be sure that there was much peeping and giggling on the part of the half-grown sisters who were denied the great privilege of the parlor and company as yet. Your grandmother sat in the kitchen knitting and trying to keep the younger children in order, when to her consternation the door opened and in walked father. 'Elizabeth,' said he, 'I hear a man's voice in the parlor. What's the trouble?' Poor mother tried to explain, and murmured something about a gentleman calling on Fanny. 'A man,' roared father, 'calling on my daughter!' and the first thing we knew, he seized the bucket of water from the kitchen dresser—we had wells in those days, and a bucket of water always stood on the dresser and started for the parlor and flung the door open. Without speaking to the astonished occupants of the room, he stalked to the fireplace and poured the water upon the blazing wood, then turned to the caller and said: 'Young man, if you have a home, go to it; this is no halfway house for young squirts. Fanny,' he said, turning to your aunt, 'go to bed, and don't let this thing occur again.' The young man left as quickly as possible, and poor Fanny retired to her room mortified.

"That's good discipline for girls," said John with a laugh. "If we had more fathers like that, we fellows would get better wives."

"And we girls better husbands," chimed in Dora. "Still, I pity poor Aunt Fanny."

"The fellow wasn't much or he'd have stuck, and not been driven off that way. I'd have made the old gentleman like me in spite of himself if I had meant business," said Will. "Oh, by the by, did your new lodger come, Dora?"

"Yes; and, Will, I never met anyone so beautiful in all my life. You'll be fascinated when you meet her."

"That's you all over, Dora; all your swans generally turn out to be

35

geese. I'll bet you a new pair of Easter gloves that she's a rank old maid with false teeth, bald head, hair on her upper lip."

"All right, Will Smith, all right. Just wait until you see her! I'll wager a new pair of embroidered silk suspenders that you're over head and ears in love with her long before that time."

"I'll hold the stakes," cried John.

They rose from the table now, and John said, with a tender glance at Dora: "I thought someone would enjoy seeing the Old Homestead. It's at the Boston Theatre tonight; don't you want to go, Dora?" Dora's eyes sparkled as he held the two tickets before her.

"Get your things on, Dora; you've just time to reach the theatre before the curtain rises," said her brother.

In a little while the house was quiet, and the mother and son settled down to the enjoyment of a quiet evening together.

CHAPTER 6

February drew slowly to a close. Boston had rain for the past three or four days in the grasp of the snow king. At 500 D Street each tenant seemed content to keep within the bounds of his or her small domain, literally "frozen up," as Mrs Ophelia Davis expressed it.

No one had seen much of the new lodger. She passed in and out each morning with a package of work in her hand; and all day long, from nine in the morning until late at night sometimes, the click of the typewriter could be heard coming from the "first front-square," which interpreted meant the front room on the second floor. Dora had been very neighborly and had called on Miss Clark frequently. There was a great fascination for her about the quiet, self-possessed woman. She did not, as a rule, care much for girl friendships, holding that a close intimacy between two of the same sex was more than likely to end disastrously for one or the other. But Sappho Clark seemed to fill a long-felt want in her life, and she had from the first a perfect trust in the beautiful girl.

Mrs Smith had furnished her rooms substantially and well, but there had been no attempt at decoration. The first time Dora entered the room after Sappho had settled herself in it, she was struck at the alteration in its appearance. The iron bedstead and the washing utensils were completely hidden by drapery curtains of dark blue denim, beautifully embroidered in white floss; a cover of the same material was thrown over the small table between the windows; plain white muslin draperies hid the unsightly but serviceable yellow shades at the windows; her desk and typewriter occupied the center of the room, and a couch had been improvised from two packing cases and a spring, covered with denim and piled high with cushions; two good steel engravings completed a very inviting interior.

"How pretty you have made it," observed Dora, looking curiously around the room.

Sappho came and stood beside her, and the two girls smiled at each other in a glow of mutual interest, and became fast friends at once.

"I always carry these things with me in my travels, and I find that I can make myself very comfortable in a short time with their help."

"I wish you would show me how to do this embroidery," said Dora, as she lifted the edge of the denim curtain before the toilet stand and critically examined it. "This is beautifully done. Where did you learn?"

37

"I will teach you with pleasure," replied Sappho; but Dora noticed that she did not tell her where she had learned.

"Do you like your work—is it hard?" asked Dora, as she idly wandered from one object to another in the pretty room, pausing beside the desk to glance admiringly at a pile of neatly written sheets, just taken from the machine.

"Oh, I like the work very well. Sometimes the dictator is obtuse, or long-winded, or thinks that the writer ought to do his thinking for him as well as the corrections; then it is not pleasant work. But, generally speaking, I prefer it to most anything that I know of. Do sit down," she continued, pushing a chair toward Dora.

"This man received sinners," read Dora from a pamphlet on the desk, as she turned to accept the offered chair. "I see that is your illuminated text for the day. Are you a Christian?" Then she saw an ivory crucifix suspended at the left side of the desk, and stopped in some confusion. Sappho dropped the dress she was mending, and for a moment her eyes took on the far away look of one in deep thought. Finally she said: "I saw you glance at the crucifix. I am not a Catholic, but I have received many benefits and kindnesses at their hands. Your question is a hard one to answer. I am afraid I am not a Christian, as we of our race understand the expression, but I try to do the best I can. For my part, I am sick of loud professions and constant hypocrisy. My religion is short, and to the point—feed the starving thief and make him an honest man; cover your friend's faults with the mantle of charity and keep her in the path of virtue."

"Then you are not one of those who think that a woman should be condemned to eternal banishment for the sake of one mistake?"

"Not I, indeed; I have always felt a great curiosity to know the reason why each individual woman loses character and standing in the eyes of the world. I believe that we would hang our heads in shame at having the temerity to judge a fallen sister, could we but know the circumstances attending many such cases. And, after all we may do or say," continued the girl softly, "the best of us, who have lived the purest lives on earth that mortal can conceive, find at last that our only hope lies in the words of the text: 'This man received sinners.' "

"You are a dear little preacher," said Sappho gently, as she looked at Dora from two wet eyes; "and if our race ever amounts to anything in this world, it will be because such women as you are raised up to save us."

Dora laughed and said, as she rose from her seat: "I think I am forgetting my errand." And making an elaborate bow, she continued: "If it please your royal highness, I present to you the compliments of the occupants of 500 D Street, with the request that you will honor us on Sunday evening, at half after seven, in the parlor of the worthy landlady of said house, where an informal reception will be held to further the better acquaintance of Miss Sappho Clark with her fellow occupants of said house. Music during the evening. Refreshments at nine sharp; after which, you are all expected to retire to your rooms like virtuous citizens."

"I herewith most gratefully accept your kind invitation," replied Sappho, with a deep courtesy.

"Until Sunday night then. I shall not see you before that. I shall be lost for the remainder of the week getting ready for company," and Dora, with a gay laugh, ran lightly down the stairs.

Mrs Smith, after many trials, found that her house contained respectable though unlettered people, who possessed kindly hearts and honesty of purpose in a greater degree than one generally finds in a lodging house. Her great desire, then, was to make them as happy together as possible, and to this end she had Dora institute musical evenings or reception nights, that her tenants might have a better opportunity of becoming acquainted with each other. She argued, logically enough, that those who were inclined to stray from right paths would be influenced either in favor of upright conduct or else shamed into an acceptance of the right. It soon became noised about that very pleasant times were enjoyed in that house; and that a sick lodger had been nursed back to health instead of being hustled into the hospital ambulance at the first sign of sickness. It was also whispered that to enjoy these privileges one must be "pretty nice," or as some expressed it: "You've got to be high toned to get in there." The result, however, justified Mrs Smith's judgment, and rooms were always hard to get at 500 D Street.

Saturday was a busy day for Dora and her mother. At these little gatherings Mrs Smith always gave her guests plenty of good homemade cake, sandwiches, hot chocolate, and on very special occasions, ice cream or sherbet. Sunday night there was to be ice cream in honor of the new lodger. "Good things to eat," said Ma Smith, as she industriously beat eggs, sugar and butter together in a large yellow bowl, "good things to eat make a man respect himself and look up in the world. You can't feel that you are nobody all the time if once in a while you eat the same quality of food that a millionaire does."

Dora lighted the lamps all over the house on Sunday night as soon as it fell dark. In the parlor there was a handsome piano lamp, which was only used on special occasions; it was lighted, and threw a soft, warm glow over the neat woollen carpet, the modest furniture and few ornaments. In a corner stood Dora's piano, given her on her sixteenth birthday by her brother. Very soon after seven o'clock the guests began to drop in; and as Dora and her mother were busy still over a few last preparations, Will and John volunteered to act as the reception committee.

The first comers were the two occupants of the basement rooms—those which would have answered for the dining room and kitchen of a moderately well-to-do family living in this class of house. Mrs Ophelia Davis and Mrs Sarah Ann White were friends of long standing. They were both born in faraway Louisiana, had been raised on neighboring plantations, and together had sought the blessings of liberty in the North at the close of the war. Mrs Davis had always been a first class cook, while Mrs White tempted fortune as a second girl. As their ideas of life and living enlarged, and they saw the possibilities of enjoying some comfort in a home, they began to think of establishing themselves where they could realise this blessing, and finally hit upon the idea of going into partnership in a laundry. After looking about them for a suitable situation for such a project, their choice finally fell upon Mrs Smith's house, because of her known respectability, and because they could there come into contact with brighter intellects than their own; for, strange to say, it is a very hopeless case when a colored man or woman does not respect intelligence and good position.

"Yes, Sister Smith," said Mrs Ophelia Davis the day she and Sarah Ann White went to engage the rooms; "yes, I'm tired of living in white folkses' kitchens. Yes, that's lots of talk 'bout servant gals not being as good as anybody else, specially cooks. Yes, I can get my five dollars a week with anyone; but if you put on a decent dress to go to church with on a Sunday afternoon, the mistress is wondering how you can afford such style and you nothing but a cook in her kitchen. Yes, I've got a silk dress, two of them, and a lace shawl and a gold watch and chain. People wants to know how I get them. I come by them honest, I did. Yes, when my old mistress left her great big house and all that good stuff—silver and things—a-laying there for anyone to pick up that had sense enough to know a good thing and get it ahead of anybody else, I just said to myself: 'Phelia, chile, now's your time!' Yes, I feathered my nest, I just did. Sarah Ann, you remember that time, honey, and how scared we were for fear some of them Union soldiers would catch us. You stuffed yourself with greenbacks, but, honey, I took those, too."

"Bless God, Sister 'Phelia," replied her friend, with a chuckle and a great shaking of her fat sides; "bless God, I forget how much I did took in that pile; but Lord love you, honey, I'se got some of that money yet."

The two women engaged the rooms and prospered in their enterprise. The clothes under their deft fingers seemed to gain an added prettiness. They became the style; and no young bride on the Back Bay felt that she was complete unless 'The First class New Orleans Laundry' placed the finishing polish on the dainty lingerie of her wedding finery.

Tonight Mrs Davis wore the famous black silk dress and gold watch

40

and chain of ante bellum days, and Mrs White was gay in a bright blue silk skirt and rose-colored silk blouse. She said that she did not believe in any of your gloomy colours; for her part, she'd be dead soon enough and have a long time enough to stay 'mouldering' into clay, without burying herself before it was time. The next arrival was the young student preacher from the 'first square back'. He was due at a prayer meeting, but when the time came for him to go there, he peeped over the banister and caught sight of Dora flitting back and forth in the entries, and then a whiff of Ma Smith's famous white cake was borne temptingly to his nostrils and banished the last scruple. He satisfied his conscience by hugging to his breast the idea that his presence was necessary to give the festivities the religious air which was needed for Sunday evening. In his Prince Albert coat and high white stock and tie he entered the parlor early, so that proper decorum might be maintained. Two dressmakers from the 'second front and back' now appeared and were made very welcome by the family; and then Sappho entered.

Her dress was plain black, with white chiffon at the neck and wrists, and on her breast a large bunch of "Jack" roses was fastened. With modest self-possession she moved to Mrs Smith's side, and soon found herself being presented to the occupants of the parlor. For a moment or two there was an unbroken hush in the room. Tall and fair, with hair of a golden cast, aquiline nose, rosebud mouth, soft brown eyes veiled by long, dark lashes which swept her cheek, just now covered with a delicate rose flush, she burst upon them—a combination of "queen rose and lily in one."

"Lord," said Ophelia Davis to her friend Sarah Ann, "I haven't see anything look like that child since I left home."

"That's the truth, 'Phelia," replied Sarah Ann; "that's something God made, honey; that ain't nothing like that grew outside of Louisiana."

"Miss Clark," said Mr. Davis, during a lull in the conversation, "I presume you're from Louisiana?"

"My mother was born in New Orleans," replied the girl.

"I knowed it," cried Mrs White, as she triumphantly glanced around the room. "Old New Orleans blood will tell on itself anywhere. These cool-blooded Yankees can't raise nothing that looks like that child; no, indeed!"

Two or three of the young friends of the family who lived in the neighborhood had now arrived, and the conversation became very animated. Then it was announced that a literary and musical programme had been provided. Dora played an opening piece, which was a melody of Moody and Sankey hymns; Will sang Palm Branches in a musical baritone voice; John contributed a poem, and two young friends gave the duet from Il Trovatore. After a little persuasion Sappho rendered the

'Chariot Race' from Ben Hur in true dramatic style, and breathing so much of the stage that the Rev. Tommy James, the young theologian, felt that possibly he might have made a mistake in going into such hilarious company on the Sabbath.

"Now," said Mrs Ophelia Davis, "I'm going to sing 'Swanee River.' None of you high faluting things can teach that song. "Dora accompanied her, and soon the air was filled with Mrs Davis' ambitious attempts to imitate an operatic artist singing that good old-time song. With much wheezing and puffing—for the singer was neither slender nor young—and many would-be fascinating jumps and groans, presumed to be trills and runs, she finished, to the relief of the company. Her friend, Mrs White, looked at her with great approval, and immediately informed them that 'Phelia made a great impression the Sunday before at Tremont Temple.

"The whole congregation was to sing Where's My Wondering Boy. 'Phelia had no paper to see the words—not as that made any matter, because 'Phelia can't read nohow—and the gentleman next us on the other side, he gave 'Phelia a paper that he had. The man wanted to be polite. Well, 'Phelia was that flattered that she just let herself go, and that man never sung another note, he was so surprised. After the second verse 'Phelia saw the distraction she was making, and she says to me, says she: 'How's That, Sarah Ann?' and I says to her: 'That's out of sight, 'Phelia' You just ought to see them white folks look! They was paralysed! Why, you could hear 'Phelia clean above the organ!" Meantime the young people in the room had gathered in a little knot, and were discussing many questions of the day and their effect upon the colored people. During a pause in the music the last remark made by John Langley was distinctly heard: "Yes, I must admit that our people are improving in their dress, in their looks and in their manners."

"What's that, John Langley?" asked Mrs Davis, as she leaned forward to catch the words of the speaker, "colored people improving in their manners? I should think they was! Don't you fool yourself 'bout that, now, will you? The other night Sarah Ann and me was going down to Beacon Street to 'liver some goods, and the car was crowded with people, and there was a pile of young colored folks on it from the West End. Some of them was standing up in the car, and every once in a while I noticed that a passenger squirm as if something had hit him. Finally I got so mad I just couldn't see along with such antics from them critters disgracing themselves and the whole of the rest of the colored population, and I just elbowed myself into that crowd of young jades or was they gals? Yes, they was young jades every one of them! Now what do you think they was doing?" she asked, as she swept her gaze over the company.

"Not being a mind reader, I wouldn't dare to say," replied John Langley, with a grin of delight.

"They was a-tramping onto the feet of every white man and woman to show the white folks how free they was. I just took my umbrella and knocked it into two or three of them that I knowed, and told them I'd tell their mothers. Improving in their manners I should think they was!"

At this moment refreshments were served, and the attention of the company was turned to the wants of the inner man.

Dora had placed a pretty little tea table at one side of the room, and Sappho had promised to pour the tea and chocolate. At a sign from Mrs Smith she took her place, and soon the steaming beverage was cheering the hearts of the guests. The young men vied with each other in serving her. The tea table became the center of attraction, in fact, for the whole room. Even the divinity student was drawn into the magic circle, and divided his attention between Sappho and Mrs Ophelia Davis, for whom he seemed to have a very tender regard.

The girl was naturally buoyant and bright, and the influence of the pleasant company in which she found herself seemed to inspire her, and yet no man would have overstepped the bounds of propriety with her in his manner. The pleasant word and jest were free from all coquetry. John was dumb before so much beauty and wit. Will was so blinded by her charms that he was scarcely conscious of what he was doing; but not a word or movement of hers was lost to him.

Dora watched the tea table smilingly. She loved to see her friends enjoy themselves. It never occurred to her to be jealous of the attention given Sappho by her brother and John Langley.

Presently there were many pleasant compliments passed on the enjoyable evening which had so quickly flown, and each gentleman proposed a toast, which was drunk in a cup of hot chocolate; and as the clock struck ten, they all joined hands and united in singing "Auld Lang Syne" and "Praise God, from Whom All Blessings Flow." The evening was over; the lights were out; but up in John's attic chamber the two young men smoked a social cigar before separating for the night.

They were silent for some time, and then Will said: "Miss Clark is a very beautiful woman; don't you think so, John?"

"Well," replied John, "beauty is not the word to describe her. She's a stunner, and no mistake,"

John went to bed; but Will sat by the fire a longer time than usual, thinking thoughts which had never before troubled his young manhood; and. unconsciously, one face—the face of Sappho Clark—formed the background of his thoughts.

CHAPTER 7

After that evening the two girls were much together. Sappho's beauty appealed strongly to Dora's artistic nature; but hidden beneath the classic outlines of the face, the graceful symmetry of the form, and the dainty coloring of the skin, Dora's shrewd common sense and womanly intuition discovered a character of sterling worth—bold, strong and ennobling; while into Sappho's lonely self-suppressed life the energetic little Yankee girl swept like a healthful, strengthening breeze. Care was forgotten; there was new joy in living. It was the Southern girl's first experience of Northern life. True, the seductive skies of her nativity had a potent hold upon her affections, but truth demanded her to recognise the superiority of the vigorous activity in the life all about her. The Negro, while held in contempt by many, yet reflected the spirit of his surroundings in his upright carriage, his fearlessness in advancing his opinions, his self-reliance, his anxiety to obtain paying employment that would give to his family some few of the advantages enjoyed by the more favored classes of citizens, his love of liberty, which in its intensity recalled the memory of New England men who had counted all worldly gain as nothing if demanding the sacrifice of even one of the great principles of freedom. It was a new view of the possibilities and probabilities which the future might open to her people. Long, she struggled with thoughts which represented to her but vaguely a life beyond anything of which she had ever dreamed.

Sappho generally carried her work home in the morning, but ten o'clock would find her seated at her desk and ready to begin her task anew. Some days she was unoccupied; but this did not happen very frequently. These free days were the gala days of her existence, when under Dora's guidance she explored various points of interest, and learned from observation the great plan of life as practiced in an intelligent, liberty-loving community. Here in the free air of New England's freest city, Sappho drank great draughts of freedom's subtle elixir. Dora was interested and amused in watching the changes on the mirror-like face of her friend whenever her attention was arrested by a new phenomenon. It was strange to see this girl, resembling nothing so much as a lily in its beautiful purity, shrink from entering a place of public resort for fear of insult. It was difficult to convince her that she might enter a restaurant frequented by educated whites and meet with nothing but the greatest courtesy; that she might take part in the glorious service at fashionable

Trinity and be received with punctilious politeness. To this woman, denied association with the vast sources of information, which are heirlooms to the lowliest inhabitant of Boston, the noble piles, which represented the halls of learning, and the massive grandeur of the library, free to all, seemed to invite her to a full participation in their intellectual joys. She had seen nothing like them. Statuary, paintings, sculptures—all appealed to her beauty-loving nature. The hidden springs of spirituality were satisfied and at rest, claiming kinship with the great minds of the past, whose never-dying works breathed perennial life in the atmosphere of the quiet halls.

Now was the beginning of the storm season in New England, and on stormy days the two girls would sit before the fire in Sappho's room and talk of the many things dear to women, while they embroidered or stitched. So they sat one cold, snowy day. The storm had started the afternoon before and had raged with unceasing fury all night—snow and rain which the increasing cold quickly turned into cutting sleet. Morning had brought relief from the high winds, and the temperature had moderated somewhat; but the snow still fell steadily, drifting into huge piles, which made the streets impossible. It was the first great storm Sappho had seen. It was impossible for her to leave home, so she begged Dora to pass the day with her and play "company," like the children. Dora was nothing loathe; and as soon as her morning duties were finished, she told her mother that she was going visiting and would not be at home until tea time. By eleven o'clock they had locked the door of Sappho's room to keep out all intruders, had mended the fire until the little stove gave out a delicious warmth, and had drawn the window curtains close to keep out stray currents of air. Sappho's couch was drawn close beside the stove, while Dora's small person was most cosily bestowed in her favorite rocking chair.

It was a very convenient stove that Sappho had in her room. The ornamental top could be turned back on its movable hinge, and there was a flat stove cover ready to hold any vessel and heat its contents to just the right temperature. Sappho was prouder of that stove than a daughter of Fortune would have been of the most expensive silver chafing dish. It was very near lunch time, so the top was turned back, and the little copper teakettle was beginning to sing its welcome song. Dora had placed a small, round table between the couch and the rocker. A service for two was set out in dainty china dishes, cream and sugar looking doubly tempting as it gleamed and glistened in the delicate ware. One plate was piled with thinly cut slices of bread and butter, another held slices of pink ham.

Sappho lay back among her cushions, lazily stretching her little slippered feet toward the warm stove, where the fire burned so cheerily and

45

glowed so invitingly as it shone through the isinglass door. She folded her arms above her head and turned an admiring gaze on the brown face of her friend, who swayed gently back and forth in her rocking chair, her feet on a hassock, and a scarlet afghan wrapped about her knees. Dora was telling Sappho all about her engagement to John Langley and their plans for the future.

"I think you will be happy, Dora, if you love him. All things are possible if love is the foundation stone," said Sappho, after a slight pause, as she nestled among her pillows. Dora was sitting bolt upright with the usual business-like look upon her face.

"I like him well enough to marry him, but I don't believe there's enough sentiment in me to make love a great passion, such as we read of in books. Do you believe marriage is the beautiful state it is painted by writers?"

"Why, yes," laughed Sappho; "I wouldn't believe anything else for your sake, my little brownie."

"No joking, Sappho; this is dead earnest. Don't you ever expect to marry, and don't you speculate about the pros and cons and the maybes and perhaps of the situation?" asked Dora, as she filled the cups with steaming cocoa and passed one to her friend.

"Dora, you little gourmand, what have you got in the refrigerator?" A box ingeniously nailed to the window seat outside, and filled with shelves, and having a substantial door, was the ice box, or refrigerator, where Sappho kept materials handy for a quick lunch. Dora closed the window and returned quickly to her seat, placing a glass dish on the table as she did so.

"It's only part of a cream pie that ma had left last night. I thought it would help out nicely with our lunch."

"What, again!" said Sappho significantly. "That's the fourth time this week, and here it is but Friday. You'll be as fat as a seal, and then John P. won't want you at any price. Take warning, and depart from the error of your ways before it is too late."

Dora laughed guiltily and said, as she drew a box from her apron pocket: "Well, here are John's chocolate bonbons that he brought last night. I suppose you won't want me to touch them, for fear of getting fat."

Sappho shook her head in mock despair. "And your teeth, your beautiful white teeth, where will they be shortly if you persist in eating a pound of bonbons every day? Think of your fate, Dora, and pause in your reckless career—forty inches about the waist and only scraggy snags to show me when you grin!"

"Thank heaven I'll never come to that while there's a dentist in the city of Boston! I'll eat all the bonbons I want in spite of you, Sappho, and if you don't hurry I'll eat your slice of cream pie, too." At this dire threat there ensued a scramble for the pie, mingled with peals of merry laughter, until all rosy and sparkling, Sappho emerged from the fray with the dish containing her share of the dainty held high in the air.

Presently lunch was over, and they resumed their old positions, prepared to "take comfort."

"You haven't answered my question yet, Sappho."

"To tell you the truth, I had forgotten your remark, Dora; what was it?"

"I suspect that is a bit of a fib to keep me from teasing you about getting married. What I want to know is: Do you ever mean to marry, or are you going to pine in single blessedness on my hands and be a bachelor-maid to the end?"

"Well," replied Sappho, with a comical twist to her face, "in the words of Uncle Gulliver, 'I might, and then again I might not'."

"What troubles me is having a man bothering around. Now I tell John P. that I'm busy, or something like that, and I'm rid of him; but after you marry a man, he's on your hands for good and all. I'm wondering if my love could stand the test."

"That's queer talk for an engaged girl, with a fine, handsome fellow to court her. Why, Dora, I'm surprised at you!" laughed Sappho gaily.

"I'm not ashamed of John P.'s appearance in company; he looks all right; but when one is terribly in love one is supposed to want the dear object always near; but matches—love matches—my child, turn out so badly that a girl hesitates to get joined to any man for better or worse, as Dr Peters says. Then I get tired of a man so soon!" She sighed. "I dread to think of being tied to John for good and all; I know I'll be sick of him inside of a week. I do despair of ever being like other girls."

Sappho laughed outright at the woe-begone countenance before her.

"It is generally the other way: the men get tired of us first. A woman loves one man, and is true to him through all eternity."

"That's just what makes me feel so unsexed, so to speak, I like John's looks. He's the style among all the girls in our set. I like to know that I can claim him before them all. It's fun to see them fluttering around him, kindly trying to put my nose out of joint. I must say that I feel real comfortable to spoil sport by walking off with him just when they think they've got things running as they wish. Yes, it's real comfortable to know that they're all as jealous as can be. But for all that, I know I'll get tired of him."

"Let us hope not, if you have really made up your mind to marry him. Dora, sometimes I am afraid that you mean what you say. I notice that you call him 'John P.' What's the P for?"

"Pollock—John Pollock Langley. His grandfather was his father's master, and Pollock was his name," sang Dora, as she rocked gently to and fro. "Now, there's Arthur Lewis," she continued; "he's jolly fun. He isn't a fascinator, or anything of that sort; he's just good."

"Who is he?" asked Sappho, with languid interest.

"Properly speaking, he's Dr Arthur Lewis. We were children together, although he is five years older than I. He's a fine scholar and a great business man. He has a large industrial school in Louisiana. He's gone up in the world, I tell you, since we made mud pies on the back doorsteps; but I never think of him except as old Arthur, who used to drag me to school on his sled."

There was a gleam of fun in Sappho's eyes, as she said demurely: "You seem to know all about him. Was he ever a lover of yours?"

"Lover! no, indeed!" Dora flushed vividly under her brown skin. "The idea of Arthur as my lover is too absurd."

"Excuse me, dear, for my mistake," said Sappho mischievously. "I didn't know but that he might be the mysterious link which would join love, marriage and the necessary man in a harmonious whole."

"Well," said Dora, after a slight pause, blushing furiously, "I don't say he wouldn't like the role. You'll see him soon; he's coming to Boston on business in a few weeks. Oh, we've had rare times together." She sighed and smiled, lost for the moment in pleasant memories. Sappho smiled, too, in sympathy with her mood.

"Ah, yes; I think I understand. Poor John!"

"John's all right. Don't shed any tears over him," said Dora testily. They sat awhile in silence, listening to the sound of the whirling frozen flakes wind-driven against the window panes. It was scarce three o'clock, but darkness was beginning to envelop the city, and it was already a pleasant twilight in the room.

"Tell me about Dr Lewis and his work, Dora," said Sappho presently. "Do you know, he interests me exceedingly."

"I don't really understand Arthur's hobbies, but I believe that he is supposed to be doing a great work in the Black Belt. His argument is, as I understand it, that industrial education and the exclusion of politics will cure all our race troubles."

"I doubt it," returned Sappho quickly, with an impatient toss of the head. "That reasoning might be practically illustrated with benefit to us for a few years in the South, but to my mind would not effect a permanent cure for race troubles if we are willing to admit that human nature is the same in us as in others. The time will come when our men will grow away from the trammels of narrow prejudice, and desire the same treatment that is accorded to other men. Why, one can but see that any degree of education and development will not fail of such a result."

"I am willing to confess that the subject is a little deep for me," replied

Dora. "I'm not the least bit of a politician, and I generally accept whatever the men tell me as right; but I know that there is something very wrong in our lives, and nothing seems to remedy the evils under which the colored man labors."

"But you can see, can't you, that if our men are deprived of the franchise, we become aliens in the very land of our birth?"

"Arthur says that would be better for us; the great loss of life would cease, and we should be at peace with the whites."

"Ah, how can he argue so falsely! I have lived beneath the system of oppression in the South. If we lose the franchise, at the same time we shall lose the respect of all other citizens. Temporising will not benefit us; rather, it will leave us branded as cowards, not worthy a freeman's respect—an alien people, without a country and without a home."

Dora gazed at her friend with admiration, and wished that she had a kodak, so that she might catch just the expression that lighted her eyes and glowed in a bright color Upon her cheeks.

"I predict some fun when you and Arthur meet. I'll just start you both out some night, and you'll be spitting at each other like two cats inside of five minutes. Arthur thinks that women should be seen and not heard, where politics is under discussion."

"Insufferable prig!" exclaimed Sappho, with snapping eyes.

"Oh, no, he isn't; Arthur's all right. But you see he is living South; his work is there, and he must keep in with the whites of the section where his work lies, or all he has accomplished will go for naught, and perhaps his life might be forfeited, too."

"I see. The mess of pottage and the birthright."

"Bless you! not so bad as that; but money makes the mare go," returned Dora, with a wink at her friend, and a shrewd business look on her bright little Yankee face. "I say to you, as Arthur says to me when I tell him what I think of his system: 'If you want honey, you must have money.' I don't know anything about politics, as I said before, but my opinion won't cost you anything: when we can say that lots of our men are as rich as Jews, there'll be no question about the franchise, and my idea is that Arthur'll be one of the Jews."

"Oh!" exclaimed Sappho disgustedly, as she resumed her lounging position.

"Sappho, how did you come to take up stenography? I should have thought you would have preferred teaching."

"I had to live my dear; I could not teach school, because my education does not include a college course. I could not do housework, because my constitution is naturally weak."

It was noticeable in these confidential chats that Sappho never spoke of her early life. Dora had confided to her friend every event of importance that had occurred in her young life; and, in harmless gossip, had related the history of all the friends who visited the house intimately; but all this had begot no like unburdening to eager ears of the early history of her friend. Wonderful to relate, however, Dora did not resent this reserve, which she could see was studied. It spoke well for the sincerity of the love that had taken root in her heart for Sappho, that it subdued her inquisitiveness, and she gladly accepted her friendship without asking troublesome questions.

"How did you finally succeed in getting work? I have always heard that it was very difficult for colored girls to find employment in offices where your class of work is required."

"And so it is, my dear. I sometimes think that if I lose the work I am on, I shall not try for another position. I shall never forget the day I started out to find work: the first place that I visited was all right until the man found I was colored; then he said that his wife wanted a nurse girl, and he had no doubt she would be glad to hire me, for I looked good-tempered. At the second place where I ventured to intrude the proprietor said: 'Yes; we want a stenographer, but we've no work for your kind.' However, that was preferable to the insulting familiarity which some men assumed. It was dreadful! I don't like to think about it. Father Andrew induced the man for whom I am working to employ me. I do not interfere with the other help, because I take my work home; many of the other clerks have never seen me, and so the proprietor runs no risk of being bothered with complaints from them. He treats me very well, too."

"I have heard many girls tell much the same tale about other lines of business," said Dora. "It makes me content to do the work of this house, and not complain."

"You ought to thank God every day for such a refuge as you have in your home."

"I cannot understand people. Here in the North we are allowed every privilege. There seems to be no prejudice until we seek employment; then every door is closed against us. Can you explain this?"

"No, I cannot, to my way of thinking the whole thing is a Chinese puzzle."

"Bless my soul! Just look at that clock!" exclaimed Dora, as she scrambled to her feet and began gathering up her scattered property. "Five o'clock, and tea to get. Sappho, you've been lazy enough for one day. Come downstairs and help me get tea. The boys will be here in no time, as hungry as bears."

Piloted by Dora, Sappho became well acquainted with ancient landmarks of peculiar interest to the colored people. They visited the home for aged women on M—Street, and read and sang to the occupants. They visited St. Monica's Hospital, and carried clothes, flowers, and a little money saved from the cost of contemplated Easter finery. They scattered brightness along with charitable acts wherever a case of want was brought to their attention.

Dora had accepted the position of organist for a prominent colored church in the city. There was a small salary attached to the place, which she was glad to receive. Sappho usually went with her to choir rehearsals, and sitting in the shadows, well hidden from view, would think over the romantic history of the fine old edifice. The building, so the story ran, was the place of worship of a rich, white Baptist congregation in the years preceding the emancipation. Negroes were allowed in the galleries only. Believing this color-bar to be a stigma on the house of God, a few of the members protested, but finding their warnings unheeded, withdrew from the church, and finally found a Sabbath home in an old building long used as a theatre. These people prospered, and grew rich and powerful; colored people were always welcome in the congregation. The society in the old church, left to itself, had at last been glad to sell the building to its present occupants. Thus the despised people, who were not allowed a seat outside of the galleries, now owned and occupied the scene of their former humiliation. It was a solemn and wonderful dispensation of Providence, and filled the girl's heart with strong emotion.

During these evenings, when she waited for the close of the rehearsals, she became acquainted with many odd specimens of the race: men of brain and thought, but of unique expression and filled with quaint humor. One of these characters was known as Dr Abraham Peters. Dr Peters was a well-read man, greatly interested in scientific research, but who had lacked the opportunity to obtain information in his youth. He had been a slave when a boy, a few years before the Civil War. Now he was the church janitor, and to eke out his scanty income kept a little bootblack stand just around the corner from the church, and knowing something of medicine and nursing the sick, had advertised himself as a magnetic physician. He displayed much skill in practice, and had acquired something of a local reputation. Dr Peters and Sappho were good friends, and he brought out all his store of knowledge, proudly displaying it for her approval.

"You see, Miss Sappho, I've knocked 'bout the world some considerable," he said one night, in his soft Southern tones and quaint Northernised dialect, as they sat in the cosy vestry waiting for the close of the rehearsal. "Being poorer than any church mouse. But I've saved something, and I know the world. Perhaps you's interested enough in an old man to want to hear how I come to advertise myself as a magnifying doctor, and where I picked it up, eh?"

"Yes," replied Sappho, "I certainly am interested in your story."

51

"Well, while they're caterwauling on that Easter anthem in ten flats, I reckon I'll have time to tell you all 'bout it. First I knowed 'bout magnetics was brought to my attention down home. Some people said I had the evil eye, and some said it was only a strong eye, but be that whomsoever, it was a bad eye, and a terror to thieves when it was my watch on the chicken houses. Magnifying and voodooing is 'bout the same thing down that tho' sense the 'surrender most all old-time doings is done 'way. 'Bout the time I realised that I had this power I had experienced religion, and had been justified and concentrated, so that I got the blessing. Them days, too, I was setting out to court my Susie (that's my wife), and all the young fellas 'round the county was approaching up to her just like crows round carry on. Sunday was the day I had most on my mind, 'cause they'd ride up and hitch their mules in a line all along the old man's fence (you see he had right smart property, and I suspect it was a mighty drawing influence on some of them shiftless fellas who hadn't enough skonsh to get their own mule team up a hill), an' that they'd sot like so many buzzards, waiting for a chance to sly Susie off to church under my nose. I had to work lively, I tell you; Susie was kind of skittish and restless, and it was first come, first served, with her, being she had her choice. Well, just at the time I got the blessing I got the insurance that Susie was going to have me. All the fellas was satisfied but Possum Tooit. Possum and me was boys together, and we'd both run each other pretty hard striving to come through first at the mourner's bench as well as to get the gal. Possum was beat when he found I had a full hand and had swept the pot."

"Oomhoo!" laughed Brother Jones, who was an interested listener to Dr Peters' story. "Oomhoo, Brother Peters; done gave yourself away. What you know 'bout full hands an' pots?"

"Who give himself away, Brother Jones? Ever hear me say, Is bettering anybody else in this church? I'm a man, sir, I'm a man! I done trespassed on the fleshpots of Egypt as much as any other man. Don't you 'oomhoo' me, Brother Jones, no sir!"

"Teach a sore place, Brother Peters, teach a sore place," laughed the brother as he walked away, his shoulders shaking like great mounds of jelly. It was some minutes before Dr Peters could recover his equilibrium and go on with his tale.

"Possum Tooit was so mad and disappointed that he finally challenged me to fight a jewel. I wasn't in no state of mind to be killed by any of his voodoo tricks, Possum being an export at putting spells and such like on anybody for from twenty-five cents up to five dollars; neither did I want Susie to think I was afraid of Possum Tooit. So that I was between a hawk an' a buzzard. Well, I accepted the challenge, and being the defendant in the matter, of course, I had the choice of weapons, and I choose rifles. We keep mighty secret 'bout the 'arrangements, and met at moonrise on a field just back of the graveyard. The seconds measured off ten spaces after we'd shaken hands, and we each stepped to our places. Though it was a solemn occasion, I wasn't scared, but Possum was a rolling up the whites of his eyes, and you could hear his teeth chatter worse than dried corn shuks. Ike Watkins was head second, and he stood between us, holding his red bandanna in his hand waiting to say the word. 'Gentlemen, is you ready?' he says. 'Let her go, Ike,' says I. 'Take aim,' says he, an' I pointed the rifle at Possum, and calling up all the power in me I threw it along the body of the gun plumb 'between Possum's eyes just above the bridge of his nose. And that was a fair target, because the bridge of Possum's nose was a miracle for size. Possum gave a yell when he felt the strength of that eye, that would a split your year-pan in two. And in two seconds he was in the worst alpaca fit you ever seen. The seconds acknowledged me the victor by a reckless invention of Providence, they being aware that the adversary wasn't hit by nary bullet, the rifles being loaded with salt for fear of mischief. Possum owned up like a man that I was more powerful than him, because of the supernatural strength in my bad eye.

"Well, I keep on praying for more faith until I got the power in my hands, and by laying them on a sick person I could 'electrocute' him instantly, and that bad feelings would disappear. People got the notion I could pray a person right out the grave, and my fame spread abroad until I began charging for my services, explaining to my patients that the dead might be raised, but not for nothing, after which I seed a falling off in my popularity. Business being pretty brief just then, I took Susie and moved up North, and went to cooking on a steamboat. I've done almost everything in this world, honey, as I told you, to get an honest living without stealing it. An' I do know," added the old man reflectively, as he stroked the grey, stubby fringe on his chin,"I do know as I'm any too good if I got pushed real hard to help myself out; humans is humans, an' I've seen many a well-intentioned fella sitting in the caboose when times was hard, and the mule mortgaged for full value to three men at once to buy meal and bread, and hog and hominy, and tobacco. But most in generally, I've got along without soiling my hands with other people's property. Well, honey, they gave me fifteen dollars a month and found, for being head cook, and I paid ten dollars a month house rent out of that. Things was pretty brief, pretty brief. Times was more and more spurious, and it was work your wits, Abraham Peters, to get a living. I just didn't know which way to turn.

"One day I got a telegraph at the other end of the route that the baby was dead and no money to pay the undertaker, and the old woman sick in the bed from worrying. The Lord just seemed to pour his blessing

53

down on us in a house full of children. After Susie'd had twenty I used to pray the Lord to stop blessing us that way, because he could see for himself that too many blessings was a getting to be a nuisance. I cooked the dinner myself that day, being the other cook was ashore, and you believe me, I sung and I prayed and I wrestled for help in that old steamboat kitchen down behind my biggest brass boiler where I was covered from prying eyes. All of a sudden I felt the power, and the Lord spoke to me and he said: 'Get up, Abraham Peters, and go out and voodoo the first man you meet.' Bless you, child, I rise up in a hurry and started out, not knowing no more than nothing what was meant by that. First man I saw when I got on deck was the captain; I went up to him, and I smiled. I must have been a pretty picture with my face all grease an' tears. I says, not thinking what words I was going to utter: 'Morning, Captain; how's your corporosity seem to segashiate?' Captain he roared; you could a heard him holler up to Boston. He slapped me on the back, and says he: 'Abe Peters, that's the darndest thing I ever heard.' With that he hauled out a five dollar bill an' gave me, an' walked off laughing fit to kill himself. By night I had twenty dollars in my pocket, and everybody on the boat was a calling me 'corporosity segashiate.' I've used that voodoo ever since, and I ain't found any white gentleman can seem to get away from it without showing the color of his money.

"One of the owners of the boat took a great liking to me, and he says to me one day, says he: 'Abe, how'd you like to work ashore so you could be nearer your family an' get better pay?' 'I like it?' says I. 'If you don't want to pulverise me, don't make me no such an offer.' He laughed a bit, and then he says: 'I've got a big building up Washington Street, and I want a trustee man to keep it, clean an' look after the tenants. I'll give you ten dollars a week.'

"I took off my cap, and I truly bowed down to that man, and I says: 'The Lord's been a working on your heart, Mr Pierson.' 'Maybe he has,' says he; 'anyhow, you can pack up and go ashore next trip; your place'll be waiting for you.' First thing I knowed I was a bossing a big job of janitorin'. Most of the people in the building was Christian Science. After they'd got a little bit acquainted with me they found out the power I had in my hands for laying on. Don't suppose you know much 'bout this Science business, do you?"

Sappho confessed her ignorance.

"Christian Science is a faith cure; that is, it's using your brains and training him to know that there's nothing 'tall the matter with you if you only think there ain't. They argue that all sickness is a mistake, because it's imaginary. I don't believe that, though, because I had the rheumatism while I was there, and the doctors started into cure me by praying and working on my body through my spirit, an' it weren't no more good than nothing 'tall. I've got as much faith as any living man, but rheumatism is one of them things that'll convince you against your will; it will draw speech out of a deaf mute and make a blind man see, when them pains is a grinding enter your bones and its worse than a saw cutting through knots in a cord wood stick. I'm free to say that curing my mind didn't have no effect on my pain, an' I just keep on seeing blue blazes and swearing like mad. I'll allow that faith can move mountains. If you believe you'll get what you wants and asks for, that's faith. That's good; that's all right. Trouble is we don't believe it according to scripture. We get mad when our prayers ain't answered, not thinking it's because we ain't got horse sense enough to use discretion in putting our faith on subjects that is approving to the Lord, and will fit in with his own ideas 'bout running the business of the universe. And that's where faith cure is weak, 'cause it's coming in 'junction with God. Faith cure won't operate on any man where it was pre-ordinated that a particular man was to die with a particular complaint. We ain't up to coming in conjunction with the Lord's business. There's a number of grand diversions to Christian Science. There's hypnotism and pessimism and a number of other isms, but they all bear the same way. The doctors kept after me 'bout my gifts of healing, and very kindly showed me wherein I could make an honest dollar, and business being business I finally determined to adopt magnifying as a perfection. I've been in the business nigh upon ten years now, an' I've picked up as good a living as any colored gentleman who has worked a sight harder and had to take piles of unregenerate sass from his boss."

That night they walked home together after the rehearsal: the four young people—Dora and John, Sappho and Will. Someone of the choir boys walking ahead of them was singing in a sweet, high tenor voice the refrain of an old love song: "Couldst thou but know how much I love you." It suited Will's mood, and voiced his dream exquisitely. Across the heavens the Northern Lights streamed in radiance. Meteors bright and shooting stars added to the beauty of the night. The moon, at its full, shed the light of day about them. The wind whispered amidst the leafless branches of the huge old trees on the Common and Public Garden as they passed them on their homeward way. Once Will took her hand in his; she let it stay a moment while she made an incoherent little speech about clouds and trees. Will said nothing. It was not time yet, he told himself. He would wait a little longer.

CHAPTER 8

Ma Smith was a member of the church referred to in the last chapter, the most prominent one of color in New England. It was situated in the heart of the West End, and was a very valuable piece of property. Every winter this church gave many entertainments to aid in paying off the mortgage, which at this time amounted to about eight thousand dollars. Mrs Smith, as the chairman of the board of stewardesses, was inaugurating a fair—one that should eclipse anything of a similar nature ever attempted by the colored people, and numerous sewing circles were being held among the members all over the city. Parlor entertainments where an admission fee of ten cents was collected from every patron, were also greatly in vogue, and the money thus obtained was put into a fund to defray the expense of purchasing eatables and decorations, and paying for the printing of tickets, circulars, etc., for the fair. The strongest forces of the colored people in the vicinity were to combine and lend their aid in making a supreme effort to clear this magnificent property.

Boston contains a number of well-to-do families of color whose tax bills show a most comfortable return each year to the city treasury. Strange as it may seem, these well-to-do people, in goodly numbers, distribute themselves and their children among the various Episcopal churches with which the city abounds, the government of which holds out the welcome hand to the brother in black, who is drawn to unite his fortunes with the members of this particular denomination. It may be true that the beautiful ritual of the church is responsible in some measure for this. Colored people are nothing if not beauty lovers, and for such a people the grandeur of the service has great attractions. But in justice to this church one must acknowledge that it has been instrumental in doing much toward helping this race to help itself, along the lines of brotherly interest.

These people were well represented within the precincts of Mrs Smith's pretty parlor one afternoon, all desirous of lending their aid to help along the great project.

As we have said, Mrs Smith occupied the back parlor of the house as her chamber, and within this room the matrons had assembled to take charge of the cutting out of different garments; and here, too, the sewing machine was placed ready for use. In the parlor proper all the young ladies were seated ready to perform any service which might be required of them in the way of putting garments together.

By two o'clock all the members of the sewing circle were in their places. The parlor was crowded. Mrs Willis, the brilliant widow of a bright Negro politician, had charge of the girls, and after the sewing had been given out the first business of the meeting was to go over events of interest to the Negro race which had transpired during the week throughout the country. These facts had been previously tabulated upon a blackboard which was placed upon an easel, and occupied a conspicuous position in the room. Each one was supposed to contribute anything of interest that she had read or heard in that time for the benefit of all. After these points had been gone over, Mrs Willis gave a talk upon some topic of interest. At six o'clock tea was to be served in the kitchen, the company taking refreshment in squads of five. At eight o'clock all unfinished work would be folded and packed away in the convenient little Boston bag, to be finished at home, and the male friends of the various ladies were expected to put in an appearance. Music and recitations were to be enjoyed for two hours, ice cream and cake being sold for the benefit of the cause.

Mrs Willis was a good example of a class of women of color that came into existence at the close of the Civil War. She was not a rare species, but one of many possibilities which the future will develop from among the colored women of New England. Every city or town from Maine to New York has its Mrs Willis. Keen in her analysis of human nature most people realised, after a short acquaintance in which they ran the gamut of emotions from strong attraction to repulsion, that she had sifted them thoroughly, while they had gained nothing in return. Shrewd in business matters, many a subtle business man had been worsted by her apparent womanly weakness and charming simplicity. With little money, she yet contrived to live in quiet elegance, even including the little journeys from place to place, so adroitly managed as to increase her influence at home and her fame abroad. Well-read and thoroughly conversant with all current topics, she impressed one as having been liberally educated and polished by travel, whereas a high school course more than covered all her opportunities.

Even today it is erroneously believed that all racial development among colored people has taken place since emancipation. It is impossible of belief for some, that little circles of educated men and women of color have existed since the Revolutionary War. Some of these people were born free, some have lost the memory of servitude in the dim past; a greater number by far were recruited from the energetic slaves of the South, who toiled when they should have slept, for the money that purchased their freedom, or else they boldly took the rights which man denied. Mrs Willis was one from among these classes. The history of her

57

descent could not be traced, but somewhere, somehow, a strain of white blood had filtered through the African stream. At sixty odd she was vigorous, well-preserved, broad and comfortable in appearance, with an aureole of white hair crowning a pleasant face.

She had loved her husband with a love ambitious for his advancement. His foot on the stairs mounting to the two-room tenement which constituted their home in the early years of married life, had sent a thrill to her very heart as she sat sewing baby clothes for the always expected addition to the family. But twenty years make a difference in all our lives. It brought many changes to the colored people of New England—social and business changes. Politics had become the open sesame for the ambitious Negro. A seat in the Legislature then was not a dream to this man, urged by the loving woman behind him. Other offices of trust were quickly offered him when his worth became known. He grasped his opportunity; grew richer, more polished, less social, and the family broadened out and overflowed from old familiar "West End" environments across the River Charles into the aristocratic suburbs of Cambridge. Death comes to us all.

Money, the sinews of living and social standing, she did not possess upon her husband's death. Therefore she was forced to begin a weary pilgrimage—a hunt for the means to help her breast the social tide. The best opening, she decided after looking carefully about her, was in the great cause of the evolution of true womanhood in the work of the 'Woman Question' as embodied in marriage and suffrage. She could talk dashingly on many themes, for which she had received much applause in bygone days, when in private life she had held forth in the drawing room of some Back Bay philanthropist who sought to use her talents as an attraction for a worthy charitable object, the discovery of a rare species of versatility in the Negro character being a sure drawing-card. It was her boast that she had made the fortunes of her family and settled her children well in life. The advancement of the colored woman should be the new problem in the woman question that should float her upon its tide into the prosperity she desired. And she succeeded well in her plans: conceived in selfishness, they yet bore glorious fruit in the formation of clubs of colored women banded together for charity, for study, for every reason under God's glorious heavens that can better the condition of mankind.

Trivialities are not to be despised. Inborn love implanted in a woman's heart for a luxurious, aesthetic home life, running on well-oiled wheels amid flowers, sunshine, books and priceless pamphlets, easy chairs and French gowns, may be the means of developing a Paderewski or freeing a race from servitude. It was amusing to watch the way in which she governed societies and held her position. In her hands com-

58

mittees were as wax, and loud murmurings against the tyranny of her rule died down to judicious whispers. If a vote went contrary to her desires, it was in her absence. Thus she became the pivot about which all the social and intellectual life of the colored people of her section revolved. No one had yet been found with the temerity to contest her position, which, like a title of nobility, bade fair to descend to her children. It was thought that she might be eclipsed by the younger and more brilliant women students on the strength of their alma mater, but she still held her own by sheer force of willpower and indomitable pluck.

The subject of the talk at this meeting was: "The place which the virtuous woman occupies in upbuilding a race." After a few explanatory remarks, Mrs Willis said:

"I am particularly anxious that you should think upon this matter seriously, because of its intrinsic value to all of us as race women. I am not less anxious because you represent the coming factors of our race. Shortly, you must fill the positions now occupied by your mothers, and it will rest with you and your children to refute the charges brought against us as to our moral irresponsibility, and the low moral standard maintained by us in comparison with other races."

"Did I understand you to say that the Negro woman in her native state is truly a virtuous woman?" asked Sappho, who had been very silent during the bustle attending the opening of the meeting.

"Travelers tell us that the native African woman is impregnable in her virtue," replied Mrs Willis.

"So we have sacrificed that attribute in order to acquire civilisation," chimed in Dora.

"No, not sacrificed," but pushed one side by the force of circumstances. Let us thank God that it is an essential attribute peculiar to us— a racial characteristic which is slumbering but not lost," replied Mrs Willis. "But let us not forget the definition of virtue—strength to do the right thing under all temptations. Our ideas of virtue are too narrow. We confine them to that conduct which is ruled by our animal passions alone. It goes deeper than that—general excellence in every duty of life is what we may call virtue."

"Do you think, then, that Negro women will be held responsible for all the lack of virtue that is being laid to their charge today? I mean, do you think that God will hold us responsible for the illegitimacy with which our race has been obliged, as it were, to flood the world?" asked Sappho.

"I believe that we shall not be held responsible for wrongs which we have unconsciously committed, or which we have committed under compulsion. We are virtuous or non-virtuous only when we have a choice under temptation.

59

"We cannot by any means apply the word to a little child who has never been exposed to temptation, nor to the Supreme Being who cannot be tempted with evil. So with the African brought to these shores against his will—the state of morality which implies willpower on his part does not exist, therefore he is not a responsible being. The sin and its punishment lies with the person consciously false to his knowledge of right. From this we deduce the truism that 'the civility of no race is perfect whilst another race is degraded'."

"I shall never forget my feelings," chimed in Anna Stevens, a school teacher of a very studious temperament, "at certain remarks made by the Rev. John Thomas at one of his noonday lectures in the Temple. He was speaking on 'Different Races', and had in his vigorous style been sweeping his audience with him at a high elevation of thought which was dazzling to the faculties, and almost impossible to follow in some points. Suddenly he touched upon the Negro, and with impressive gesture and lowered voice thanked God that the mulatto race was dying out, because it was a mongrel mixture which combined the worst elements of two races. Lo, the poor mulatto! Despised by the blacks of his own race, scorned by the whites. Let him go out and hang himself!"

In her indignation Anna forgot the scissors, and bit her thread off viciously with her little white teeth.

Mrs Willis smiled as she said calmly: "My dear Anna, I would not worry about the fate of the mulatto, for the fate of the mulatto will be the fate of the entire race. Did you never think that today the black race on this continent has developed into a race of mulattos?"

"Why, Mrs Willis!" came in a chorus of voices.

"Yes," continued Mrs Willis, still smiling. "It is an incontrovertible truth that there is no such thing as an unmixed black on the American continent. Just bear in mind that we cannot tell by a person's complexion whether he be dark or light in blood, for by the working of the natural laws the white father and black mother produce the mulatto offspring; the black father and white mother the mulatto offspring also, while the black father and quadroon mother produce the black child, which to the eye alone is a child of unmixed black blood. I will venture to say that out of a hundred apparently pure black men not one will be able to trace an unmixed flow of African blood since landing upon these shores! What an unhappy example of the frailty of all human intellects, when such a man and scholar as Dr Thomas could so far allow his prejudices to dominate his better judgment as to add one straw to the burden which is popularly supposed to rest upon the unhappy mulattos of a despised race," finished the lady, with a dangerous flash of her large dark eyes.

"Mrs Willis," said Dora, with a scornful little laugh, "I am not unhappy, and I am a mulatto. I just enjoy my life, and I don't want to die before my time comes, either. There are lots of good things left on earth to be enjoyed even by mulattos, and I want my share."

"Yes, my dear; and I hope you may all live and take comfort in the proper joys of your lives. While we are all content to accept life, and enjoy it along the lines which God has laid down for us as individuals as well as a race, we shall be happy and get the best out of life. Now, let me close this talk by asking you to remember one maxim written of your race by a good man: 'Happiness and social position are not to be gained by pushing.' Let the world, by its need of us along certain lines, and our intrinsic fitness for these lines, push us into the niche which God has prepared for us. So shall our lives be beautified and our race raised in the civilisation of the future as we grow away from all these prejudices which have been the instruments of our advancement according to the intention of an all-seeing omnipotence, from the beginning. Never mind our poverty, ignorance, and the slights and injuries which we bear at the hands of a higher race. With the thought ever before us of what the Master suffered to raise all humanity to its present degree of prosperity and intelligence, let us cultivate, while we go about our daily tasks, no matter how inferior they may seem to us, beauty of the soul and mind, which being transmitted to our children by the law of heredity, shall improve the race by eliminating immorality from our midst and raising morality and virtue to their true place. Thirty-five years of liberty have made us a new people. The marks of servitude and oppression are dropping slowly from us; let us hasten the transformation of the body by the nobility of the soul."

"Yes," said Mrs Willis with a smile, "that is the idea exactly, and well expressed. Now I hope that through the coming week you will think of what we have talked about this afternoon, for it is of the very first importance to all people, but particularly so to young folks."

Sappho, who had been thoughtfully embroidering pansies on white linen, now leaned back in her chair for a moment and said: "Mrs Willis, there is one thing which puzzles me—how are we to overcome the nature which is given us? I mean how can we eliminate passion from our lives, and emerge into the purity which marked the life of Christ? So many of us desire purity and think to have found it, but in a moment of passion, or under the pressure of circumstances which we cannot control, we commit some horrid sin, and the taint of it sticks and will not leave us, and we grow to loathe ourselves."

"Passion, my dear Miss Clark, is a state in which the will lies dormant, and all other desires become subservient to one. Enthusiasm for any one object or duty may become a passion. I believe that in some degree passion may be beneficial, but we must guard ourselves against a sinful growth of any appetite. All work of whatever character, as I look at it, needs a certain amount of absorbing interest to become successful, and it is here that the Christian life gains its greatest glory in teaching us how to keep ourselves from abusing any of our human attributes. We are not held responsible for compulsory sin, only for the sin that is pleasant to our thoughts and palatable to our appetites. All desires and hopes with which we are endowed are good in the sight of God, only it is left for us to discover their right uses. Do I cover your ground?"

"Yes and no," replied Sappho, "but perhaps at some future time you will be good enough to talk with me personally upon this subject."

"Dear child, sit here by me. It is a blessing to look at you. Beauty like yours is inspiring. You seem to be troubled; what is it? If I can comfort or strengthen, it is all I ask." She pressed the girl's hand in hers and drew her into a secluded corner. For a moment the floodgates of suppressed feeling flew open in the girl's heart, and she longed to lean her head on that motherly breast and unburden her sorrows there.

"Mrs Willis, I am troubled greatly," she said at length.

"I am so sorry; tell me, my love, what it is all about."

Just as the barriers of Sappho's reserve seemed about to be swept away, there followed, almost instantly, a wave of repulsion toward this woman and her effusiveness, so forced and insincere. Sappho was very impressionable, and yielded readily to the influence which fell like a cold shadow between them. She drew back as from an abyss suddenly beheld stretching before her.

"On second thoughts, I think I ought to correct my remarks. It is not really trouble, but more a desire to confirm me in my own ideas."

"Well, if you feel you are right, dear girl, stand for the uplifting of the race and womanhood. Do not shrink from duty."

"It was simply a thought raised by your remarks on morality. I once knew a woman who had sinned. No one in the community in which she lived knew it but herself. She married a man who would have despised her had he known her story; but as it is, she is looked upon as a pattern of virtue for all women."

"And then what?" asked Mrs Willis, with a searching glance at the fair face beside her.

"Ought she not to have told her husband before marriage? Was it not her duty to have thrown herself upon his clemency?"

"I think not," replied Mrs Willis dryly. "See here, my dear, I am a practical woman of the world, and I think your young woman builded wiser than she knew. I am of the opinion that most men are like the lower animals in many things—they don't always know what is for their best good. If the husband had been left to himself, he probably would not have married the one woman in the world best fitted to be his wife. I think in her case she did her duty."

"Ah, that word 'duty.' What is our duty?" queried the girl, with a sad droop to the sensitive mouth. "It is so hard to know our duty. We are told that all hidden things shall be revealed. Must repented and atoned for sin rise at last to be our curse?"

"Here is a point, dear girl. God does not look upon the constitution of sin as we do. His judgment is not ours; ours is finite, his infinite. Your duty is not to be morbid, thinking these thoughts that have puzzled older heads than yours. Your duty is, also, to be happy and bright for the good of those about you. Just blossom like the flowers, have faith and trust." At this point the entrance of the men made an interruption, and Mrs Willis disappeared in a crowd of other matrons. Sappho was impressed in spite of herself, by the woman's words. She sat buried in deep thought.

There was evidently more in this woman than appeared upon the surface. With all the centuries of civilisation and culture that have come to this grand old world, no man has yet been found able to trace the windings of God's inscrutable ways. There are men and women whose seeming uselessness fit perfectly into Destiny's web. All things work together for good. Supper being over, the elderly people began to leave. It was understood that after nine o'clock the night belonged to the young people. A committee had been formed from among them to plan for their enjoyment, and they consulted with Ma Smith, in the kitchen, as to the best plan of procedure.

"The case is this," said the chairman, who was also the church chorister: "Ma Smith has bought four gallons of ice cream, to be sold for the benefit of this fair. It's got to go, and it rests with us to devise ways and means of getting rid of it."

"Set up a dance," suggested Sam Washington, a young fellow who was the life of all social functions.

"Dance!" exclaimed Ma Smith, "not in this house."

The choirmaster surreptitiously kicked Sam on the shins, as he said soothingly: "Under the circumstances I see no other way, as we've got to sell the cream, and there's no harm in dancing, anyway."

"You ain't going to object to our dancing, are you, Ma? It's all old fogyism about dancing being a sin," chimed in Sam.

"Oh, but my son, I've been a church member over thirty years, a consistent Christian, and I never was up before the board for behavior unbecoming a professor. Think of the disgrace on me if the church took it up," she expostulated tearfully.

"Look here, Ma, the deacons and ministers are all fooling you. It's the style for church members to go to the theatre and the circus, to balls and everything you can mention. Why, I've seen our own pastor up to see the Black Crook, and laughing like all possessed at the sights. Fact!"

63

"Why, Samuel!" said Ma Smith, "how can you stand there and tell me such awful stories?"

"Not a bit of a story," declared the brazen-faced Sam, "it's as true as gospel. I'll find out what seat the minister gets next June when the circus comes into town, and I'll get a seat for you right behind him. If you've never been to the circus, Ma, and to see the seven-headed lady and the dancing mokes, you ought to go as soon as possible. Think of the fun you're missing."

"Oh!" groaned the good woman in holy horror, "how you do go on."

"But that ain't nothing to the ice cream," continued Sam, "and them girls in there have got to be warmed up, or the cream will be left, and there won't be a thing doing when the committee calls for the money."

"That's so," replied Ma Smith, beginning to weaken in her opposition.

"Well, mother," said Will, who had been an amused listener to the dialogue, "we'll have the dance, and it shall be my dance for my company. No one shall trouble you; you will have nothing to do with it."

"Well, if you say so, Willie, it's all right," replied his mother with a fond smile; "you are master in this house."

In the meantime the furniture in the parlors had been moved out by other members of the committee, and in one corner a set of whist players were enjoying themselves at ten cents a head for a thirty minute game, which ended at the stroke of a small silver bell, their places being taken by others.

Already it was getting very warm in the crowded rooms. The doors leading into the entry had been thrown open, and couples were finding seats in convenient nooks waiting for dancing to begin. The girls were thinking of ice cream. Rev. Tommy James gravitated toward Mrs Davis's corner. She had not gone out with the other matrons.

"I enjoy a real good time as much as anybody," she said, "and when it comes to dancing, you can't lose your Aunt Hannah."

The Reverend Tommy was always at his ease with Mrs Davis. She led him along paths which caused him no embarrassment.

He knew that she looked up to him because of his education and his clerical dignity. On his side, he admired her rugged commonsense, which put him at his ease, and banished the last atom of his "ladylike" bashfulness. Early in the winter he had been brought to realise the nature of his feeling for Mrs Davis, by seeing Brother Silas Hamm, recently left a widower, and having ten children, making a decided stampede in the widow's direction. Reverend Tommy was grieved. To be sure, she was old enough to be his mother, but she had many good points to be considered. She was a good worker, experienced in married life and ways of making a man comfortable. Then her savings must be considered. When

Tommy reached this last point he always felt sure that she was the most desirable woman in the world for a young minister. He felt hopeful tonight, because he had seen Brother Hamm and his bride in church the Sunday before. Mrs Davis opened the conversation by speaking of the bride and groom.

"Hamm and his bride looked mighty comfortable in church Sunday, didn't they?"

"He did. I'm glad he's settled again. It is not good for man to be alone."

"Deed I'm glad, too."

"You—well, well, I'm real glad to hear you say it."

"What for?" asked the widow coyly, looking down and playing with her fan.

"I—I didn't know how you and Brother Hamm stood."

"Stood! Well, I never."

"I thought Brother Hamm had been trying to get you," whispered Tommy, sitting closer and putting his arm across the back of her chair.

"Lawd Mr Jeems, how nervous you does make me. Do take your arm away, everybody'll be looking at you, honey. I'm surprised at your thinking I'd look at Hamm and all them children. Massy knows what the woman he's got is going to do with him." But she looked so mild and smiling that Tommy went into the seventh heaven of delight, and so lost his head that when he heard the call "Another couple wanted here!" He took Mrs Davis on his arm and stood up on the floor, forgetful of the fact that he was within a few months of his ordination. A good-natured matron not connected with the church had volunteered to supply the lack of an orchestra. Waltzing was soon in full blast, and the demand on the ice cream cans was filling Ma Smith's heart with joy, tempered with inward stings of conscience and fear of the Steward's Board. Dora was dancing assiduously and eating ice cream at John's expense, he meantime saying that if she kept on she would turn into a frozen dainty, to say nothing of a frost in his pocketbook. Dora declared that it was for the good of the cause, and he'd "just got to stand it." She was wildly happy because of the tender familiarity between her brother and her friend. A long stemmed rose that Will wore in his button-hole had been transferred to Sappho's corsage. Dora smiled as she caught the half-puzzled, half-wondering expression on her mother's face.

It was approaching twelve o'clock when it was proposed to wind up the festivities with the good old 'Virginy' reel. Sam Washington was the caller, and did his work with the fancy touch peculiar to a poetic Southern temperament. He was shrewd and good-natured, and a bit of a wag. He knew all the secret sighings of the ladies and their attendant swains. A lively girl whom everyone called 'Jinny,' remarked to Sam, referring to the fact that Sam was on probation: "Your class leader won't recommend you to the Board for membership after tonight."

"Now, Jinny," replied Sam, stopping in his business of arranging couples, "don't make yourself obnoxious bringing up unpleasant subjects. I'll take my medicine like a man when the time comes; but I'd sure bust if I didn't get loose tonight. I'm in good company, too," he grinned, nodding toward Reverend Tommy and Mrs Davis, who were just taking their places on the floor. "If this is good for Tommy, it is good enough for me."

All reserve was broken down the instant the familiar strains of the Virginia reel were heard. The dance was soon in full swing—an up and down, dead-in-earnest seeking for a good time, and a determination to have it if it was to be got. It was a vehement rhythmic thump, thump, thumpity thump, with a great stamping of the feet and cutting of the pigeon wing. Sam had provided himself with the lively Jinny for a partner, and was cutting grotesque juba figures in the pauses of the music, to the delight of the company. His partner, in wild vivacity, fairly vied with him in his efforts at doing the hoe-down and the heel-and-toe. Not to be outdone, the Rev. Tommy James and Mrs Davis scored great hits in cutting pigeon wings and in reviving forgotten beauties of the 'walk'. Tommy hadn't enjoyed himself so much since he came up North.

"Yes," said Sam, "this beats the cake walk all holler. Now then, one more turn and we're done. Forward on the head; balance your partner; swing the next gent; swing that lady. Now swing your rose, your pretty rose, your yellow rose of Texas. All promenade."

Everybody declared it had been a wonderful evening. "Thank the Lord it's over," said Ma Smith to Mrs Sarah Ann White, who was helping her in the kitchen.

"Well," said the latter, pausing in her work with her arms akimbo, "such sights as I've seen tonight I never would have believed. 'Phelia Davis, what ought to be a mother in Jerusalem, kicking up her heels in your parlor like a colt in a corn field; and that Tommy seems, no more fitting for a minister than a sucking babe, a-traipsin' after her like a baldheaded rooster."

CHAPTER 9

Will Smith sat the next evening in his room trying to engage his mind and chain his wandering thoughts upon an important prize thesis. As a brilliant philosophical student destined to shine in the future in the world of science, he had been requested to become a competitor for the prize. Ever and anon his attention wavered, and finally he threw his books and papers to one side with a sigh, and rising to his feet paced the floor impatiently. Two soft eyes looked into his; the low music of a gentle voice seemed all about him.

"Pshaw!" he exclaimed impatiently, "I have laughed at others only to become more of a drivelling idiot than any of the men I have ridiculed. I never thought mere beauty in a woman could move me so." The smile induced by pleasant thoughts lingered on his face as he threw himself upon his couch and tried to bring order out of the chaos of his thoughts. Smith's hopes were all for a finishing course at college, and then a course in philosophy at some good German university. Philosophy was a mania with him. In vain had bishops and clergymen of all denominations warned him that his mania might become a passion, which would draw him from a right conception of the Word, and dull his appreciation of the beauties of Revelation. Will contended that religion and the natural laws were not antagonistic, and that being convinced and thoroughly grounded in his faith, he but discovered fresh evidence of infinite perfection in the doctrine of his Master when he sought to expand his faculties and illuminate his mind by seeking a clearer perception of the interesting relation which weak humanity bears to the glorious mysteries of life and the grandeurs of creation.

He laughed at the idea of Latin and Greek being above the calibre of the Negro and likely to unfit him for the business of bread-getting in the peculiar position in life to which the Negro, as maintained by some, was destined from the beginning. With him Latin and Greek represented but tools which he used to unlock the storehouse of knowledge. The development of his race was a matter of first importance to his mind. The only way to bring the best faculties of the Negro to their full fruition, he contended, was by the careful education of the moral faculties along the lines of the natural laws. No Negro college, he argued, ought to bestow a diploma upon man or woman who had not been thoroughly grounded in the rudiments of moral and natural philosophy, physiology, and political economy.

At twenty-five, Smith found himself about to realise his hopes. He was fitted to enter Harvard University and graduate after a short course there. His articles in local magazines had attracted the favorable notice of scientific men, and one wealthy gentleman had offered him a course at Heidelberg after graduation. Emerson's words on character were an apt description of the strong personality of this man: A reserved force which acted directly by its presence, and without (apparent) means.

His sister's friends possessed no attraction for him; he treated them as little girls, looking down upon them from the superior height of his twenty-five years with a gentle condescension, tempered always by the natural chivalry of a generous nature toward the weak and helpless. He was a favorite with women, old and young, in spite of his careless, half-haughty ways. Many a sigh was wafted after his handsome, unconscious self, as a pretty maiden who had fancied that she had at length conquered the unconquerable, saw her chains fall from him as lightly as a cobweb is brushed away. What had come to him now at the glance of a soft, fawn-like eye, the touch of a hand, a caressing smile, the sound of a sweet voice? Sappho had been with them two months, but Will felt that he must have known her for years. Suddenly he passed from youth to manhood, and realised man's destiny. He had assisted his mother and sister with happy pride, but now the desire to shield, to protect, to love one being supremely above all others, rose and surged within him with a mighty strength.

Although love had come to Smith like a flood sweeping all barriers before it, yet the very strength of his desire for her love but served to restrain decided action. He approached the desired end slowly and carefully, not to defeat his own plans. He was well aware that Sappho's nature was a rare one, dwelling much upon lonely heights, the home of extraordinary moral sensitiveness and high intellectual development. Again he saw her advancing toward him in the mazes of the dance: her hand lay in his; her soft hair brushed his face; her sweet breath came to him from smiling rose-leaf lips, and intoxicated his senses.

The star-like beauty of immortal eyes, fringed by long, curling lashes, flashed at him from the four corners of his dingy room. What tender thrills of sympathetic feeling had seemed to enfold his senses as he gazed into their limpid depths—what beauty and strength lurked in the mobile, sweetly smiling mouth. The delicately moulded chin on which the God of Love had left his impress, might have served as the model for a sculptor. She and no other should be his wife—God willing.

Propinquity is responsible for many matches. It was pleasant for Sappho, when she returned mornings from delivering her work, to find her fire burning briskly and the room well warmed. It was a comfort to her not to have the ugly problem of ashes, wood and coal to solve. Not that she was too proud, or that she thought housework of any kind beneath her; but what woman does not feel it a relief to find the machinery of the home running smoothly without her aid. She thought nothing about ways and means, taking it for granted that there was nothing unusual in finding things pleasant, and she congratulated herself on being so fortunate in having heat included in Ma Smith's modest charges for lodging. Upon her return one morning, as she mounted the stairs to her room she saw from the light reflected that her door was open. Someone within the room was singing in a fine baritone voice a verse of an old song:

> Of all the days that are in the week,
> I dearly love but one day.
> That is the day that comes between
> Saturday and Monday.
> For then I dress all in my best
> And roam with my dear Sally;
> She's the darling of my heart,
> And she lives in our alley.

She pushed the door open and entered. Her cheeks were glowing from her walk in the bracing morning air, but her face assumed a serious, questioning look as she discovered Will just finishing up his self-imposed morning task. He gave an extra flourish to the brushes to cover his confusion and annoyance, and kept right on polishing off the little heater with his dubious-looking black cloths well filled with stove polish.

"Well!" she exclaimed.

"Good morning," returned Will, with a businesslike flourish of his cloth, as, having finished the stove, he proceeded to touch up the bright piece of zinc under it. 'How will she take it?' he asked himself.

"Well!" she repeated.

"Quite well, thank you," said Will, this time with a quizzical grin on his face.

"I had no idea you were the fireman, Mr Smith."

"No? In the words of Dr Peters, 'I do most anything in the world, honey, to get an honest living without stealing it.' "

Will had donned one of his mother's ample kitchen aprons for the protection of his clothing. The bib was pinned well up in front across the broad expanse of shirt bosom; the ample folds of the apron-skirt enveloped his limbs to his ankles; the long strings, crossed in the back, met in front in a huge bow knot. There was a streak of smut across one eye, and the side of his nose was polished to perfection. The picture was

69

too much for Sappho, and peal after peal of laughter shook her slight frame.

"Oh, Mr Smith," she said, when she could find breath, "you do look so funny!"

"It was ever thus from childhood's hour," quoted Will, marching up to the mirror to survey his beauty spots. "I do look rather fetching," he continued, with a confidential smile at his laughing companion.

"Do you do this every day?" asked Sappho, suddenly sobering down.

"Do what every day?"

"Why, make my fire?"

"It's not your fire any more than anyone else's fire."

"I'm very sorry."

"Sorry! Sorry about what? It isn't a crime, is it, for a man to make a fire for his women folks?"

"But I'm not your 'women folks.' "

"Look here," said Will in an aggrieved tone, balancing a hod of ashes in one hand and a pile of stove brushes in the other, "are we going to quarrel?"

"There is no reason why we should if we agree," said Sappho, smiling gravely.

"That means that we shall not quarrel if I agree to whatever you are going to propose. What is it you want to say?" he asked, becoming grave in his turn. "Is it that I have behaved unmanly in visiting your room in your absence? Why cavil about a little thing of that sort? I do this for you as I would for Dora."

"Oh, if you look at it that way," she began, a trifle confused by his apparent unconsciousness.

"How else ought I to look at it?"

"How horrid you are."

"Horrid! I don't see what I've said that is so very dreadful."

"You speak so—well—so cross."

"I speak like a man talking to a silly girl."

"Now you are rude again, calling me names."

"Children must be kept in their places," he said banteringly.

"You're making fun of me."

"Of course I am. What do you expect?"

"But you must not make my fire again."

"I am sorry you found it out, I didn't intend you to know it."

"I can't pay for having the work done, and it is not proper for you to do it; there is no reason why you should do such work for me."

"Suppose we pretend you are my other sister. That will make it all right, won't it?"

"No," came firmly from Sappho's lips, "no more fires."

"See here, I've hit it! Pretend I'm your father."

"Ridiculous!"

"What, neither brother nor father? How'd it do to imagine that you're my mother? You can't find fault with that, surely."

"How silly you are."

"No like me for sonny?" queried Will, with a sad shake of his head.

"If you don't leave this room instantly, William Smith, I'll call your mother," replied Sappho, laughing in spite of herself.

"The best pretence, though, would be sweethearts," he continued, as though she had not spoken.

"Sweethearts!"

"Yes, sweethearts."

"You must be very sure of your power, young man. You need a lesson in diffidence."

He held her gaze for a moment, and there was so much earnestness in the persistent dark eyes that she blushed furiously. He turned and abruptly left the room. No more was said about the fire, but Will continued to perform common everyday duties for her the same as for his sister. She did her part, too. Many an evening he found her helping Dora, darning socks or replacing lost buttons. Will's manner had changed toward her from that day; from easy familiarity it changed to a mixture of timid reserve and marked deference. Sappho noticed it, but somehow she liked it better. It spoke to her silently of tender, sacred thoughts. Tonight he thought of the scene just pictured, as he sat there in his room. She and none other should be his wife—God willing.

In another part of the house Ma Smith sat before the fire in her chamber and meditated on many things. The knitting with which the busy hands were always engaged when at leisure, dropped in her lap, and lay there unheeded. She thought of the incident of Sappho and the rose of the night before, and the merry, teasing look that had flashed out at her for one instant from Dora's laughing eyes. Could it be possible that she was about to lose her son? Dora's engagement to John Langley had been a source of great satisfaction to her; the old fashioned notion was still strong within her that it was the right destiny for girls to marry, and that the only cause for a mother to grieve in the idea of marriage for her daughter was the awful chance of that daughter's remaining single. The girl's life should be lost in that of the wife and mother. Such an end to maidenhood was a happy achievement for the girl and a glory to her family. But with her boy it was different. He was her first born, and memory was busy tonight with the past.

Her Will with a wife! Herself a grandmother! To renew at this age the joys which had been hers when first he lay within her arms a soft morsel of humanity, with sweet brown face and melting black eyes that mirrored themselves within the citadel of her heart. Ma Smith had known much sorrow in her life. She could tell you of hard times when it seemed that the combined efforts of her husband and herself would not avail to keep the wolf from the door. She knew what it was to bake and brew, to mend and make over, to minister to the needs of childhood with increasing maternal cares near at hand. With all this, the offered work which added a few dollars to their little store was always gladly accepted. But she would tell you also that she would not have given one hour of those days, with all their privations, for the happiness that she enjoyed when in the privacy of a humble home. She counted her good fortune—an honest husband and two beautiful children. "Yes," she was wont to say, "we had a hard time, and sometimes the waters of affliction seemed about to sweep us from our foothold, but somehow just when everything was darkest we could see the light of prosperity shining through the clouds, and we would take courage, bless the Lord, and keep on struggling."

Tonight she lived those struggles over again, and tried to imagine what it would be to have another share the love and reverence of the idolised son. At first it seemed that she could not endure the thought; but then she remembered how happy she had been in her married life, and prayed the Lord to deliver her from selfish desires. Who was she to stand in the way of her son's happiness—a son whom she loved? Sappho Clark was beautiful; she believed her to be a girl of exemplary conduct. Sappho was always deferential to her, giving to the elder woman the gentle deference which, coming from youth, is so dear to those advanced in years. So with a heart overflowing with love, and filled with kind and tender thoughts, it was no mystery where the pretty old face had caught its added charm of heavenly brightness. So Dora found her when she returned from spending the evening with some young friends.

"Why, mummy dear, I declare you are growing younger and more handsome every day. We girls must look to our laurels if you keep on growing so pretty."

"Well, my love, I have been thinking of your father tonight, and how happy we were when you and Will were wee tots."

Dora knew well what had set her mother thinking. She appreciated her feelings. She knew that her mother had always felt that no woman could be good enough for Will's wife. She felt instinctively that her mother had faced the difficulty alone that evening and conquered it, effacing herself and her desires for the happiness of her son. With her usual impulsiveness Dora threw herself on her knees beside her mother's chair, and drawing her face down to her, kissed the wrinkled brow and smoothed the soft white hair.

"Mummy, dear," she said, "you have made up your mind to give him up to Sappho if things turn out that way?"

"Yes, my dear," replied her mother, with her hand upon the dark braids beside her. "I will not say that it was not a struggle, but mothers know, if they stop to think, that they must lose their babies sometime. Your father and I made a home for ourselves, so I must look forward to the time when you young birds will want to build a nest away from me. But what is the matter with you, Dora? you look worried. Is anything wrong?"

"Oh, no," replied the girl, as she rose from her knees by her mother's side and began putting her things away and preparing for the night. "Isn't it strange what a queer old world this is? If you are happy I am not, or vice versa. It does seem that one thing or another is always happening to vex a body. And the worst of it is that it may happen that we are impatient and unhappy about things that are trivial. I don't feel sweet-tempered tonight, and really, I can't tell why."

Ma Smith glanced at her daughter sharply but said nothing, as Dora thrust her bare feet into bedroom slippers and proceeded to undo the thick masses of curling brown hair, and brush and arrange it for the night. The mother knew that her daughter would unburden her mind presently, and so she waited patiently. It was not like Dora to be petulant and have moods. She was a happy, healthy, active girl with a kindly disposition,

"Ma," said Dora after a silence, "why is it that Southern colored people seem to be so prejudiced against the Northern colored people? I always fancied that we were all in the same boat, and that mere accidental locality was not to be considered."

"That is true, my dear. But it must be that you imagine the prejudice to exist that you mention. Surely we have outgrown such ideas, as a race, by this time."

Dora shook her head obstinately. "I fancied that the Wilsons slighted me tonight, and that they would have been better pleased if John had chosen a Southern girl."

"You are over-sensitive, Dora."

Dora did not reply, and after a moment's silence continued: "John said that he had not met a decent-looking woman who was Northern born, and that when he did see a pretty colored girl on the street he knew without asking that she was a Southerner."

"That was rather thoughtless in John, but I don't think he meant to hurt your feelings, daughter."

"I cannot imagine what has got into him lately; he's not like himself. Oh, I do wish I was handsome like Sappho Clark. All the men are wild over her."

"Well, my dear, you don't harbor hard feelings against Sappho on that account, do you? That would not be like you, Dora, and would

73

grieve me very much."

"Sappho is the best and dearest girl on earth, and I only hope that Will may be so lucky as to marry her. And, mummy, I hope Will will speak to her right off, so as to get the matter straightened out. There won't be a blessed man left to us girls if she remains single long."

Her mother smiled. "Daughter, I want to say just a word to you about our conversation: Don't allow jealousy to lurk in your heart; don't brood over unkind words; cast them from you. And I would have you remember, also, that sectional prejudice has always been fostered by the Southern whites among the Negroes to stifle natural feelings of brotherly love among us. Dissension means disunion. Carry these thoughts always in your mind, and act accordingly. Do not allow yourself to be made unhappy."

Meanwhile on the floor above them Sappho turned restlessly on her pillow, thinking of a noble head and bright dark eyes. She knew that Will Smith loved her. What woman does not feel the subtle intertwining of a kindred spirit linked to her own by the decree of Destiny, long years, perhaps, before either restless soul has entered upon its earthly pilgrimage. She was not happy in her knowledge. Under cover of the friendly darkness she gave up the long struggle for self-control, and indulged in the grief that she knew was hers for all eternity. Oh, for death, the solitude of the grave and self-forgetfulness.

"What have I done, what have I done to suffer thus? To give up all joy, and have only misery for all my life. I love this man; I know it now! I want his love, his care, his protection. I want him through life and beyond the grave, we two as one—my husband. Oh, my God, help me, help me!" Heavy sobs shook her frame. Broken exclamations fell from her lips. "I cannot. It must not be! So good, so noble! Oh, the happiness of home and love! Must I be shut from them forever?"

Far into the night the agony of sobs continued. At last with a murmured prayer for help she fell asleep.

CHAPTER 10

The days went on apace at No. 500 D Street, but a spirit of restlessness seemed to pervade the atmosphere; expectancy was on tiptoe. Everyone was absorbed in preparations for the fair. Such a time had not been known for years among the colored people. Every available individual was pressed into the service.

Naturally many factions had arisen, and a fierce but friendly rivalry divided the different societies within the church. Some of these were none too cordial to the outsiders who had joined them, and whom they dubbed in derision "the colored 400."

"I'd just like to know," said Sister Mary Jane Robinson, with a hand on each hip, "I'd just like to know who asked the '400' for any other help? I've been a member here for more than thirty years, and this church has lived without him."

This was one morning directly after service, while the good sisters were waiting for class to begin. As the fair was the all absorbing topic at present, conversation naturally ended in going over all the interesting details connected with it.

"Lord, Sister Robertson, what mortal difference does it make as long as the church gets the money? The more helpers we has, the easier it makes it for us," replied Sister Scott, as she endeavored to pour oil on the troubled waters. Sister Robinson was a veritable firebrand; she spoke first and thought afterwards.

"That's that Mrs Willis with her 'High Church' notions," continued Sister Robinson. "Sister Smith has made her president of the fine arts and fancy work department. Wasn't any of the members of this church good enough, and they didn't know enough to attend to that business! That's that piano and that silver set and that are gold watch and chain that's going to be voted for. If that stuff don't be left right here in this church that's going to be trouble. And as for that diamond pin, that's to go to the one who sells the most admission tickets. Well, now, if the hard working sisters of this church what sweats over the washtub earning and honest living don't deserve it, then what's the matter? Yes, I wants to know what's the matter?" Here the irate woman sawed the air with hand and arm as she laid down the law on the back of the nearest settee. By this time a group of sisters attracted by her loud tones had gathered around, anxious to learn what the trouble could be.

"Well, honey," said one meek-looking woman, "don't let's bury trouble. The way the committee has fixed the business I can't see how that can be any monkeying with the voting or selling of the tickets. I do declare, my dear, I think the right ones will get the prizes."

"I'm a doing my level best," said another sister with hands hard and horny with toil. "I'm a-doing my level best to get that diamond pin for my Mandy. I've got William Vanderbilt and Charles Sumner Astor Gould and the twins all out selling tickets among my white people. And I tell you, sisters, you's all going to have a hard time to get away with you Aunt Hanner Jackson this time."

The family surname was Jackson, but Mrs Jackson liked to name her children for all the celebrities that she heard of, and sometimes it made a bewildering combination when one found that William Vanderbilt was represented by a sprightly little Negro boy with crispy hair and beadlike black eyes.

"That silver service is just my size," here chimed in another sister, "and it's going hard with anyone what tries to get it 'way from me; I'm selling tickets to beat the ban. I've done picked out a sideboard for it down to Osgood's. I can get it for a dollar down and a dollar a week, and expected to have it if it takes me all the summer and winter to pay for it."

"Talking 'bout the prizes, ain't you?" spoke up another sister who had just joined the group, "that gold watch and chain is just what Jim Anderson wants. 'Jim,' I says to him, 'that's your chance for a good easy way to get you a watch.' He's just raising heaven and earth are getting votes for himself."

"Hope you all won't be disappointed," here Sister Robinson broke in again, "but if you listens to me you'll watch them high-toned colored folks you all's been getting to help you. They never come around people that they don't hold on a 'quality with themselves' 'though it means something. These educated folks is always looking to make something. Most of them's too lazy to work. They wouldn't touch a flatiron or a washtub with a ten foot pole, and they'd rather live on dried codfish for a month than to do their own scrubbing. If any of them whitefolk say colored ladies gets them prizes, I'm going for to take out my letter, and put my work into some church what will 'preciate it; you here me?"

"Now sisters," chimed in the meek one again, "none of you ain't said a word 'bout trying to get one of the prizes for your pastor. I do think that's a little bit selfish in us. Suppose we give him the piano."

"Hump!" grunted Sister Robinson," when I joined this church I joined the meeting house and not the minister! I reckon he kind just look out for himself. Besides he's got a organ and don't need a piano. He gets his salary, don't he?" she queried, as she glared at the group about her. Taking their silence for consent she continued in a firm voice: "He's too much everything to everybody, and that wife of his is too white for me. I used to be taking fresh eggs and ham and chickens out to that house all the time, but recently I'se been reasoning with myself, and I came to the conclusion that I won't do it no more. Can't tell what is the matter with these colored men; a good wholesome-looking colored woman with kinky hair don't stand no living chance to get a decent-looking man for a husband, and I for one don't have time for those men."

"Pretty much so, pretty much so!" came from various ones in the group.

"Lord knows, Sis Robertson," said Sister Scott, "maybe you is right; and if that's any monkeying going on we's all going to support you in whatever you thinks is the best course."

"All right," replied Sister Robinson, considerably mollified by this concession. "I'll just take good care that none of us gets imposed on. 'Phelia Davis an' Sarah Ann White has got charge of the refreshment table and the salads, but if I don't knock him silly with roast pig, corn dodgers an' boiled cabbage, then I'm a sinner!"

Sister Robinson walked away, followed by a number of admiring satellites. Sister Scott and Sister Jackson were left alone.

"Good Lord!" said Sister Scott to Sister Jackson, "Good Lord! Mandy Jackson, did you hear Mary Jane Robertson talk? That ain't nothing the matter with her, only she's afraid that somebody's going to hold the money draw fastened against her. I tell you them '400' folks she's running will keep a close watch on her and how much money she takes in at the 'old Southern dinner table,' you here me!"

"And I for one am glad of it," replied Sister Jackson. "Mary Jane Robertson thinks she owns this church and everyone in it since Mr Jacobs left John Robertson that five hundred dollars, and they bought that house out of town."

"Bless your soul, honey, that's just so. I never see what a little posterity makes some people have a swell head. I tell you, honey, we'd better all of us keep our eye on the money draw.

When folks gets to buying houses—um, child, watch them!"

On Monday evening the fair opened. At five o'clock in the morning all the women who could get there made their appearance at the church, where the janitor was waiting to receive them. The first floor of the building contained a large lecture room, three classrooms, the pastor's study, a dining room and a kitchen. Each chairman of a committee had a certain space assigned to her by Ma Smith; then that committee took charge and proceeded to beautify the spot and arrange their wares for inspection. Ice cream, oysters, salads and temperance drinks were to be served in a fairy-like grotto formed by grouping evergreen trees together. Among the trees small tables were to be set, making a charming solitude a deux. Electricity, cunningly concealed in rose-colored shades, was to furnish the lighting. Pretty girl waiters, in white dresses and fancy caps, completed a fascinating picture. This section was under the immediate direction of Mrs Ophelia Davis and Mrs Sarah Ann White.

"You hear me, Sarah Ann," said Ophelia Davis to her friend, "you hear me, that Mary Jane Robertson means trouble. She's down on the aristocracy; she don't 'tend to give the minister a show over them prizes, and you and me's got to keep a whip hand over her somehow. The minister's going to get a new suit of clothes out of this, and you and me's going to have that piano! Lord knows whether there'll be one brick of this church left on another when this fair is done, but she ain't going to walk on me, you here me. I'm watching her, and if she runs up against me that'll be trouble."

Meanwhile Mrs Robinson and her coterie stood around and looked at the unique ideas for a fair which had been developed, and wondered how it was that the '400' people and their followers always had such a happy knack of getting everything just right. Her committee had intended to have nothing but a plain dining room, but after seeing the gorgeous display made by Mrs Davis and Mrs White, a hurried meeting was called to consult about ways and means of defeating the enemy. All the other women stopped their work, too, and came to admire the effects gained by the introduction of the lights and the tete-a-tete tables.

"A very happy thought," said Mrs Willis, as she glanced approvingly about her. "Where did you get the idea?"

"I got it up to Miss Mason's when Molly Mason was married."

"That's where you lived so long, wasn't it, Mrs Davis?" asked one of the girls, as she paused a moment in her work of arranging festoons of evergreens, and stood back to note the effect.

"I lived there and nowhere else the first fifteen years I was up North," replied Mrs Davis proudly.

"Were they very wealthy? Do you ever see them nowadays?" asked Mrs Willis.

"Miss Mason was worth her millions, and Molly was her only child," replied Mrs Davis, now fairly launched on her favorite subject. 'The Mason wedding' had passed into a proverb among the young people who were acquainted with Mrs Davis. "You see, when Molly was married, Miss Mason took it into her head to have a caterer from Boston do the work of feeding the guests. She was living in Worcester then. Even the servants were invited to the wedding. She had a house that matched her money, you may just reckon, and the whole of her lawn was used for feeding and for dancing. There were two acres of land, nothing but lawn, an' all among the trees you could see little tables set out and plenty of lanterns, although in the dancing pavilion they just connected a gas pipe with the main one, and had the place lit with gas just as if you was in the house."

"You ought to ask them to contribute to the fair, and help you out with your table," remarked Mrs Willis.

Mrs Davis cocked her head on one side and said, with a knowing wink at Mrs Willis: "Now, ain't you talking, honey, and maybe I should write to her and tell her all 'bout Mary Jane Robertson. Yes, you hold on child, till you sees me paralyse her."

"Did you go to the wedding, Mrs Davis?" asked Sappho, who, being something of a stranger, did not know all the little points about the wedding.

"Who, me?" exclaimed Mrs Davis. "Yes, I just did! Lord, child, but Miss Mason's a lady. She don't know how to be like some of your Northern people. These ladies up here are so afraid that the black'll rub off. Down South the big white folks has hired so many black mammies that they don't know nothing else for their children. It don't matter how black you is if you willing to keep in the mud. Up here it's different; you can do all right and live all right, but don't put your hand on a white man or woman, or they'll have a fit for fear the black'll rub off."

"I suppose you went to the wedding dressed to kill," said one of the girls.

"Lord, child, I had to have a new light silk for that, I tell you. And such a time as I had when I went to get me a pair of patent leather shoes. Clorindy, gal," she called to a young woman who was placing trees in position, "what kind of way do you call that to put them trees? You ain't got a bit of eye for being an artist, your perpendicler is all crooked. Bring me a chair that, one of you gals, and let me fix that tree right." Having straightened out the matter of the trees, she returned panting and puffing to the refreshment bar. "As I was saying, the man said he didn't have a shoe in the shop that would fit me. I told him I knowed better; he just said that because I was a coloured woman. Then he went to the show window and took out a pair, and told me to sit down and he'd try them on me and see if they'd do, and if they would I might have them, and he'd get another pair that'd do for signs just as well as them. I told him I didn't care a bit if they was signs; why didn't he trot them out when I asked him for them first? 'Well,' he says, 'they's number elevens, and I didn't want to insult you.' 'Insult nothing,' says I. 'As long as I can get them on.' They fitted me all right, only they kind of cramped me across my bunion. I always has a hard time with that darned bunion of mine. I managed to wear them, though I'm free to say that I never felt as though I got my money out of the darned things. As I was saying, I was cook, and the second girl was colored, too. We just hired an open buggy to drive to the church in—I believe in doing things right—and I tell you the white folks was dumb when we drove up that night to the church door and stepped out of the carriage onto the strip of carpet under the awning, for all the world just like quality. We got 'long all right tell we struck the entry, then Sally kind of hung back when she saw a big usher looking for all the world like a picture book, standing there and telling us to wait our turn to be seated in the family pew. Yes, indeed! Bless your soul, Miss Mason had done put us into one of the family pews. I'm used to them sort of things myself, but you see, Sally she's kind of low down corn-shucker, not used to nothing 'tall, and I keep my eye onto her. I could see it into her face that she intended to give me the slip an' bolt and hide herself. 'Oh, Miss Davis,' says she, 'has we got to walk all the way up that aisle with one of them white gentlemen?' 'Yes, Sally, we has, and it won't kill us neither to be like live gentry for once in our lives.' Just then one of them made for me, and I only had time to whisper: 'Brace up, Sally, and be a woman,' when I found myself walking up the aisle on that white man's arm, as big as Cuffy, and a-sweating too."

"What became of Sally?" asked Sappho.

"Bless your soul, Miss Sappho. When she sawed me go she just broke and run down them steps plum into the street, and made tracks for the house all dressed as she was in white chiffon, and when I got back that she was standing up in the middle of the kitchen floor grinning like a Chessy cat. 'Miss Davis,' says she, 'Miss Davis, I wouldn't have walked up that church aisle with that white gentleman for a thousand dollars, no I wouldn't.' I was so mad with that fool girl that I just itched to spank her well. How we to advance any if we don't 'brace our opportunities, I'd like to know?"

All the committees worked willingly, and soon every one of the departments had been provided with appropriate enclosures like quaint pictures set in exquisite frames. The bare walls disappeared, and the whole place burst into beauty bewildering enough to draw the money from the pockets of the spectators who would come with the evening to help a worthy charity. Mrs Robinson, with her 'old fashioned busy bees', as they called themselves, had hurriedly decorated the dining room with American flags and Christian Endeavour banners. The long, white-covered tables looked very inviting, and the motherly women in black dresses, white aprons and bandanna handkerchiefs tied into fantastic head coverings, added another charm which their soft Southern accent completed. Late in the afternoon the tired workers examined the results of their labours with much satisfaction.

CHAPTER 11

On Monday evening at 7 P.M. the doors of the fair were opened. In the center of the hall the prize piano was advantageously placed; and Dora, as the organist of the church, displayed its merits in a few well-chosen numbers. There were selections given also by a banjo, guitar and mandolin club of local reputation. Cozily ensconced behind a bower of tropical plants and flowers, they discussed popular selections in a manner which displayed most favourably the really fine musical ability which each one of them possessed. In another corner of the hall, under a tent which represented an Indian lodge, was a great and mysterious attraction: Madam Frances, spiritualistic soothsayer and marvellous mind-reader, had offered her services to the committee, and would send out bulletins, at so much a letter, on subjects supposed to be unknown to all the world but the persons themselves. The young people were in a flutter over this particular feature, the men less so than the women. Who could tell what might happen through her agency? Long delayed questions might be asked; unknown feelings might be revealed to anxious hearts. One might buy a lucky charm and present it to his inamorata, and by contact with it her coldness should vanish. Henry might receive a letter whose sweet perfume should banish the thoughts of Susan and turn his wandering heart to its first allegiance. Oh, happy race, which even now, when life is but a bare existence, though torn by howling mobs and scourged by fire, finds pleasure in the simple pastimes of innocence.

Superstition is supposed to be part of the Negro's heritage. They have brought much of it from their native Africa. It gives color, picturesqueness—light and shade we may say—to the darkness of life and complexion which so far has marked the Negro for its own. Claiming kinship with the Egyptians and other black races of the Eastern continent, the Negro is thought to possess wonderful powers of necromancy. Races are like families. The East Indian shows remarkable ability to awaken the superstitious fears of a community in his native country; so with the Egyptian; so with the Negro. But transplant them on a foreign shore and much of their supposed power vanishes. So with the Negro. We hear much of spells and charms being put upon unpleasant neighbors; wonderful stories of lizards being taken from the leg or arm of an enemy, placed there by the arts of the voodoo doctor and cured by the same gifted party. But if we notice, these wonderful and terrorising acts were never perpetrated against the inhuman master or mistress of the isolated plantation, never upon enemies wearing a white skin, but always upon the humble associate and brother in bondage. Be these things true or false, the Negro no longer holds the distinction of being the only race that believes in the pretensions of those who claim to be able to look into the future with mesmerised sight favored by hidden powers, that have a knowledge of coming events. In these days of palmistry, phrenology, card reading, mind-reading, lucky pigs, rabbit's feet worn on the watch-chain for luck, and four-leaved clover encased in crystal and silver for the same reason, who shall say that the Negro has not lost his monopoly of one great racial characteristic?

Madam Frances was supposed to be skilled in the occult arts which were once the glory of the freshly imported African. Wonderful tales were. told of her ability to foretell the future. Her services were of great value to the managers of the fair, for her fame had been rumoured abroad, through the members of the church, and it was popularly report-ed that some of the richest people in the city would visit the fair, if for nothing but to test the ability of this woman. And as one gazed upon her, he might be pardoned for thinking that within that dark house, mould-ed upon symmetrical lines, and appearing as though cut from purest ebony, albeit somewhat thin and spare, as became one past the meridian of life and now upon the road leading downward into the shadows of the last valley through which we must pass on our outward journey toward the spheres of celestial light, dwelt a rare mind. How did she look?

I knew a princess; she was old,
Crisp-haired, flat-featured, with a look
Such as no dainty pen of gold
Would write of in a fairy book.

Her face was like the Sphinx's face, to me,
Touched with vast patience, desert grace,
And lonesome, brooding mystery.

Nothing of loveliest loveliness
This strange, sad princess seemed to lack;
Majestic with her calm distress
She was, and beautiful, though black.

A quaint conceit which gave great pleasure to the children, big and little, was the pretty great-nephew of the seeress who, dressed in cos-tume, represented Mercury and carried messages to the fortunate ones remembered by the mystic powers of Futurity. Alphonse was a beautiful boy about eight years old, with golden curls and dark blue eyes that looked out on life from beneath their sweeping lashes with a glance all too melancholy for one of his tender years. There are children who seem to have been born with the shadows of life heavy upon them. So it was with little Alphonse. He passed from groups of merry young people and pleasant elders who, attracted by the beauty of the weird child, sought to beguile him with soft caress and loving touch. He would stand quietly waiting until the speaker had finished his question, would answer carefully, and suffer the caresses as though accepting them as a part of his duty, and would return to the tent and his aunt, evincing no desire for the frolic and fun which belongs to the golden days of childhood. Many influential whites were present in order to display their philanthropic interest in the welfare of the colored people. They gazed with surprise upon the child, and could not be convinced when told that he was a Negro, and identified by ties of blood with the blackest men and women in the crowded company. In a distant corner Sappho sat keeping a strict account of the moneys received. Occasionally she would leave her seat and mingle with the crowd. Gowned in a pure white china silk with a bunch of her favorite Jacks in her corsage, she, moved "a daughter of the gods divinely fair." And many a thought came into the heart of one learned doctor as he gazed on the child and the beautiful girl, and then upon faces ebony-hued but bright and sparkling with the light of freedom and intelligence. In that moment a cloud passed from before his mental vision, and he beheld in all its hideousness the deep sore which is eating into the heart of republican principles and stamping the lie upon the Constitution. Expediency and right must go hand in hand. There is no room for compromise.

Sappho was tired, and one of the young girls in her Bible class, noticing the weariness of her attitude, insisted upon assuming the duties of cashier for an hour. She gladly availed herself of the girl's offer, and turned with a sigh of relief to find a secluded seat where she could watch unobserved the passing of the gay throng. As she turned a hand was laid gently on her arm, and Will Smith's gay voice sounded in her ear: "Whither away, fair lady?"

Sappho smiled back into the debonair face as she replied: "Just to the fairy grotto to rest a while."

"I will accompany you, fair queen," hummed Will, as he drew her hand within his arm and moved slowly through the crowd toward the refreshment room. No more was said until they reached the spot; then Will seated her at one of the most secluded tables, placing himself upon the opposite side.

"Lord love you, Sarah Ann, just see that couple!" said Mrs Davis to

Mrs White. "If that ain't a match then no matter. See him look at her! I'se going to wait on them myself; and Sarah Ann, you keep these young squirts busy in some other corner; there ain't nobody going to spoil sport if I can help it."

Mrs Davis bustled over to the young people and literally beamed upon them. "Good evening; now Mr Smith, what be you an' Miss Sappho going to have? You see I've just come over to wait on you myself."

"Good evening, Mrs Davis; you are looking as bright and charming as a rose. How are the refreshments going?"

"Charming!" responded Mrs Davis, secretly delighted at the compliment. "Ain't you ashamed to talk like that to an old woman? You young fellas gets worse every day. Y'see Miss Sappho laughing at you! Well, thank God, we's doing well tonight, took in a pile of money so far. Mary Jane Robertson thinks she's going to down me in this here refreshment room, but just you wait 'till Friday night!"

"What about Friday night?" asked Sappho.

"Nothing, only I've got a big surprise waiting for Mary Jane Robertson."

"Friday will be a mighty unlucky day for Sister Robinson, eh?" laughed Will.

"That won't be a thing doing for her, honey, you'll see. I'se going to paralyse her!"

"I'll bet my money on you every time, Mrs Davis," laughed Will. "I have every confidence in your business sagacity. I feel sorry for Sister Robinson."

"She'll need your sorrow," replied Mrs Davis. "Mary Jane Robberson's jealous, and when people gets jealous they can't do the best thing in the best place. I ain't jealous of nobody, and I'se just sitting back here watching her kill herself, as cool as a sitting hen. I had a letter from Miss Mason, an' she says as how she's going to stand by me. You know what that means, don't you, hone? Oysters, coffee, ice cream and cake for two," she murmured, repeating Will's order. "My head's level, that ain't a thing the matter with it," she finished, as she turned to execute the order.

A silence fell between the two as they sat within the shadow of the trees, content to be with each other. Will was happy to have the privilege of feasting his eyes upon the lovely face opposite him, which dimpled and blushed in such a charming manner beneath his glance. Never before had she seemed to abandon herself so completely to the influence of his passion; but tonight she laid aside her coldness and seemed ready to accept the homage which he was longing to lay at her feet. The girl felt it.

'Why', she asked herself, 'why should I always walk in the shadow of a crime for which I am in no way to blame? Why deny myself all the pleasures of a home and love with such a man as he who will offer me the noblest heritage of woman?'

The more she thought, the stronger became her resolve not to fight against fate, but to accept the goods the gods provided without question. She would rise above maddening fears, penance for involuntary wrongs, the sackcloth and ashes of her life, and be as other women, who loved and were beloved. So she smiled on Will bewitchingly; sallies of wit and fun flashed from her pretty lips in a way which was as fascinating as bewildering. Will knew her to be well educated, but had never supposed that she possessed the exquisite art of repartee. Tonight he caught glimpses of an ideal woman and wife, and the glimpse intoxicated him. Now Love was kind.

They had very nearly finished their lunch when the room was invaded by Dora, followed by Dr Lewis, who had arrived from New Orleans the last of the previous week.

"Oh, here you are, Sappho, I've been looking for you everywhere. Have you had one of Madam Frances' predictions? She is creating a sensation."

"No," replied Sappho, "I have not. Have you one? Is it good?"

"Yes, I have one. For my part I think it's rubbish. Just listen," and she read from a slip of paper in her hand:

All that glistens is not gold;
Often have you heard this told.
Despise the false; welcome the true,
So shall you receive your due.

"Now whatever in the world does she mean by all that?"

"Where's John?" asked her brother rather abruptly; "has he had a message, too?"

"Yes; and he's so mad that he won't give anyone a decent word," replied his sister. "I'm sure," she continued, "if I felt as hateful as John Langley has acted tonight, I'd stay at home."

"Do you remember how his message read?" asked her brother.

"Yes," said Dora, "it was something like this: 'He who expects gain shall lose. Be faithful to the object of your choice, or merit the fate reserved for fickleness and deceit.' "

"Can't blame him for feeling funny over such a fortune as that, can you, Lewis?" asked Will, turning to his sister's companion.

"God, no!" replied the doctor. "If he would only prove unfaithful to the object of his choice how happy some other fellow might be."

Dora looked at her companion with scorn on her countenance. "I just think I hate you sometime, Arthur Lewis!" she exclaimed, as she turned to leave the room.

"Oh, I say, Dora, do have something before you go," urged the unlucky fellow, as he followed his angry companion toward the door.

"No, I won't have anything. I do believe you just love to see John Langley quarrel with me, but it won't do you a bit of good, Arthur Lewis, not a bit."

As they vanished from sight Will turned to Sappho and said: "Dora and John worry me Miss Clark; I fear that there is trouble ahead for my little sister if she marries him, and I could find it in my heart to wish that her choice had fallen on Lewis. He is a thoroughly good and capable man, and loves the girl devotedly."

"Let us hope that all things may turn out for the best," replied Sappho.

"I don't know why I should worry you with this, Miss Clark," said Will, as he turned toward her with a light in his eyes which a man gives to but one woman in the world. "Miss Clark—Sappho—"

"Ah, here you are." This time it was John Langley who had broken in upon the lovers. He came up to them smiling, polished, bland. Sappho wondered why she had never noticed how very disagreeable John Langley's smile was. She shuddered a bit as he drew nearer to them. Behind him walked the little Mercury, and in his hand he held a white missive just drawn from the small black velvet bag which hung at his side.

"Mercury wanted to find you, Miss Clark, and as I had a message for you from your mother, Will, I ventured to interrupt your earnest conversation. I hope I don't intrude." He bowed with easy grace to Sappho and bade her good evening, at the same time taking the chair which Will vacated as he rose to go to his mother.

"Thank you, John. No, you do not intrude. Miss Clark, I shall see you again shortly, I hope. I would very much like to finish our conversation."

Sappho bowed and he turned away. She followed the retreating figure with her eyes; John watched her jealously, and the child stood and watched them both. Finally with a sigh she opened the note, but before reading it turned to murmur a gentle apology to Langley.

"Oh, never mind me," he returned pleasantly; "if you get such a mongrel mixture as the one sent to me, I shan't envy you the pleasure you'll get out of it."

"It wasn't pleasant, I remember. Dora told us about it."

"Pleasant! A regular death's head at a feast, I call it. Do read yours, Miss Clark, and see if you haven't something better."

"Let me see: 'The mysterious stars bespeak for you better luck than you have already had. Harassed and perplexed by fickle Fortune, love shall find a way.' "

"Bravo!" cried John. But how could it be otherwise? If the same blood which inaugurated the Trojan wars, of which fair Helen was the object, still runs in the veins of the gods of love and fortune, they could not resist the influence of so much youth and beauty as we are blessed with here tonight,"

"And what shall I say in reply to so gallant a speech, Mr Langley? To my way of thinking, such words should be uttered to one alone. You must have forgotten Dora." Sappho turned to the waiting child and drew him into her lap.

"Because a man is engaged to one girl does that spoil all the pleasure which lies in meeting others? One woman can never tie my wandering fancy; my heart is large enough to appreciate the charms of the fair sex wherever discovered. Dora don't like it, I know, but she'll get used to it after we are married," he said, recklessly.

Sappho kissed the child on her lap, and placing the postage for her letter in his hand, told him to run away. "Truly, Mr Langley, you appear in a new light. Why do you tell your thoughts to me, who am Dora's friend? I do not wish to hear them."

There was a mocking smile on his face as he turned to her from watching the child. "A pretty boy that. His is beauty of a rare kind. Do you know, I fancy that he resembles you."

"Really, Mr Langley, you grow very strange in your conversation. I shall have to beg you to excuse me," and with a haughty little bow she left the place.

John watched her departure with a slight smile on his face. "Oh, beauty is the wine of life, fair woman, for me," he hummed beneath his moustache. The smile was still on his face as he ordered a cup of coffee and proceeded to drink it leisurely.

The fair had been very popular, and most successful from a business point of view. The week was now drawing to a close. The community was buzzing over the rivalry between Mrs Robinson and Mrs Davis. Racy developments were looked for on the closing night. Every woman had ranged herself on one side or the other, and not a few of the men had been led by their vigorous wives to declare themselves for a chosen leader.

Friday night was to end the sale of votes on the prizes. Saturday was to be devoted to counting up the votes, so that at nine o'clock that night the successful winners could be announced. The pastor was asked to allow the fair to run another week, but he declined emphatically, saying that so many controversies had grown out of it that another week would seriously deplete his membership and bring disaster upon the cause of religion. So that idea was abandoned. Wednesday Mrs Robinson was ahead on the piano but behind on the dining room receipts. Thursday night Mrs Davis was ahead on the piano but behind on the receipts in the refreshment room. So luck fluctuated until the rivals found themselves neck and neck, so to speak, at eight o'clock on Friday night. Anyone who had watched Mrs Robinson would have noticed that her face wore a satisfied smirk which told that she anticipated an easy victory, and the knowing ones of her satellites told each other that "Sis Robertson was all right."

Mrs Davis viewed the action of her rival with solid countenance, from which the envoys of the other side, who stood about trying to catch a word to repeat to their champion, could gain no comfort. To her trusted henchmen she whispered: "Yes, you watch me keep them guessing. I'm going to show them, shortly, that the 'race am not to the swifter nor the battle to the stronger, but to her what endureth until the end'."

As half-past seven approached various savory smells could be traced to the 'old Southern dining room', but above all the enticing scents which were ever introduced to aggravate the palate of the lover of good living, the knowing ones could trace the odour of a rare and tempting dainty—the opossum! Yes, Mrs Robinson had conspired with her Southern friends and received a tempting animal direct from the old Dominion," and on this eventful night she stood in the middle of the dining room triumphantly directing the placing of the dish upon the main table, which was carefully arranged with covers laid for twenty-five persons. The ordinary patrons of the room were turned from the door, and even the pastor was not allowed to enter, being told that the dining room had been engaged for an hour by a private party. At eight o'clock a message was brought to her by a lad stationed at the outside entrance to the vestry, and Mrs Robinson immediately hurried to the door to receive a sleighload of young white ladies and gentlemen who had come from among the wealthy people of the city, for whom Mrs Robinson was a faithful servant, to help her triumph over her enemies. With head thrown back and held very high, and satisfaction beaming from her countenance, the good sister marched in at the head of the company like a successful warrior on his return from victory. The assembled company made way, gazing with awe upon so many representatives of wealth and influence. Then they were lost within the sacred precincts of the dining room, into which Mrs Robinson ushered them. The pastor was sent for presently, and attended by the most prominent trustee on the Board. He waited upon the guests who had so honored his flock. During the interview which ensued, the door was closed to the gaze of the inquisitive crowd, but after half an hour the good man came forth with the guests and proceeded to show them the points of interest in the fair. A few minutes before nine they took their departure, seemingly well pleased with what they had seen.

"Well, Sis Davis," said one of the brothers when the door closed upon the visitors and the company felt at liberty to enjoy itself after its own fashion. "Well, sister, that rather gets ahead of you. Sis Robberson's got you dead sure this time."

He laughed with a good-natured chuckle which was meant to be very aggravating.

"Who me?" snorted Mrs Davis, as she turned upon the questioner with a stony stare. "White folks don't scare Ophelia Davis. I'se seed them before in my life, and I've eat at the table with them. Didn't have to have the door shut on me to keep me out the dining room because they was feared the black'd rub off. I think too much of my white people to trot them up here to this one cent fair."

"No use, Sis Davis, we's got you," laughed another member who had just come up. "Robberson's smart."

"Smart!" cried the irate woman, now thoroughly angry. "You-alls having your hallelujah meeting too soon. Don't holler 'tell you knows what you hollering 'bout. I ain't beat tell nine o'clock sharp, when the polls is closed."

"Five minutes is all you's got, anyhow. Can't change much in five minutes," laughed another.

Just at this moment a messenger boy made his way from the door and was conducted to the judges' seat. He handed them an envelope which upon being opened was seen to contain two bits of paper.

"Please step this way, Mrs Davis, and make your mark for value received," called out one of the judges.

Mrs Davis was escorted to the table by a curious crowd, anxious to know the meaning of this latest sensation. The judge stood up after she had signed, and said: "Ladies and gentlemen, knowing the interest that you take in all that relates to the two ladies who are rival candidates for the piano, and also for the ten dollars for the largest amount taken at a refreshment table, I beg leave to state that one hundred and fifty dollars have been contributed by Mrs Mason and Mrs Molly Mason Farnham, to be used for buying votes in the favor of Mrs Davis in the contest for the piano, and to swell the receipts at her refreshment tables. As I hold my watch in my hand it is now one minute of the closing hour of the polls. Any more votes?" He paused and looked around. "No more? Then I have the honor of informing you that the polls are closed. No more tickets can be bought, and I may as well say right here that Sister Davis will have the most votes; she'll stand at least five hundred ahead. Now I propose that we give three cheers for Sister Davis."

And they were given with a will, led by the pastor, who stood upon a chair and swung his bandanna handkerchief wildly in the air.

Mrs Davis was greatly excited. "Sis Robberson's got me, has she? Beat, am I? How 'bout it, honeys, how 'bout it?"

Sister Mary Jane Robinson was carried home sick.

The next night brought a great crowd to see the distribution of the prizes. The fun waxed warmer and warmer as each name was called. When young Mandy Jackson was called to receive the diamond pin, her twin brothers turned handsprings in the aisle, and yelled out: "Hi, Mandy, you a peach! We-uns did the business for you, you bet."

Sister Susanna Johnson received the much coveted silver set, and thought with pride of the handsome sideboard, and made up her mind then and there to give the Stewardess Board such a tea as they had not had for many a day, before another week rolled over her head.

Jim Anderson walked up to the judges' stand feeling very bashful and with a fearful grin on his face, when his name was called for the gold watch and chain.

"Wet it, Jim! Wet it!" cried one of his friends.

"Set them up, old man!" roared another, as Jim returned to his seat. "Don't be 'shamed; do the right thing by the boys."

Jim Anderson was angry. He was a trustee, and was looked up to by all the young members as an exemplary Christian. Jim made up his mind not to stand it, and he paused on the way to his seat and offered to take the speaker and "set him up" by standing him on his head if he'd only come out where he could get at him, "making a fool of him right out in church."

This stopped the fun in that direction, for Jim was a beef-lugger at the market, and they had a wholesome regard for his muscle.

But when Mrs Davis was called for the piano and the ten dollars, the excitement broke out with renewed vigour: "Speech! speech!" resounded from all over the hall.

"You must say a word to your friends, sister," said the pastor. Then she stood up.

"Friends, I'm much obliged to you for making all this noise over me, but being a lonesome old woman, I cannot make no speech. I'll just say that's nothing mean 'bout me. I don't feel good because some of us is took sick. Now, pastor, I want you to take this ten dollars over to Sis Robertson and tell her we's quits, and I forgive her for all her mean feelings to me. Will you do it?"

The pastor promised, and for a while pandemonium reigned. Then the pastor said a few words about how good it was "to dwell together in brotherly love." Sister Sarah Ann White said: "The brothers had nothing to do with it, it was Ophelia Davis and nobody else."

Mrs Davis, true to her word, had not forgotten the pastor; and all the women, mindful of the feeling engendered by Mrs Robinson against him, had secretly gone about among the '400,' and money enough had been contributed to buy him a fine new Sunday suit, made up in the latest clerical fashion. After all the prizes had been presented, the women formed in a body, and headed by Ma Smith, marched up to the judges' seats and presented him with the result of their good feelings. So everybody was made happy.

It was estimated that the proceeds of the fair exceeded the eight thousand dollars hoped for, and no church had more sincere cause to rejoice on the next Easter Sunday than the body of people comprising the church on X Street, who on that memorable day consecrated anew to God their house of worship free from all encumbrances.

CHAPTER 12

John Langley occupied an office in the business portion of the city among the most reliable lawyers in the profession. He held that association with success would in the end bring the desired quality to any one. He had never been moved by a generous heart impulse in his whole life. Actual need found no pity dwelling in his breast. The comfortable home which the thrift of Smith had founded and the industry of the family had fostered to prosperity, influenced his devotion to Dora to an extent which if realised by her would have led to his instant dismissal by that impetuous young lady. According to his way of thinking, the wife ought to contribute as much to the expenses of the household, by having a comfortable nest-egg before marriage, as the husband. He listened to the romantic story of the Montfort family with eagerness, and while regarding it as a fanciful creation of the mind, yet he felt that he must look it up and be very sure that a dollar could not be gained from it, before he marked it in his mind as valueless. He meditated on the subject constantly, but with the shrewdness characteristic of his nature, carefully concealed his thoughts from every one. He had no idea where he should begin to unravel this great mystery of family connections lost within the fog-banks of life in London, but he intended to try.

Langley's nature was the natural product of such an institution as slavery. Natural instinct for good had been perverted by a mixture of 'cracker' blood of the lowest type on his father's side with whatever God-saving quality that might have been loaned the Negro by pitying nature. This blood, while it gave him the pleasant features of the Caucasian race, vitiated his moral nature and left it stranded high and dry on the shore of blind ignorance, and there he seemed content to dwell, supinely self-satisfied with the narrow boundary of the horizon of his mental vision.

He remembered little of his parentage, but what had most impressed him was that somewhere in the dim past a woman, presumably his mother, had boasted that through her he was a direct descendant of the North Carolina Pollocks. So he clung to the name, and called himself John Pollock Langley. Neither the Smiths nor he connected his name in any way with the Montfort story; it was a mere coincidence.

If taken in his first state, fresh from the woods and streams of his nativity, the Negro be subjected to the saving influences of the Christian home where freedom and happiness, education and morality abound, the Anglo-Saxon would lose the main arguments which he uses against the black brother; rather would he bow humbly in recognition of the ebony-hued miniature of God. Subject the Anglo-Saxon to the whip and scourge, grind the iron heel of oppression in his face until all resemblance to the human family is lost in the degradation of the brute, take from wives and mothers the sacredness and protection of home in the time before birth, when moral and intellectual development are most dependent upon pre-natal influences for the advancement of generations to come; join to all this the uncontrolled bestial passions of humanity, and what have you? Classic features and a godlike mind? No, rather the lineaments of hideous despair, fearful and hopeless as the angel forms that fell from heaven to the black gulf of impenetrable hell.

Up from the South there came one morning early in March the report of another lynching. The skies were heavy with grey, storm-laden clouds, not darker nor more threatening than the dire and bloody news the daylight ushered in. For a month or two peace had seemingly reigned in southern latitudes, but it was the slumbering of passion, not its subsidence. At table, in the cars, at the workshop, men read with sick hearts the description of another illegal act of distorted justice, wherein the sufferings of the poor wretches were depicted only too truthfully for the peace of the community:

Jim Jones, a burly black Negro accused of the crime of rape against the person of a beautiful white woman, was taken from his home by a number of our leading citizens, and after being identified by his victim, was carried into the woods, where, before an immense concourse of people, he was bound to a tree, pieces of his flesh were stripped from his body, his eyes were gouged out, his ears cut off, his nose split open, and his legs broken at the knees. After this the young woman stepped forward and poured oil upon the wretch, and the wood being piled about him, she applied the torch to light the fire which was to consume the black monster. Leaving some of the party to watch the funereal pile, a posse went into the city and brought to the scene of vengeance Sam Smith, Bill Sykes and Manuel Jackson, who were accused of hiding the guilty wretch from the justice of the populace. These three men were hanged to the nearest trees in full sight of the burning wretch, who made the day hideous with his cries of agony. We think the Negroes of this section have been taught a salutary lesson.—Torchlight

The American Colored League was made up of leading colored men all over New England. These men were in communication with the colored people in every section of the country, for there is no community of colored people so remote that a branch of the great National League of American Colored Men cannot be found within easy reach of all. To the

Boston branch of this society the people of all sections of the country look for aid and comfort, not because of any acknowledged superiority of its members, but solely on account of the advantages which they are supposed to enjoy under the beneficent rulings of the grand old Commonwealth of Massachusetts. We do not claim for Massachusetts, in her policy toward the Negroes within her gates, freedom from prejudice or error. There is prejudice enough, heaven knows, prejudice which is fed every day by fresh arrivals from the South and by intermarriage between Southern women and the sons of Massachusetts. But Massachusetts is noted for being willing to see fair play: she hears the complaints of the Negro, and listens with attention to the accusations of the Southern whites, weighs the one against the other, and, naturally enough, the scales tip in favor of the white brother. From one class the Negro suffers in the state and is contemptuously flouted; from another he receives the hearty word of encouragement, backed by the all-powerful dollar which goes to feed such universities as Hampton, Tuskegee, and the like.

News of the latest horrible event had just reached the officers of the American Colored League. A call had been issued through the church and press for a public indignation meeting at the church on X Street, and John, as one of the executive committee of the League, was turning over in his mind ways and means of making it a success. With pencil in hand and paper before him he sat thinking. Outside, the sound of the typewriter clicking away for dear life came to his ears, mingled with the whistle of the office boy as he shuffled in and out, attending to his morning chores. John hired a white office boy and a white stenographer, not because he would not have liked to patronise his own people, but because he thought that it would be pleasanter for his patrons to meet their own race when business compelled them to visit him, and because he wished everyone to realise that so, at least, had no prejudice in his heart toward anyone. This was what he told the committee from the League when they waited on him and asked him to give the office work to two worthy representatives of their race, and pointed out to him that it was his duty so to do as a leading man of influence among them. Some of the committee were unkind enough to say that they believed that Langley was as prejudiced toward black people as any Anglo-Saxon; but as he denied it most emphatically, there was nothing more to be said about the matter, though many colored men voted him a "sneak" in private, and had a watchful eye on all his movements.

Usually John had no difficulty in fixing his attention on the humdrum routine of the office, but today his thoughts wandered. Sappho Clark had touched a vein in his nature which was a revelation to himself. Sensuality was prominent in the phrenological development of his head, although no one of his associates would have called him a libertine. Nevertheless,

94

there it lurked ready to assert itself when conditions were ripe to call it into action. Sappho represented the necessary conditions. Her beauty intoxicated him; her friendlessness did not appeal to his manliness, because, as we have intimated, that was an unknown quality in the makeup of this man. Her coldness urged him on; and Jealousy, the argus-eyed attendant of Love, and its counterfeit—Infatuation—warned him that Will's love was returned, and made him impatient to force upon her an acceptance of his own devotion, at whatever cost. He did not contemplate marriage, because he intended to marry Dora for mercenary reasons. But to his mind that was no obstacle to the consummation and lifelong duration of an illicit love. He had detected in Sappho's personality a coldness more in accordance with the disposition of women of the North than with that of one born beneath the smiling skies of the languorous Southland. Where, with such a face and complexion, had she imbibed a moral character so strong and self-reliant as her conduct had shown her to possess? Not by inheritance, if he read the signs aright. Then, he argued, if she had acquired that stately, cold, dispassionate bearing by force of habit only, the time would surely come when unexpectedly the true nature would reassert itself. Ah, he could wait. Meantime he could watch for opportunities to coax the unwilling bird within the net.

"Gentleman to see you, sir," announced the office boy, laying a card on the table before him. Langley glanced at the card and then said: "Show the gentleman in, and remember I'm 'engaged' to anyone who calls while he is here." As the boy left the room he thought to himself: "I wonder what brings the Hon. Herbert Clapp here today. Something uncommon, I warrant."

Langley arose to receive his visitor with an easy grace which was a distinguishing point in his personality. Men would tell you privately—keen, far-sighted politicians—that they believed Langley to be 'tricky', but that he had such a pleasant way with him that you would give in to him when you knew, within your own mind, that he would 'do' you out of a case in court or a hundred dollars with the suavity of a Lord Chesterfield; or, as one politician expressed it: "He has such an oily way with him that a man forgets to fire him until it is too late." He received his guest politely, bade him good morning in a cordial voice, seated him in the easiest chair which the cozy office contained, and, before his hat had fairly reached a resting place, had produced a box of fine cigars, and made him comfortable.

"Deuced pleasant office you have here, Langley," remarked the visitor as he lit a fragrant Havana and proceeded to enjoy himself.

"Oh, it isn't bad," replied Langley, "though if my practice allowed it I would be glad to take more commodious quarters." John had helped

95

himself to a cigar, and was now contemplating the ceiling through rings of curling smoke. Apparently he watched a belated fly trail its body slowly over the white space, but really his mind was alert and watchful to find a clue as to the nature of the business which had caused this man to call upon him. Mr Clapp had visited him twice before since he had been in business, and each time his call had brought substantial profit, in a political way, to his little bank account.

"Horrible thing, this latest case of lynching," Mr Clapp remarked after an interval of silent enjoyment.

"Yes," replied John, "pretty bad. Isn't it most time for the Administration to take it up? You can't expect us to stand this sort of thing always, and not strike back."

"What'd you gain by doing that?" questioned Mr Clapp.

"I'll tell you," replied John, looking earnestly at his visitor, "there are thirty-five thousand of us in this state alone. We can be organised, if the work is done by the right ones and in the right way. We can help start a new party, if nothing more."

"That won't do any good, John, we can down you. Colored people won't stick together; and then where'd you be?"

"We'd stick all right if once we got started," returned John doggedly.

"No you wouldn't; you're so confoundedly jealous of honours. Each one of you wants all there is for himself, and you never know when to get off, individually. We white men know this, and it is easy to upset your plans."

"I know that there is a great deal of truth in what you say, but that won't always be the case with us; we are growing away from it more and more every day; and with the missionary work that the League is doing, we expect to fight you one of these days, and knock the party clear over the ropes."

"You'll never do it!" declared Mr Clapp.

"Time will tell. You don't expect to succeed in keeping us out of employment, shoved in a corner to starve and to be burnt alive, without getting square sometime, do you? There would be some satisfaction in throwing you fellows out and putting others in, if a new party is the outcome of the issue, and seeing some of you, who have your pockets filled with the salaries which the Government has heaped upon you, shoved out of a job and your vast schemes for growing richer, at the expense of the lives of just such poor unfortunates as the Negroes you are allowing the South to burn in order to keep in power, blown to the devil. We can at least do that much."

"I didn't expect such talk from you, Langley," said Mr Clapp, his lips tightening in a tense line about the mouth.

"I suppose not. I've always been pliable, like the rest of the race.

96

Things are changing."

"The dollar will fetch you every time, John."

"Not this time, anyhow," was the dogged reply.

"Pshaw! You people are standing in your own light."

"Yes, I think we are. Been doing the same old thing for the last thirty-five years."

"What do you mean?" demanded Mr Clapp, growing white with suppressed passion. "Is that a reflection?"

"Don't lose your temper, Colonel; the man who gets mad always gets the worst of it," replied John blandly. "I want to ask you a question: Did you ever hear of such a thing as a man being robbed and murdered in the house of his friends?" He looked Mr Clapp squarely in the eye. The latter shifted uneasily in his seat.

"That's what's been done to my people."

"Well, you can't complain; you've had all you're worth."

"Had all we're worth! Yes, you give us a bootblack stand in the corridor of the State House, and think we are placated."

"You can't expect anything more until you have earned it. Besides, you're incompetent to fill any higher position. I have had a number of your best men tried in clerical positions, and you always fail to compete favourably with an ordinary white clerk. You can't ask the people to pay for ignorant incompetents."

"Ha, ha, ha!" laughed John, as he lay back in his chair and winked at the Colonel, "that's a good one! What do you think I've been doing since I've been in the law business in this city? Why, the greenest ward-healer knows that neither a white nor black man is competent to fill an office if the heads of the department where he is employed wish to get rid of him. The civil service is a good thing, but even that can't save a man from becoming incompetent when his resignation is desired by any one in authority. That's no argument at all. And as for our earning our rights— we didn't earn them at Wagner and Fort Fisher and at Fort Pillow; we haven't held the casting vote, and floated you from poverty into affluence."

"But the South, man!" exclaimed the Colonel, pounding the table before him with his fists until the dust sprang from the covers of the volumes lying there, "the South has rights as well as you. They are white men, man; you can't expect us to leave them out. All sections must be satisfied, and if you love your country as you should, you will be willing to sacrifice a little for the good of the whole. It won't hurt you; you can't miss luxuries and positions that you have never been used to!" The Colonel was shouting at the top of his lungs. John sat calmly waiting for the storm to subside.

"Then what I have heard so often is true, that the South is in the saddle."

"Eh?" said the Colonel, subsiding limply into his chair and wiping his heated face on his handkerchief. "Well, I might as well own it, to you; I know it will go no further. It is so in great measure, Langley. That is the reason we want your people to go slow. This is a great country. Each man is for the good of his own section. Can't blame them, can you?"

"No; and neither can you blame us for trying to get the best we can for the good of our race. You'll find we mean to do it."

"You mean to do it—yes, but the white man rules in this country every time, John, because he's born for the business, and it's just as well for you to keep the few friends you've got, and not drive them away because you're sore over your disappointments. You know nothing about business, you've no capital, no money, and we've got you every time."

"Threats do not frighten me, Colonel; nearly nineteen hundred years ago Christ sat at supper with his friends, and one of them, with a kiss still warm on his lips, betrayed him to crucifixion. What have we to expect from our friends?"

"Now, look here, Langley, don't say hard things, and don't get mad. I will admit every word that you say. It is all true, damn it!" he exclaimed as he arose to his feet and began walking up and down the floor with rapid strides. "I imagine I should feel even worse than you do if I were one of your race, but you see things are as they are, and why not make the best of a bad matter? Your people can't help themselves. If you rose in the South and appealed to arms you would soon be exterminated; for of course the South is our brother, and in an uprising of that sort, the National arms would necessarily be directed against the 'rioters,' as they would be termed. Individually, I might feel the justice of your cause; others might feel with me; but expediency would make me fight against you. And that brings me to my errand here today. It is the duty of every one of us to wait for justice, and not to countenance excitement and bloodshed. I assure you upon my honor as a man, that if the colored people are only patient for a while longer, this thing will be settled amicably. We have great plans for pacifying the South, and if we have the help of every good citizen we shall sooner be able to bring about a season of peace and prosperity, not only to the colored people, but to the whole country."

"Talk's cheap. I've heard that old gag so many times that it's grown stale."

"But we intend to do the right thing this time."

"It ain't in you to do the right thing by us. It is as natural for you to cheat us and maltreat us as it is for boys to pull out the wings and legs of flies. You say now you've got no power to stop lynching. If you haven't the power before election, where will you get it after the votes are in? No, sir; it's votes you want, and after you get them, and all the subsidies, corporations, and trusts are riding easily on the front seat of the coach for another year, you won't know us; and robbing and killing the black man can go right on."

"You talk like a fool, John Langley. You're jeopardising the best chance you ever had since Lincoln issued the Emancipation Proclamation."

"That's all right. Promises are like pie crust, made to be broken. You may be the best we can do, and the best is poor. Colonel, you just make up your mind to one thing: we're coming high this time. It's going to cost you something; yes, sir, right smart."

"I tell you, Langley, we have a hard fight to give your people even the little that they do get. It's your duty to listen to reason in this matter. What do you want, anyhow?"

"We want our men given something beside boot blacking in the employment of the state. We want our girls given a chance as clerks; that's what we want. Anything unreasonable in that?"

"No; that isn't unreasonable, but all the other employees would kick."

"Let them kick. Turn them out and get others; the civil service lists are always full." John faced the angry man with grim determination on every feature. He thought to himself: "The Colonel wants something done, and he might as well know that it's going to take a good thing to get me on his side."

"All right! I see what's the matter with you; you want to fight!" exclaimed the angry Colonel. "All right! be pig-headed; don't listen to reason; plunge the country into a race war in spite of all we've done for you, especially for your leaders; and when your race is exterminated, put the blame where it belongs. I wash my hands of the whole business I... "

"Oh," replied John, with a conciliatory air, "I don't want to see bloodshed any more than you do, and I am just as ready to accept amicable terms for my race as you are to offer them. I only want to convince you that we can do something if conditions are right."

"You're all right, John, my boy," returned Clapp, as he slapped Langley on the back, apparently very ready to grasp the olive branch of peace. "You stick to the party and the party'll stick to you. We don't want to quarrel, do we?"

"No, that won't pay," said John.

Each man now resumed the seat which he had vacated under the excitement of the moment, helped himself to another cigar, and again contemplated the ceiling through rings of smoke. John noticed that the fly had made the circuit of the ceiling, and was moving toward him from the opposite side of the room. After a moment's silence the Colonel said:

"Your folks are going to have a meeting about this last atrocious affair, aren't they?"

"Yes; I was just looking over the list of speakers as you came in."

"I suppose they're pretty mad?"

"Yes; pretty hot."

"By the way, Langley, your name is up for the place of City Solicitor, to fill the vacancy made by the death of Calvin. I suppose you'll accept it if you pull it off?"

This was the first that John had heard about any such place being offered to him, but he took it as a matter of course, and his eyes sparkled as he replied: "That would suit me to a T."

"That settles it, then; it's a go. Now I tell you what you do," he continued between the puffs of fragrant smoke; "you hold that meeting down among your people to a calm level. Don't let your fire-eaters like Judge Watson raise the devil of a row, and throw dirt on the party. You keep that end down and I'll work the papers."

"Just so," replied John.

"How's the city election going down your way, anyhow?" asked the Colonel, after a few more explicit directions to Langley concerning the work he would have him do.

"Pretty fair. Some of the voters want to take their own heads, but they can be managed."

"Well, here's an order on the committee for money waiting to be used in your district in an emergency. Draw when you need it." Then he arose from his chair to take his leave. "Mighty good cigars you keep, John."

"Help yourself, Colonel, help yourself."

The Hon. Herbert Clapp graciously took a half-dozen and stored them away in a capacious coat pocket. After a few more commonplace remarks Langley accompanied his visitor to the door, they shook hands, and the interview was ended.

CHAPTER 13

When Judge Watson, the president of the League, reached his office on that eventful March morning, he found his desk deluged with telegrams from all over the country. From the South the cry was: "Can nothing be done?" "Where is Massachusetts? Has our old friend been turned against us at last?"

"For God's sake help us!" "How long, O Lord, how long!" "Let the voice of the League be heard from every city, town and village in the Union. Speak, and let our voices be heard!"

Such were the messages that compelled the hoary-haired veteran of a hundred anti-slavery meetings to crush back the sobs which arose in his throat as he, too, reiterated the cry of an afflicted people: "How long, O Lord, how long!" That day the executive committee of the League met and asked themselves what could be done. "Nothing," was the final decision after debating the question, "but to agitate." This plan they proceeded to put into execution. Notices were sent all over New England of a gigantic public meeting to be held at the church on Tenth Street, on the Tuesday evening following. The press, with one or two exceptions, sided either openly or secretly against the Negroes, North and South. "Ah, ah!" they cried, "see how the Negro abuses the great privileges which we have bestowed upon him." In view of this fact, the League decided that a conservative white man should be asked to address the meeting, along with men imbued with the old abolition spirit, and in this way each side could have a chance to represent the subject as seen from its point of view. "Let us, once and for all, look at the question dispassionately; if the fault be ours, let us acknowledge it like men, and seek to amend it; if it belongs to others, may God help them to do right."

The excitement among the colored people was intense: prayers were held in all the churches the Sunday preceding. Telegrams were received from the branches of the League all over the state that delegates would represent them. The meeting would be a great expression of public opinion.

Dr Arthur Lewis was head of a large educational institution in the South devoted to the welfare of the Negroes. Every year he visited the city, and assisted by a quartet of singers, who were also members of the school, collected large sums of money from the best class of philanthropic citizens, who gave to the Negro not only because they believed he was wronged, but also because they believed that in great measure his elevation would remove the stigma under which the Southern white laboured. For the loyal white man there would be no greater joy in life than to see his poetic dream of superiority to all other governments realised in the "land of the free and the home of the brave." He knows that this can never be while the Negro question keeps up the line of demarcation which marks the division of the North from the South. True and loyal son of his country, he would sacrifice any race, any principle, to bring about this much-desired consummation; so he contributes his money to build up manufacturing interests at the South to his own material disadvantage in the North: to develop uncultivated land there, and to educate the Negro with the hope that in the general advance the latter question may be buried from public notice, if not obliterated. Delusive hope that grasps at shadows.

That momentous Tuesday evening rolled quickly round. The committee asked that the meeting should open at half-past seven, on account of the time needed by the speakers, and long before the hour appointed the large edifice was filled to overflowing. And what a crowd! They came from towns remote, from the farm, from domestic service in the homes of wealth and from among the lowly ones who earn a scanty living with scrubbing brush and pail. Doctor, lawyer, politician, mechanic—every class sent its representative there to help protest against the wrongs of down-trodden manhood.

The platform was heavily draped in American flags supplemented by wide bands of mourning. Pictures of the anti-slavery apostles peered out at the audience from the folds of the national colors. Speakers and representative citizens were seated upon the platform, and visiting delegates occupied seats in close proximity. The choir had volunteered its services, and, after a prayer by the pastor, rendered Mrs Julia Ward Howe's 'Battle Hymn of the Republic' in masterly style. In listening to the martial strains the pulse of the vast concourse of people was strained with excitement and expectation. The stillness was intense as the grey-haired president of the League and chairman of the meeting arose in his seat and passing to the desk, rapped for order.

"Fellow citizens and men and women of my race: The occasion for this meeting is one of great solemnity. Forty years ago, when as a young man I sat at the feet of Sumner, Phillips, Garrison, Pillsbury, Charles Lenox Remond, Nell, Robert Morris, Fred Douglass and all the mighty host of anti-slavery fathers, we thought that with the abolishment of slavery the black man's destiny would be accomplished, and fixed beyond a peradventure. Today a condition of affairs confronts us that they never foresaw: the systematic destruction of the Negro by every device which the fury of enlightened malevolence can invent. In what ever direction we turn, the clouds hang dark and threatening, This new birth of the black race is a mighty agony. God help us in our struggle for liberty and manhood. Agitation and eternal vigilance in the formation of public opinion were the weapons which broke the power of the slave-holder and gave us emancipation. I recommend these methods to you today, knowing their value in the past...Up then and act! Thy courage wake! Combat intrigue, injustice, tyranny. And in thine efforts God will be with you."

He then called upon the Hon. Herbert Clapp, as a representative of the party and of the sentiment of the best white people of the country, to address the meeting.

The political contingent gave him a hearty welcome as he moved with stately tread to the front of the platform. He said:

"The topic to be discussed is a very serious one, and I feel deeply how incompetent I am to deal with it, how incompetent most of us are to attempt the solution of the question before us. As a white man looking upon the South as my brother, and desiring to see the welfare of that section secured along with the rights of the brother in black, I feel the responsibility which rests upon me tonight to be fair and just, impartial to both sides in what I may say. I ask you tonight as rational people to look at this question from both points of view; to be calm and logical; to be willing, as just men of intelligence and judgment, to see and acknowledge wrong wherever you find it among your own people, and to be willing to consult as to the best method of procedure to rectify mistakes which if corrected may lead to an amicable adjustment of all difficulties in the South. As a friend of both sides, I ask you to do this.

"I am not here to apologise for the South; she has her ills and her sins. What section has not? Let us thank God that sectionalism is dead.

"Now then, let us try to appreciate the relations of the Negro at the South. All history shows that two races, approaching in any degree equality in numbers, cannot live together unless intermarriage takes place or the one is dependent and in some sense subject to the other. Miscegenation by law will never take place in the South. No matter how much we people of the North may differ with our brothers of the South, this point will always remain fixed. Miscegenation, then, being out of the question, nothing remains for the Negro but to be dominated by the white man there. I hold that the Negro in American civilisation is a problem of a vast deal more import than we are inclined to believe. The problem is national, not sectional. The sin of slavery was the sin of the nation, and that sin stands before us today full of menace, full of peril to the whole people. The Southern brother claims, and with some justice I think you will allow, that under the influence of scalawags and carpet-baggers, mostly composed of unprincipled Northern white men, the Negro has opposed, politically, everything that he thinks the white man wants.

Upon this subject Prof. H. M. Brown, a Negro and member of the faculty of Hampton Institute, says: 'The greatest enemy to the Negro and the greatest obstacle to his progress is the politician, and the Negro politician is the worst of all.'

"You cannot deny that the well-behaved Negro has the respect of the community in which he lives at the South. Witness the death of a highly respected Negro in Georgia a short time ago. He never dabbled in politics, and his death was deplored by white and black alike. In thirty years forty per cent of the illiteracy at the South among the colored people has disappeared, due no doubt to environment and emulation of the whites. All kinds of employment, trades, professions, etc., are open to the Negro at the South, and you know that counts for a great deal. Here at the North the pressure is so great from the white labourer that we are forced, to some extent, to bar against the colored brother. I am ashamed to say it; but let us state the case truthfully, if at all.

"To come to the case in hand, I wish it to be distinctly understood that I am absolutely opposed to mob law. But there is an unwritten law, not peculiar to any section, which demands the quickest execution, in the quickest way, of the fiend who robs a virtuous woman of her honor to gratify his hellish diabolism. Human nature is the same throughout the civilised world. If in return for all the benefits conferred upon the Negro at the South, which I have enumerated previously, they give us the heinous crime of rape, what shall we say? Where find excuses for such ingratitude? Surely as men we must have sympathy for the pure and virtuous woman who carries with her a living shame, in a living death, in a life all too long for its miseries, if it lasts but for a day."

As he finished and returned to his seat, a sigh like a broken moan seemed to come from the very heart of the multitude, but not a movement broke the stillness. The Hon. Herbert Clapp felt that his part of the exercises was a failure. After a pause, the chairman introduced Dr Lewis as a leading representative of the race whom they would, doubtless, be glad to hear express his views upon the momentous question under consideration. He was received with liberal applause, and said:

"I agree with our friend the Hon. Herbert Clapp in about all that he has said in relation to the grievous matter before us. I think that he has stated the case as impartially as it is possible so to do. The moment there is a lynching in the South, it is made the pretext for many press comments and public meetings among ourselves, and a general agitation of the question in the wrong way. The result is that you people at the North get a wrong idea of the matter. The published accounts of your meetings here do us at the South, who are working along the best lines that we know of for the elevation of the race, an injury, and often retard us greatly in the accomplishment of our designs. Take the Black Belt, and within its circumference you will find the densest ignorance, as well as bright intelligence of no ordinary quality. Among those people you will find the vicious ones who would rather drink, carouse, and fight than do a day's work to keep themselves from the penitentiary. Such men can be bought, bribed, worked upon for the furtherance of any planar scheme that may suggest itself to the wily brain of the unscrupulous politician. These men are dangerous to the peace of the community, and it is such men who commit the deeds of violence with which the country is horrified at short intervals. If we cannot reach these men individually, we hope to reach their children. Thus we have planned that with the aid of our universities we shall at length root out evil and ignorance, and in the future give our race a clean, pure citizenship. As our friend has stated—politics is the bane of the Negro's existence. Those of us who eschew that subject, let matters of government take care of themselves, while we look out for our own individual or collective advancement, find no difficulty in living at the South in peace and harmony with our neighbors. If we are patient, docile, harmless, we may expect to see that prosperity for which we long, in the years to come, if not for ourselves then for our children. I am an optimist in regard to the future. I have great hopes of the better class of Southern people themselves.

"Let us remember that the South was more conquered than persuaded. The Confederates did not surrender their convictions with their swords. Immediately after the war Henry W. Grady would have been looked upon as a monstrosity. It was a severe blow to the South when the slave gained his liberty. As the South gains wealth and resources I think that the problem will grow less difficult. It is the idea of the Negro holding political preferment that is so hard for the North and South to swallow. But if we give them time and do not hurry them, they will grow gradually accustomed to the new era. Convince the South that we do not want social equality, neither do we wish to rule. We want nothing but our God-given rights as men.

"I believe in the humanising influence of the dollar judiciously expended for educational advantages, holding it better and wiser to tend the weeds in the garden than to water the exotic in the window. We should strive to obtain the education of the industrial school, seeking there our level, content to abide there, leaving to the white man the superiority of brain and intellect which hundreds of years have developed."

He ceased speaking and sat down amid murmurs of applause, mingled with disapprobation. Some among the audience began to grow restless. Was this what they came to hear—an apology, almost an eulogy upon the course pursued by the South toward the Negro? Other speakers—white and colored—followed; then the chairman introduced our friend John Langley. He came to the front of the platform with his usual graceful bearing. He was well known among the people, especially the younger contingent, and was received with liberal applause.

"My friends," he said, "I shall not detain you with any lengthy remarks upon the situation, because there are speakers to follow me. I am glad of the opportunity to say what I think about lynch law: It is a terrible thing to contemplate. The crime which provokes it is still more terrible, to my thinking. I utter no eulogy upon the position of the South toward the Negro, neither do I harbor undue resentment for the grievous wrongs which I feel they have, in some measure, heaped upon us. I am willing to leave the punishment of criminals, the suppression of mob violence, with the national government, being convinced that in good time the government so trusted will acquit itself with equity toward my race. You have listened to the speeches made by our friend, the Hon. Herbert Clapp, and our brother, Dr Arthur Lewis, upon whose word we can implicitly rely, because he works, lives, and moves among the very happenings of which we know nothing save by reading. It is discretion to act coolly, calmly and deliberately; to look at all sides of a question before we jump at conclusions. I can see nothing to be gained, if, as we have been advised, we took up arms in defence of our rights of citizenship. Extermination would speedily follow. Let us not invite destruction. But we have opportunities of advancement. Let us seize them. Let us await the issue of events with patience, trusting in the fealty of our party leaders, putting faith in their sagacity to push our claims and redress whatever grievances we may have, at a seasonable time. We thoroughly understand the attitude of the whites. Let us not offend the class upon whom we depend for employment and assistance in times of emergencies. By so doing, if we cannot have amity we can have peace."

CHAPTER 14

Scarcely had the speaker taken his seat amid suppressed murmurs of discontent, when a tall, gaunt man of very black complexion arose in his seat among the delegates, and in a sonorous bass voice uttered the solemn protest of Patrick Henry, so famous in history: "Gentlemen may cry 'Peace! peace!' but there is no peace."

In an instant confusion reigned. Women fluttered their handkerchiefs, and above waves of applause and cheers could be heard cries of "Hear, hear!" "Platform! platform!" The chairman rapped for order, and when he could make himself heard, asked the delegate to come to the platform; another speaker was waiting, but the audience would be glad to hear anything he might have to say. As he passed up the aisle and mounted the steps of the rostrum, the people saw a man of majestic frame, rugged physique and immense muscular development. His face was kindly, but withal bore the marks of superior intelligence, shrewdness and great strength of character. He might have been a Cromwell, a Robespierre, a Lincoln. Men of his physiological development—when white—mould humanity, and leave their own characteristics engraved upon the pages of the history of their times.

"Friends," said he, when he stood before them, "I come from Williamstown, in the western part of this state, to be a delegate at this meeting. Here are my credentials to show that I am in good standing in the League where I belong." He handed his papers to the chairman. "I want to impress that fact upon the minds of this assembly, because I am going to tell you some awful facts before I get through." He paused, and with his handkerchief wiped the tears and perspiration from his face "Friends, I am thirty years old and look fifty. I want to tell you why this is so. I want to tell you what brought me here. I want to tell the gentlemen who have spoken here tonight that conservatism, lack of brotherly affiliation, lack of energy for the right and the power of the almighty dollar which deadens men's hearts to the sufferings of their brothers, and makes them feel that if only they can rise to the top of the ladder may God help the hindmost man, are the forces which are ruining the Negro in this country. It is killing him off by thousands, destroying his self respect, and degrading him to the level of the brute. These are the contending forces that are dooming this race go despair!

"My name is Lycurgus Sawyer; Luke they call me for short. When I was about ten years old my father kept a large store in a little town in the state of Louisiana. I had two brothers and a sister. My mother was a fine woman, somewhat better educated than my father. Through her influence he went into this business of trading, and soon had the largest business and as much money as any man in the county. Father didn't care to meddle with politics, for, with the natural shrewdness of many of us, he saw that that might be made an excuse for his destruction. When I was about ten years old, then, a white man in the village, seeing the headway my father was making in accumulating property, opened a store on the same street. Father said nothing, but his customers still continued to trade with him, and it seemed that the other man would be compelled to give up. About this time father received threatening letters ordering him to move, and saying that in case he did not do as ordered he would lose his life. Mother was frightened, and advised father to get out of the place, but he, anxious to save some part of his hard earnings, waited to sell his stock and houses before seeking a home elsewhere. One night a posse of men came to our house and began smoking us out. You don't know anything about that up here, do you? Well, you'll get there if things keep on as they're going. My father had arms. He raised the window of his sleeping room and fired into the mob of cowardly hounds. Thoroughly enraged, they broke open the doors back and front, seized my father and hung him to the nearest tree, whipped my mother and sister, and otherwise abused them so that they died next day. My brothers were twins, still so small that they were but babes. The mob took them by the heels and dashed their brains out against the walls of the house! Then they burned the house. I saw all this, and frenzied with horror, half-dead with fright, crept into the woods to die. I was found there by a colored planter named Beaubean, who lived in the next township. He pitied me and took me home. That, gentlemen, was my first experience of lynching. Do you think it is possible to preach 'peace' to a man like me?"

The house was filled with the cries and groans of the audience. Sobs shook the women, while the men drank in the words of the speaker with darkening brows and hands which involuntarily clinched themselves in sympathy with his words.

"But that is not the only story I can tell. Here's another. I will tell it to you, and you can digest it at your leisure.

"Monsieur Beaubean was an educated man, descended from a very wealthy family. His father had been his owner. When the father died he left to his son, born of a black mother, an equal share of the estate along with his legitimate heirs. They made no objections, so he got it.

"Monsieur Beaubean had married a quadroon woman of great beauty—Louisiana abounds in handsome women of color; they had two children, a boy and a girl. She was three years old when I went to live with them. I remained in the family twelve years. I learned many things there;

along with the trade of blacksmithing I learned to esteem myself as a man.

"I cannot describe to you the beauty and loveliness of that child. As a boy I worshipped her, and as a man I loved her; not with the hope of ever having a return of the feeling she had aroused in me, but as a faithful dog that would lay down his life for those who shelter and care for him, so I felt to Beaubean's family, and especially to that child. When Mabelle, as we called her, was old enough, she was sent to the Colored Sisters' School in the city of New Orleans. It was my pleasant duty to drive her into the city each day and go for her at night.

"Monsieur Beaubean had a half-brother—a white man—who was very wealthy and stood very high in politics. In fact, he was in the State Senate. I noticed that he seemed extremely fond of Mabelle. One day, after she had passed her fourteenth birthday, she had a holiday from school, and went with some school fellows to visit a companion who lived in the city. They returned at night without her, saying that she went into a store with Monsieur Beaubean's brother, and they had not seen her since.

"Can you imagine what a night was passed by that family? No, you cannot, unless you have been through the same experience. The father went in one direction and I in another. All night long we searched the city streets; nothing could be heard of her. Finally we went to police head-quarters and secured the services of a detective. After three weeks of incessant searching we found her a prisoner in a house of the vilest character in the lowest portion of the city of New Orleans—a poor, ruined, half-crazed creature in whom it was almost impossible to trace a resemblance to the beautiful pet of our household. These arms bore her forth from that vile den and restored her to a brokenhearted parent. I think that I must have gone mad. If I had had the man there and then that committed the crime." He raised one gaunt arm above his head, and standing in that attitude seemed the embodiment of vengeance. "I would have taken him by the throat and shaken him." He hissed the words through clenched teeth. "I would have shaken him as a dog would a rat until he was dead. DEAD! We took her home, but I believe that her father was a madman from the time he placed his eyes upon her until he was murdered. And who do you think had done this foul crime? Why, the father's half-brother, uncle of the victim!

"Crazed with grief, Monsieur Beaubean faced his brother and accused him of his crime. 'Well,' said he, 'whatever damage I have done I am willing to pay for. But your child is no better than her mother or her grandmother. What does a woman of mixed blood, or any Negress, for that matter, know of virtue? It is my belief that they were a direct creation by God to be the pleasant companions of men of my race. Now, I am willing to give you a thousand dollars and call it square.' He handed Monsieur Beaubean a roll of bills as he spoke. Beaubean seized them and hurled them into the villain's face with these words: 'I leave you to carry my case into the Federal courts and appeal for justice.' Unhappy man! That night his house was mobbed. The crowd surrounded the building after firing it, and as an inmate would show his head at a window in the struggle to escape from the burning building, someone would pick him off. So it went all that night. I seized Mabelle and wrapped her in a blanket. Watching my chance I stole from the house after the fire was well under way, and miraculously reached a place of safety. I took Mabelle to the colored convent at New Orleans, and left her there in the care of the sisters. There she died when her child was born."

As the speaker stood silently contemplating his weeping, grief convulsed audience, a woman was borne from the auditorium in a fainting condition. John Langley from his seat on the platform leaned over and asked an usher who the lady was. "Miss Sappho Clark," was his reply.

Amid universal silence, the silence which comes from feeling too deep for outward expression, the speaker concluded: "A tax too heavy placed on tea and things like that, made the American Colonies go to war with Great Britain to get their liberty. I ask you what you think the American Colonies would have done if they had suffered as we have suffered and are still suffering?

"Mr Chairman, gentlemen call for peace, and I reply: 'Peace if possible; justice at any rate.' Where is there peace for men like me? When the grave has closed over me and my memories, I shall have peace.

"Under such conditions as I have described, contentment, amity—call it by what name you will—is impossible; justice alone remains to us."

CHAPTER 15

Someone at this moment began to sing that grand old hymn, ever new and consoling:

"Jesus, Lover of my soul,
Let me to thy bosom fly;
While the nearer waters roll,
While the tempest still is nigh."

When quiet once more reigned, amid intense silence the chairman arose and introduced Mr William Smith as the last speaker of the evening. Tremendous applause greeted him, for he was known to be an able and eloquent debater.

"Friends," he said, "I shall not attempt a lengthy and discursive argument; I shall simply try to answer some of the arguments which have been advanced by other speakers. I have no doubt that they have spoken their honest convictions. Now let us look at the other side of the question.

"We know that the Negro question is the most important issue in the affairs of the American Republic today. We are told that there are but two ways of solving the vexed question of the equality of the two races: miscegenation by law, which can never take place, or complete domination by the white race—meaning by that comparative servitude.

"Miscegenation, either lawful or unlawful, we do not want. The Negro dwells less on such a social cataclysm than any other race among us. Social equality does not exist; no man is forced to receive another within the environments of intimate social life. 'Social position is not to be gained by pushing.' That much for miscegenation. The question now stands: Which race shall dominate within certain parallels of latitude south of Mason and Dixon's line? The Negro, if given his full political rights, would carry the balance of power every time. This power the South has sworn that he shall never exercise. All sorts of arguments are brought forward to prove the inferiority of intellect, hopeless depravity, and God knows what not, to uphold the white man in his wanton cruelty toward the American Ishmael.

"We are told that we can receive education only along certain elementary lines, and in the next breath we are taunted with not producing a genius in science or art. A Southern white man will tell you that of all politicians the Negro is the vilest, ignoring the fact that for corrupt politics no race ever can or ever will excel the venality of a certain class of whites. Let us, for the sake of illustration, glance at the position of the Irish element in politics. They come to this country poor, unlettered, despised. Fifty years ago Pat was as little welcome at the North as the Negro at the South. What has changed the status of his citizenship? Politics. The Irishman dominates politics at the North, and there is no gift within the power of the government that does not feel his influence. I remember a story I heard once of an Irishman just landed at Castle Garden. A friend met him, and as they walked up the street said to him: 'Well, Pat, you are just in time to vote for the city government election.' 'Begorra,' replied Pat, 'and is it a government they have here? Sure, thin, I'll vote against it.'

"The Irish vote, then, is massed at certain strategic points in the North, and its power is feared and respected. The result has been a rapid and dazzling advance all along the avenues of education and wealth in this country for that incisive race. To the Negro alone politics shall bring no fruit.

"To the defence of slavery in the past, and the inhuman treatment of the Negro in the present, the South has consecrated her best energies. Literature, politics, theology, history have been ransacked and perverted to prove the hopeless inferiority of the Negro and the design of God that he should serve by right of color and physique. She has convinced no one but herself. Bitterer than double distilled gall was the Federal success which brought Negro emancipation, domination and supremacy.

"Disfranchisement is what is wanted by the South. Disfranchise the Negro and the South will be content. He, as the weaker race, can soon be crowded out.

"Many solutions of the question of Negro domination have been advanced; among them the deportation of the Negro to Africa has been most warmly advocated by public men all over the country. They argue that in this way the prophecy of the Bible will soonest be fulfiled; that 'Ethiopia shall stretch forth her hand and princes shall come out of Egypt.'

"The late Henry Grady told us that in the 'wise and humane administration, in the lifting the slave to heights of which he had not dreamed in his savage home, and giving him a happiness he has not yet found in freedom—our fathers left their sons a saving and excellent heritage (slavery).' Another man, also a Southerner, has told us: 'In education and industrial progress this race has accomplished more than it could have achieved in centuries in a different environment, without the aid of the whites. The Negro has needed the example as well as the aid of the white man. In sections where the colored population is massed and removed from contact with the whites, the Negro has retrograded. Segregate the colored population and you take away the object lesson.' Here, then, is the testimony of two intellectual white men as to the dependence of the Negro upon his proximity to the whites for a continuance of what advancement he has made since the abolishment of slavery. Is such a race as this fit at the present time to carry enlightenment into a savage and barbarous country? Can the blind lead the blind? Would not the Negro gradually fall into the same habits of ignorance and savagery from which the white slave trader so humanely rescued him when he transported him into the blissful lap of American slavery? The Negro cannot be deported.

"It is being argued that the Negro is receiving education beyond his needs or his capacity. In short, that a Negro highly educated is a Negro spoiled. I agree with the gentleman on the other side that education alone will not produce a good citizen. But, of those who would curtail his endeavours to reach the highest that may be opened to him, I would ask: Of what use has education been to you in the upbuilding of the social and political structure which you designate the United States of America? What are the uses of education anyhow?

"To those who know the constitution of the brain as the organ of the moral and intellectual powers of man, education is of the highest importance in the formation of the character of the individual, the race, the government, the social life of any community under heaven. The objects presented to the mind by education stimulate in the same manner that the physical elements of nature do the nerves and muscles—they afford the faculties scope for action. Education is knowledge of nature in all its departments. The moment the mind discovers its own constitution and discerns the importance of the natural laws, the great advantage of moral and intellectual cultivation as a means of invigorating the brain and mental faculties, and of directing the conduct in obedience to the laws of God and man, is apparent. It is important that the Negro should not be hampered in his search after knowledge if we would eliminate from his nature any tendency toward vice that he may be thought to possess, and which has been largely increased by what he has imbibed from the example and the close 'immoral association' which often exercised between the master and the slave. From my own observation I should say that in this country today the science of man's whole nature—animal, moral and intellectual—was never more required to guide him than at present, when he seems to wield a giant's power, and in the application of it to display the selfish ignorance of an overgrown child.

"We come now to the crime of rape, with which the Negro is accused. For the sake of argument, we will allow that in one case out of a hundred the Negro is guilty of the crime with which he is charged; in the other ninety-nine cases the white man gratifies his lust, either of passion or vengeance. None of us will ever forget the tales told us tonight by Luke Sawyer; the wanton passions he revealed and which it has taken centuries of white civilisation to develop, disclosing a dire hell to which the common crime of the untutored Negro is as white as alabaster. And it is from such men as these that the appeal comes for protection of woman's virtue! Do such examples as these render the Negro gentle and pacific? No; he sees himself travelling for years the barren Sahara of poverty, imprisonment, broken hopes and violated home ties; the ignorant, half-savage, irresponsible human animal who forms the rank and file of a race so recently emancipated from servitude, sees only revenge before his short-sighted vision.

"Rape is the outgrowth of a fiendish animus of the whites toward the blacks and of the blacks toward the whites. The Southern white is unable to view the feared domination of the blacks with the dispassionate reasoning of the unprejudiced mind. He exaggerates the nearness of that possibility, which is not desired by the blacks, and, like the physician sick of a mortal disease, is unable to prescribe for himself, and cannot realise that the simple remedy, gently applied, will lift him from his couch of pain. Lynch law prevails as the only sure cure for the ills of the South.

" 'Lynchings are justifiable on two grounds,' says a thoughtful writer: 'First, if they are consonant with the moral dignity and well-being of the people; and secondly, if they stop, and are the only sure means of stopping, the crime they avenge.'

"Lynching does not stop crime; it is but a subterfuge for killing men. It is a good excuse, to use a rough expression, to 'go a-gunning for niggers.'

"Lynching was instituted to crush the manhood of the enfranchised black. Rape is the crime which appeals most strongly to the heart of the home life. Merciful God! Irony of ironies! The men who created the mulatto race, who recruit its ranks year after year by the very means which they invoked lynch law to suppress, bewailing the sorrows of violated womanhood!

"No; it is not rape. If the Negro votes, he is shot; if he marries a white woman, he is shot; if he accumulates property, he is shot or lynched—he is a pariah whom the National Government cannot defend. But if he defends himself and his home, then is heard the tread of marching feet as the Federal troops move southward to quell a 'race riot.'

"The South declares that she is no worse than the North, and that the North would do the same under like provocation. Perhaps so, if the offender were a Negro. Take the case of Christie Warden and Frank Almy, which occurred in New Hampshire only a few years ago. Where could a more atrocious crime be perpetrated? The refinement of intellectual pursuits, the elegancies of social intercourse, were the attributes which went to make up the personnel of the most brutal murderer that ever disgraced the history of crime. Centuries of culture and civilisation were combined in his make-up. The community where the girl lived and was respected and beloved did not lynch the brute. The white heat of passion led men to lay aside all pursuits for days in order to hunt the criminal from his hiding place. New Hampshire justice gave him counsel and every means to defend himself from the penalty of his horrid crime. That was in the North!

"Human nature is the same in everything. The characteristic traits of the master will be found in his dog. Black, devilish, brutal as they may picture the Negro to be, he but reflects the nature of his environments. He is the Hyde who torments the Dr Jekyll of the white man's refined civilisation!

"My friends, it is going to take time to straighten out this problem; it will only be done by the formation of public opinion. Brute force will not accomplish anything. We must agitate. We must appeal for the justice of our cause to every civilised nation under the heavens. Lift ourselves upward and forward in this great march of life until Ethiopia shall indeed stretch forth her hand, and princes shall come out of Egypt?"

When he had finished there was not a dry eye in that vast audience. Every heart followed the words of the pastor as with broken utterance he invoked the divine blessing upon the meeting just ended. Slowly they dispersed to their homes, filled with thoughts that burn but cannot be spoken.

The papers said next day that a very interesting meeting occurred the night before at the church on X Street.

CHAPTER 16

Many things troubled John Langley. The fact that Dora and he seemed to have lost the close relationship which had distinguished the first period of their engagement, and that she now studiously avoided him and accepted with alacrity all the attention which her childhood's lover so ardently showered upon her, did not disturb him so much as the utter indifference of Sappho Clark. How to bend her to his will was the thought which absorbed his waking hours and haunted him even in sleep. She should not escape him; on that he was determined.

This morning as he walked down town to his office he turned over various plans in his mind, and finally determined to go that very day and consult Madam Frances, who had been voted such a tremendous success at the fair which had just closed. John believed that the seeress could help him, and he was not so polished and refined as to hesitate to use such means to accomplish an end.

When he reached the office he noticed that an invitation to a dinner given that very evening by the Canterbury Club lay upon the desk; in his absorption in other things he had forgotten the dinner. He pushed his work at the Court House to a quick finish and retraced his steps to the office, and telling the boy that he would not return before three o'clock, hurried toward the quarter of the city in which the fortune teller lived.

J. Street is in the very heart of what is called the Negro quarter of the West End; it is also popularly known among colored people as 'the Hill'. Here Madam Frances lived in a small ten-foot wooden building which she hired.

'The Hill' has been the scene of many stirring incidents in the peculiar history of the colored people. On the J. Street side the old St. Paul's Baptist Church is situated. This historic old building was the first church the colored people owned in Massachusetts. There were five brothers—black men—bearing the name of Paul, who were educated in England in the reign of George III. One of them—Thomas—determined to return to England and beg for funds to build a colored church in America. He was well received and his mission was successful. Twenty years ago an old Negress—a centenarian—was living who had herself picked up bricks in the streets of Boston in the early morning, and carried them to the spot where the building was being erected. She did this because although too poor to give money toward furthering the enterprise, she felt that she must contribute in some way to the erection of this first colored house of worship in this part of the country. This same woman remembered seeing Thomas Paul bring into the church a large bandanna handkerchief filled with the English gold he had begged abroad, the first Sunday the building was used for worship.

St. Paul's Church became the sacred edifice where the desire for freedom was fostered in the heart of the Negro. There such men as Garrison and Phillips defied the vengeance of howling mobs that thirsted for the lives of the Negro champions.

O glorious times! Who can think of them without a quicker heartthrob and a wildly fluttering pulse? O honored men! O happy dead, gone to receive the reward promised to all who do the work of the Master. As we read of the deeds of such men the question will obtrude itself: Is it the foreordained destiny of some to achieve greatness? And if not foreordained, would these same great ones remain inert and impotent like the mediocre majority? Many of us strive to do what we can, but our efforts do not seem to amount to much. In the present emergency which confronts us as a race, no leader has yet pressed forward to take command, as in those glorious old days; no Sumner to receive upon his precious body the stripes intended for the poor, downtrodden black man.

God rest us all—we know not what we are
What nature wills, not what we wish, are we.

Let us press forward and take courage and do the little that we can, leaving the rest to God. The hand of the Divine Architect will fit each life into its own niche, to form an intricate whole of preconceived beauty.

Near the head of G. and P. Streets stands the well-known Twelfth Baptist Church, a split from St. Paul's, and world renowned under its beloved pastor and founder, Leonard Grimes. Just across the way, on P. Street, was the home of the venerable and honored Lewis Hayden. The history of Massachusetts is forever linked with that of the Anti-slavery Movement, and the Anti-slavery Movement is entwined about the familiar street corners of the old West End.

John reached the house and rang the bell of the quaint abode. A colored girl, who was evidently a servant, answered the ring, and told him that Madam Frances was now at lunch, and would not be at liberty until an hour later. However, he might come in and wait, if he wished, and she would ask the Madam to see him before her usual time. On second thoughts, she did sometimes see people before her hours (this was after John had discreetly slipped a small piece of silver into her hand). She waited on him up the narrow stairway and seated him in a small back room adjoining the audience room.

117

John took a seat a little behind the door, thereby being completely sheltered from observation. Indeed, a person passing the door on entering or leaving the building would not be likely to see him, and would declare the room empty; but from his seat he commanded a full view of the passageway. He had looked the bare and sparsely furnished room over and settled back in his chair for a tedious period of waiting when the door of the next room opened and his attention was attracted by the sound of a voice which he thought he knew: "That money will do what you wish for the boy, Aunt Sally, and"—then the door was closed. John started to his feet in great excitement. Surely he knew that voice! Again the door must have swung open, for he caught the words of the conversation distinctly: "There is no need for him to know—let him continue to think"—he heard no more. Again the door closed. It must have been fully five minutes that he stood intently listening, but nothing more rewarded him. Suddenly the door opened and shut and then he heard the quick, light footfall of a woman and the frou-frou of silken skirts, together with a delicate perfume that he recognised. He drew back as far as possible behind the shelter of the door, and then as he judged from the sound that she was upon the stairs, he ventured from his hiding place, and finding the entry clear, peered over the banisters just in time to catch a full view of the beautiful face of Sappho Clark. As she passed out she had dropped her handkerchief; John picked it up; there in the corner were her initials: 'S. C.'

He returned to his seat in the bare little room, holding the delicately scented piece of cambric in his hand with the feeling of a man who is on the verge of discovering something of importance to himself. He was confused and uncertain in his thoughts, but when he could command himself sufficiently to reason, he felt that it was very foolish of him to wonder at Sappho's presence there; all girls were eager to consult those who could unveil for them anything pertaining to the future. How silly for him to make a mystery of a common happening; still he was restless, disquieted; vague suspicions assailed his mind.

Madam Frances' niece! What could be her motive in hiding her relationship to the old fortune teller? That she had one he was confident. The child, too! She appeared never to have seen him before the fair. They had acted in concert. Madam Frances and the boy seemed not to know Sappho, and by their manner denied all previous knowledge of her. Here was something to unravel. But he was used to solving mysteries; it was his business. He would constitute himself a committee of investigation, he told himself; he owed it to the community, to himself, to the Smith family, who were so fond of her. So he planned that the sin of another poor human soul, a vague fraud against no one in particular but society in general, doing wrong to no one, should be suddenly stripped of its coverings. He mused here alone, buried in deep thought, forgetful of the hour and his surroundings. Uncanny shadows were filling the corners of the bare little room when an idea came to him which fairly made him shiver. He could feel the blood recede from his face under the excitement of the moment and grow cold in his veins. "Heaven above!" he whispered, "it cannot be possible that what I suspect is true—that child—his resemblance to her—this woman the child's great-aunt and also Sappho's aunt—the secrecy!"

As he sat there engrossed in speculation the maid who had answered his ring came into the room to tell him that the Madam would see him. He still held the handkerchief in his hand, and said as he held it toward the girl: "The lady who just went out dropped it. I think she called Madam Frances 'Aunt Sally'."

"Oh, yes," replied the girl, as she took it from him. "I will give it to Madam. Miss Clark comes here a great deal. She is Madam Frances' niece."

John's thoughts were in a whirl as he followed the girl to the door of the room Sappho had just quitted. Why had he never heard of this relationship before? He was quite certain that the Smiths knew nothing of it, or he would have heard it spoken of about the house or at the fair. There was a mystery, then, about her. Just at this point he awoke to a realisation of the fact that he was within a darkened room. It took a moment for his eyes to become accustomed to the semi-twilight of the apartment, and then he seated himself in a chair beside a small table which the girl pointed out to him before she left the room, and which was evidently intended for visitors.

"How do you do?" said a voice, and turning in the direction from whence it came he beheld the wrinkled, black face, and gaudily turbaned head of Madam Frances. As he returned her greeting another voice said:

"How do you do? Lord love you, how do you do?"

Then he saw that a large green parrot was perched on the back of the chair in which Madam Frances was seated. On the table beside him was a silver dish holding two large sea-green stones, in the depths of which one could easily trace the outlines of white coral islands, birds, beasts and reptiles. In one corner of the room was a large screen covered with unbleached cotton. The table beside Madam Frances held a curious instrument which resembled a ship's compass, and on its surface the signs of the zodiac came and went at the will of the seeress. Many curious things were in this darkened room, and no matter how much one might wish to disbelieve the power of this woman to foretell the future, he could not fail to be impressed with the surroundings. And, after all, our surroundings influence our lives and characters as much as fate, destiny or any supernatural agency.

119

Madam Frances held out her hand for her fee, and as he laid a silver dollar across her palm, she said:

"She will escape you, and you will lose the other one, too. Better stop now, and keep the one you hold."

"Keep the one you hold, fool, fool, fool!" screamed the parrot's shrill voice.

"You come to me for advice about certain property that you would like to get. There is money all about you, piles of it. You will meet one soon who will tell you something of importance concerning a large sum of money. You say you did not come here to find that out. But it is here, and the dial does not lie."

She pointed to the face of the compass-like instrument before her. John felt very uncomfortable as the old woman peered at him from eyes which, while they seemed almost sightless, yet impressed one as being able to pierce the secrets of the soul.

"There are three things you wish to ask about," she continued. "Look on the screen and behold the answer to a question."

John looked toward the screen and saw what appeared to be dim shadows forming there, which gradually took on the shape of a banquet table, and seated around it was a company of men, among whom he recognised himself and his friends William Smith and Dr Lewis. "When you are at that table, in the company of those men, you shall have the answer to one of the questions you would ask me. Look again," she said, and John saw to his amazement that the cloth of which the screen was made had resumed its color, and another shadowy outline was beginning to form. As he gazed in wonder the outlines took shape before his astonished eyes, and he saw the altar of a church. Before a priest a man and woman knelt in bridal dress. The man placed a ring upon the woman's finger. As the picture faded the faces of the couple were turned toward him for one moment, and he recognised Sappho Clark and Will Smith.

"Look again," said the voice of the seeress. He did so, and saw before him a noble ship; on her deck stood a man and a woman. The picture faded before he could distinguish the features of either party. "These are all I am permitted to show you now," said Madam Frances. "These pictures contain the answers to your questions."

"Do I understand them to mean that I shall be defeated in my plans? That I shall not enjoy a part of the wealth which you see about me?"

"You will be defeated, and you will not enjoy the wealth that is about you; unless—" she paused, shook her head, mumbled some unintelligible jargon, as if conversing with the unseen, again shook her head.

"If not a sharer of the wealth you see, what will my fate be, and in what line shall I prosper? Surely you can tell me something about my success in life."

"Enough has been shown to you. Why persist? But look again, if you will not be advised."

Again he looked at the screen, and saw dark outlines resolve themselves into shapes. He saw what appeared to be a field of ice and snow, vast and unbroken—terrible in its dreary isolation. It faded, and he turned to the fortune teller in desperation.

"What has such a scene to do with me?"

"Remorse, remorse! Who can tell the end of life?" mumbled the crone, as if in self-communion. At length she seemed to come to herself, and said in clear accents: "If you would let an old woman advise you, I should say choose the right path, no matter what the cost. But men are foolish always, foolish always for a pretty face."

She touched a bell on the table beside her, and the boy Alphonse came from behind the curtain and gravely motioned the visitor to follow him out.

"For a pretty face," croaked the parrot, rousing himself from a nap as John left the room. As he descended the stairs the words of the parrot followed him:

"Fools, fools; all men are fools for a pretty face!"

John cursed his own folly in seeking the fortune teller's aid as he went slowly back to his office, puzzling over the things he had seen and heard. He was a well-read man, and tried to account for these strange things. He knew from reading, the mediumistic powers of all created things; he knew something of the wonderful agencies of electricity and magnetism. The appliances in the room had suggested magnetism as the medium; "yet," he argued, "the same phenomena might have been produced by the power of hypnotism." He knew enough of the latter to practice it in a way for the amusement of his young friends, but had thought himself impervious to its influence.

But with all his reasoning he could not convince himself that there was not an intelligence—invisible and intangible—that had presented to him those soul-disturbing manifestations.

CHAPTER 17

The Canterbury Club of Boston, which held its annual dinner on this particular evening, was composed of the flower of Boston's literary elite. At the rooms of the club men deep in scientific research touched elbows with the advanced theological scholar and the political economist. Side by side with the vital questions of the hour in the world of progress—wireless telegraph, the philosophy of trusts! The rise and fall of monarchies, the restoration of Greek art, the philosophy of lynching was beginning to engage the attention of two hemispheres, and information was eagerly sought from every reliable source.

Now it happened that the remarkable ability of Smith in dealing with the acknowledged difficulties of the question had been spoken of to some of the members by the Hon. Herbert Clapp, the president of the club. It had already entertained Dr Lewis, on account of his great work as an educator among his people.and John Langley because he was an important factor in his line, doing the work necessary to the life of any organisation interested in active politics with which men of a delicate moral susceptibility could not be approached. It was voted to invite young Smith to this dinner as a fresh and interesting specimen of the Negro. Many fat contributions found their way annually into the treasury of the African School of Industrial and Agricultural Development, which was under the able management of Dr Lewis, through the influence of this club. He had accomplished great things; had made himself the center of this terrible human tragedy in the heart of the Black Belt, where the college was situated; but the deadly antagonism of the South made even his iron-hearted stoicism bow to its tyrannical decrees, insomuch that he had been forced to compromise, and the educational advantages allowed the pupils had been curtailed to suit the views of those who placed a low estimate on the ability of the Negro, in spite of the many bright examples of superior intellectual endowments which exist among them. Such ideas as Dr Lewis set forth in his many brilliant speeches in behalf of his people were logical, and showed a mind capable of grasping the needs of the moment—an infinity of powerful thought under a tyrannous self-suppression.

"One man's meat is another man's poison." The colored people north of Mason and Dixon's line are conspicuous for their advancement along all the lines which are distinctive features in the formation of the polished exterior of the good citizen of such a republic as ours. Among the best circles of this community are found the highest types of intellectual, moral, religious and social improvement. What becomes of such a class as this when hampered by rules and laws made to fit the needs of the Black Belt? Laws of life and living which cannot be forced, and ought not to be forced, upon the large class of colored citizens who embody within themselves the highest development of American citizenship? We believe that the spirit of fair play is not yet dead in our beloved country. We believe that there still exists beneath the seething cauldron of prejudice with which the South would deluge the advance of the Negro, brave hearts that will answer the cry of distress with patriotic alacrity, and these same brave hearts will demand for every black face, North and South, the fullest opportunity to develop whatever is best within him.

The young men had planned to go together. Their entrance created a diversion; the English member of Parliament who was the guest of honor was much surprised, although too well-bred to show it. Certainly they were fine specimens of the genus homo, whose physique demanded more than a passing glance of admiration. Curious thoughts came to Mr Withington, the English guest; certain truths which, if applicable to England, seemed doubly so to this country, so new and untried, as it were, in the changes and subtle uncertainties of government and revolutions:

> And a proud yeomanry, its country's pride
> When once destroyed can never be supplied.

Will the Republic learn the value of the black children of her adoption when it is too late?

The presence of these young Negroes was generally received as a pleasant innovation among that company. There was a senator from Alabama present among the invited guests, and for a moment he felt his color rise and all the peculiar feelings of his section protest and clamour to make themselves heard when he found that he must perforce be brought into social contact with the despised ex-slave representatives. But he remembered, in time to save himself from ridicule, that he was in Massachusetts. "What matter?" was his inward thought. "Some day we shall change all this."

The first course was about over before Will had a chance to look about him. He did not feel at all overpowered by the grandeur displayed. The great room with its high walls and ceiling of magnificently carved mahogany, the massive brass chandeliers, composed of hundreds of tiny electric lights which threw their sparkling rays upon the exquisitely appointed table, with the priceless ware in which the meal was served, the heavy scent of roses which perfumed the air, the silent waiters gliding in and out among the guests—all seemed the fantastic creation of a dream.

His neighbour happened to be Mr Withington; his vis-a-vis, a noted editor; farther down the table he recognised a foreign secretary of legation; and so on. Conversation soon became general; flashes of wit, satire, and discussions of rare value to the student—a sumptuous feast of good things. Above the click of glasses he caught snatches of conversation:

"You may search through science and find no evidence of the presence of God in the universe," declared the sharp, decisive voice of a free thinker, who was plunged in the midst of an argument with a noted theologian of the Episcopal faith. Will listened intently for the answer. It came instantly:

"How could it be otherwise? God has a subjective existence to man; therefore man must get outside of himself to know God; in fact, man must die to attain God."

"Ah, there you go, with your mythological argument! You cover the clear statement of a fact with a veil of mysticism."

"Very true; but what is the soul, mentality, existence itself, but a living mysticism?" replied the clergyman.

The whole room had become interested by this time, and watched the play of cultured thought and keen argument with great relish.

"It is only when the subjective part of man exists as a distinct entity, then, that you think the presence of God is made clear to him?"

"Yes," replied the clergyman; "for the final end of man is the beginning of spirituality, or the true knowledge of God."

"Ah, but if we let reason speak, we find the flaws in your theory, and your ground becomes untenable. I look forward to the day which coming years shall usher in, when all the discoveries which are being made each year, and the general diffusion of scientific knowledge, shall revolutionise thought, and place God and man on an entirely different plane from that which they now occupy."

"And what is this reason or thought which you feel will do so much? It is but a loan from the Almighty, whose existence you affect to doubt. Man has no title to the property until he has permission to hold it eternally."

"And then?"

"He must have satisfied the Almighty that he is worthy."

Presently Will plunged into the conversation, impelled thereto by a certain philosophical reference with which he was familiar, and which he had studied with great interest.

"What do you think of reason and religion, Mr Smith?" asked the free thinker, impressed with the intelligence of his comments. "Are you one with the rest of your race in believing all this talk of spirituality?"

"I believe that reason and religion must act together to discover the perfect power and glory of God," replied Will modestly. All eyes were for the moment bent upon him. "There is perfect harmony between them; and it is our own shortsightedness which causes us to doubt."

"Do you not believe that by seeking knowledge, and dedicating life to the welfare of mankind and obedience to God in our several vocations, our best faculties will be gratified? Wealth, fame, health, and all other good things will flow in a stream, and our delight remain permanent?" asked Dr Lewis at this stage of the argument,

"Not necessarily obedience to God," replied the free thinker. "Certain causes bring certain effects, without reference to a presiding deity."

"That's it!" said the Southerner, soft voice, to his next neighbour. "Negroes are all alike with regard to religion; ignorant, thieving, dirty and lazy, but withal crammed full of religious enthusiasm. You should know them as I do—shouting, screaming, frothing at the mouth with the outpourings of the 'spirit', and as soon as they are outside of the church door, robbing hen-roots and watermelon patches. Bah!"

Low as his words were spoken, they caught the ear of Will. His flashing black eyes were turned upon the speaker as he said with a courtly bow:

"Granted that all you say is true, still the Negro does not sin against ages of accumulated knowledge of right and wrong. It is not absolute incapacity in the Negro either, but mere want of information, arising from lack of intelligent exercise of the perceptive faculties. These faults you speak of are but the remnants of an old irresponsible life. The majority of our race has turned aside forever from the old beaten paths of slavery into the undiscovered realms of free thought and free action. Some of the race may abuse the newly acquired liberty by petty pilfering or an overflow of religious enthusiasm, but the Negro has changed, whether you realise it or not; times have changed, and the Negro with them."

There was a murmur of applause as he finished speaking.

"Well," returned the Southerner, "we will grant that some of you are making progress, but you cannot claim that as a race you are capable of becoming such examples of manhood as you and your friends. To most of you the mystery of government will always remain a mystery, and the hope of assimilating many things which are second nature to the white man, will never become a reality to your race."

"I believe that the same rules which govern all races will be applicable to mine," returned Will. "If men are rude and foolish, down they must go. When at last in any race a new principle appears, an idea, that conserves it. Ideas only save races. If the black man is feeble and impotent, unimportant to the existing races—not on a parity with the best races, the black man must serve and be exterminated. But, if he carries within his bosom the element of a new and coming civilisation, he will survive and play his part."

"Hear, hear!" cried the foreign secretary of legation, applauding vigorously, delighted at the strong, combative style in which the brave young fellow met the ancient enemy of his race. "No race is hopelessly lost to the world of progress that produces such manly specimens within fifty years of emancipation."

"England is troubled over the fact that the two races do not mix, and to all appearances never will," now joined in Mr Withington. "There seems to be no common ground between them; they cannot live together harmoniously. Can you, gentlemen, explain this to me? I should like to carry back with me, when I return, a clear realisation of the facts in the case as viewed by each party to the question. That is part of my mission in this country."

"It is true," said Dr Lewis, "that our condition is alarming to a degree. Over ten thousand graves made since the war by mob violence, are dotting the South, and of these ninety per cent are the graves of black men."

"You do not get these facts abroad because newspaper reports are doctored by local Southern writers who participate in the lynchings. Free speech and public discussions are not allowed. In the South you must think and speak as the mob dictates," here chimed in John Langley.

"But surely you have constitutional equity before the law? You can gain redress from the Federal government?"

"Constitutional equity is a political fiction," laughed Will.

"Reconstruction is a failure, then?" asked Mr Withington.

"Reconstruction is not a failure, although the whole South will tell you so, and the North is being persuaded to so believe; the Negro was the living force which rent asunder the old methods of the slave-holding states and brought them out into the healthful light of decent, God-fearing living. But they are trying to take all the credit for the good we may have done them, from us. The lines are drawn more sharply than before the emancipation. Constitutional amendments are dead letters; the ballot box is nil," replied Will.

"All of which goes to show that race is stronger than law," broke in the Southerner.

"Rather that barbarism is superior to civilisation."

"What about the crime of rape?" asked Mr Withington.

"In nine cases out of ten," replied Lewis, "you will find that .the Negro is guiltless of this awful crime. It is brought forward to alienate the sympathy of all decent men from us. It is a crime that strikes the home ties, and as such is the most deadly weapon that has yet been used against us. We invite investigation in this direction, and you will then find that it is not a characteristic of the black man, although if is of the white man of the South."

"You cannot prove your assertions!" exclaimed the Southerner, white with passion.

"I can."

"Name a case."

"John Thomas of Georgia."

"He was guilty, and deserved his fate. You, gentlemen, must have heard the story of the atrocities committed by that man. The woman's husband was brutally murdered and she was assaulted. We made the fate of the black devil a terrible example for the rest of his kind in Georgia."

"Do you not know that that story has been proven false all through? It was this way, gentlemen: After the man Thomas was lynched, the colored people were convinced of his innocence. A sum of money was raised by subscription to hire the services of a reputable detective to investigate the matter. He visited the scene of the alleged crime, and it was found that Thomas worked for Cragen on his farm. Thomas heard that his mother was sick, and wished to visit her. Having no money, he applied to Cragen for his pay. This enraged the latter, and he drew his revolver to shoot the Negro. Quick as a flash Thomas seized an axe which happened to be lying near, and struck Cragen, killing him instantly. He then fled to the woods. Mrs Cragen says that Thomas did not assault her; she never saw him."

"And for defending himself they lynched him?" said Mr Withington, with a look on his face which expressed incredulous astonishment, combined with disgust.

"Yes; that was the detective's report, given under oath. What the man suffered at the hands of the lynchers could only be equalled by the sufferings of the martyrs of Negro's time. If every case of Negro lynching could be investigated, we should discover fearful discrepancies between the story of the mob and the real truth."

"That does not prove that white men are ravishers," said the Southerner, returning to the charge.

"Oh," replied Will, with a significant shrug of the shoulders, "take the representatives of my race who are with you tonight. How did we get our complexions, soft curls and regular features? Our ancestors were black, flat-featured, and had many other racial marks. Your race does not intermarry with Negroes, does it? That being the case, the answer is self-evident."

"Do you not think, then, that under the circumstances the Government ought to assist the Negro to leave the country?" asked Mr Withington.

"Never!" cried Will, with glowing countenance. "Never! Here where we have been so outrageously maligned, let us refute the charge like men!"

"That sounds well," said the Southerner with a sneer, "but how will you do it?"

"By using the methods of the South," replied Will quickly; "create sentiment for the race and against its detractor."

"And if you get nothing else out of it, the agitators will do a good business and fill their pockets with money."

"Agitation will do much," said Will calmly, unruffled by the other's display of anger. "It gave us freedom; it will give us manhood. The peace, dignity and honor of this nation rises or falls with the Negro. Frederick Douglass once said: 'Ultimately this nation will be composite. There is a strong demand—a growing demand—for a government capable of protecting all its citizens—rich and poor, white and black alike.' The causes for such a government still exist. It remains to be seen if the prophecy will be fulfiled."

One of the founders of the American Academy at Rome was present, and conversation now turned upon the development of American talent in art. The political aspect of Great Britain in South Africa and the complications likely to arise there from was another interesting topic, but under it all the sentiment expressed and the words spoken by the representatives of an humble race that night lingered in the heart of each scholar and thinker who had heard them.

Will had a pressing engagement, and was obliged to excuse himself to the president of the club. He withdrew as quietly as possible. Those nearest him shook him warmly by the hand, and told him that they hoped to hear from him again, and soon, on the same interesting topic.

Mr Withington now attached himself to John Langley for the remainder of the evening, seeming well pleased to find himself in such company. As they bade each other good night at the close of the festivities he said to John, as he placed his card in his hand:

"I leave tomorrow for Canada, on business connected with the Home Office. I may never return to this country, but I want you to believe that I am deeply interested in the welfare of your people. Write to me whatever comes up of importance to the race, and I will do what I can to make sentiment in my own country for you, and as far as money will go, you shall have the benefit of the help it will give."

John bade him goodbye, and even his conservative heart was warmed by contact with so good a man. After he had reached his room he took the card from his pocket, and before putting it in a place of safety read the address:

Charles Montfort-Withington, MP.
Berkshire,
England.

For a long time he sat there staring at the card in his hand. Where had he heard that name before? Charles Montfort! Why, it was the family name of Mrs Smith! Instantly the words of Madam Frances came to his mind, and a great light seemed to illuminate his thoughts: 'When you are at that table in the company of those men, you shall have the answer to one of the questions you would ask me.'

How often he had listened to the story told by Ma Smith with an incredulous smile. It had seemed to him the idle boasting of a mind entering its dotage. Charles Montfort—and from England! Heavens! If there should be truth in this fairy tale!

CHAPTER 18

The days passed very quietly at 500 D Street. The excitement occasioned by the fair, and the extraordinary agitation which had attended the meeting of the American Colored League, had somewhat abated. Softer thoughts and feelings had taken possession of the public mind, for it was very near to the celebration of Easter. The two girls, Dora and Sappho, felt restrained in their intercourse because, although by tacit consent nothing was said of John's treacherous conduct toward Dora, each knew that the other had discovered it. Dora felt aggrieved and ill-treated; and who could blame her? Dr Lewis was drawn into the trouble through his attachment to Dora. He pitied her injured feelings; he knew that if she were free and he offered her his love, it would be accepted, and he was not too proud to have done this if it had been an honourable act. He knew that it would not be an honourable act to ask her to break her promise to Langley at this stage of the drama, but within his heart hope grew stronger each day. He saw that John was hopelessly infatuated with Sappho; he saw Dora knew this and resented the wrong done herself, although as yet she could hardly put her thoughts into words. Daydreams began to break in upon the dull monotony of his methodical existence. He watched the signs of growing discontent with all a lover's impatience to grasp the happiness which he felt would, after a time, be his. He was willing to work, to wait, to serve, if only he might claim her love at last. Oh, the nobleness of a good man's love! If women would but prize it, how many more happy homes we should see, and how much brighter the world and life would be. Toward Langley he was savage; and then, too, he was puzzled.

One night they were all invited to attend a reception given at the house of a friend. He was with Dora and John. Dora addressed a remark to John, and receiving no answer, turned to look in his face for the reason. His gaze was fixed upon Sappho, who was surrounded by every eligible man in the house. And such a look! Love, hatred, tenderness—the gamut of passion was disclosed by the look bent upon the unconscious girl before them. Dora shuddered as if a chill had struck her, and turning to Lewis held a cold and trembling little hand appealingly toward him. He took it gladly into his firm and loving clasp, and tenderly asked her if she would like to go home. She grasped the offer instantly with evident relief. She left John's side to seek the ladies' dressing room for her wraps; he, absorbed in thoughts of Sappho, did not miss her presence. Lewis sent word to Will that he was taking Dora home because she was feeling very tired. He apologised to the hostess, engineered all the delicate details of social life with neatness and dispatch, and met the harassed girl at the foot of the staircase, ready to lead her home without arousing disagreeable comment.

"What does the beggar mean?" he asked himself more than once that night. "He does not seem inclined to give Dora up, and yet he is completely gone over the other one." But, like a prudent man, he said nothing; he kept his own counsel and watched.

Since the meeting at which Sappho had fainted, the girl had grown more silent and depressed. People said: "Yes, she is beautiful, but so cold and silent."

She and Will had scarcely spoken since the night of the fair, but each felt and knew that it would be but a short time before the story of their love must be settled for good and all. So the days crept by and brought the crisis of these lives, so strangely interwoven.

Easter Sunday fell early in April that year. The city had donned its gayest attire to welcome the return of the celebration of Christ's triumphant resurrection. The morning service was ended. The exultant organ peals, the glorious strains of hymns of victory poured forth by highly trained voices in hundreds of augmented church choirs all over the city, still seemed to vibrate upon the listening air even after the churches had given up their crowds of worshippers. Sappho had been to the mission church of St. Augustine, on P. Street, at the West End. Here the good Fathers of the Mission of St. John had reared a church, and elected to bend their efforts particularly to the salvation and upraising of the poorest of God's children. This church, with its beautiful silver chimes, given by a wealthy Boston woman in commemoration of the life and services of the lamented Bishop Brooks, is destined to stand for ages as a memorial of the deeds of philanthropy which have always been a distinguishing feature of the true spirit of Massachusetts. The sound of the bells lingered with her like a benediction. For the first time in weeks a tranquil mind was hers. The spirit of the day was upon her in full measure; to her the risen Christ was a reality, and his triumph over sin and death was to her bruised spirit a promise and a blessing. Stepping lightly along she gained the Public Garden and crossed the rustic bridge, skirting the lake as she walked toward the Arlington street entrance. Many admiring glances followed the graceful figure, clad in its fresh, jaunty, tailor-made suit of grey. The strong wind kissed the pure face and gently lifted the clustering curls from the white brow, where Cupid lurked in every curve and delicate thread of gold. The Garden was very beautiful this year; it had blossomed with more than its usual luxuriance for the annual festival. Beds of crocuses, gaudy tulips and hyacinths dotted the landscape side by side with the modest violet and exquisite pansy. God's smile was everywhere. April's sun and showers had blessed the earth, and "cold Nature, by his amorous kiss stung sweetly, stirred his limbs and felt A thrill of immemorial bliss."

Someone sat upon a garden seat awaiting her coming. Far down the mall he spied the solitary figure. It was she herself! As he gazed upon the advancing figure of the girl he loved he felt his heart swell within him, and tender thrills of joy filled his soul, too full for utterance. He noticed that she wore a bunch of violets today, instead of her favorite Jacks. They were more in keeping with the sentiment of the day. There they rested in a splendid cluster upon her breast—modest and beautifully fragrant. "As sweet as a violet herself," he thought, as he murmured to himself:

> The breeze runs riot with thy charms,
> O faint, delicious, springtime violet!

As a man Will Smith was not ashamed of the passion which consumed him. An honourable love has its own subtle charm. Now was his opportunity! The almost deserted paths were secure from intrusion. She was not indifferent to him; today should end suspense. He would have her answer.

Sappho caught sight of him directly she entered the path. She hesitated, turned, then stood still, as if conscious of his resolution. He saw her hesitation, and read her thoughts by virtue of that harmony which is love's perfection. He arose and stood before her, hat in hand. His apparent coolness and self-possession did what he intended it should: restored her calmness; and when she placed her hand in his and responded to his cheery greeting, she was herself again.

"Do not hurry away," he said, as she turned as if to resume her walk. "Let us sit a moment and enjoy this charming view of beautiful Boston."

She stood a moment gazing at the fair prospect spread out before them.

"How peaceful, beautiful and calm the landscape seems. If earth be so fair, what must be the beauty of heaven?" she said, after a slight pause.

"Indeed, yes," replied Will, as he glanced at the fair face beside him with something like awe. For a moment he felt that he stood in the presence of a saint; earthly passion seemed out of place.

After a moment's silence she seated herself, mechanically protesting that she had promised Dora to help her with her Sunday school class at half-past one.

"Never mind," said Will, "it is real Sunday school work for you to

132

look after me a bit. I'm sure I need Bible lessons." At this they both laughed, and then Sappho asked:

"Where ought the lesson to be?"

She saw instantly by the change in his expression that she had given him his opening, and immediately lost the self possession she had just gained.

" 'And Jacob loved Rachel; and said, I will serve thee seven years for thy younger daughter,' " quoted Will softly, as he looked at the gentle face and downcast eyes beside him. Sappho said nothing, but gazed intently at the landscape with unseeing eyes, as she nervously clasped and unclasped her delicately gloved hands. Suddenly she felt one small hand drawn within a strong, warm clasp.

"There are shadows on your face; why are they there? You think all kinds of sad thoughts. Tell them to me, Sappho."

"Nay,"she said at length, "why should I? They are not clear even to myself. You would not understand my vagaries. Why should you be bothered with them?"

"Because, Sappho, my beautiful one, my darling, I love you—surely you know it. I have loved you from the first moment that I saw you. Be my wife, my blessing."

She did not answer; her face had grown very white.

"Have I frightened you? Do not think me cruel, Sappho; you do not know how much I love you."

She was still silent, but another look satisfied him that she was not angry. The gloved hand stopped fluttering, and lay quietly within his clasp.

"You do not think me presumptuous? You are not angry? Tell me that you love me."

"Wait one moment," she said; and then he saw that she was trembling violently.

"Don't you care for me a little?" he asked anxiously, "or have I been living in a fool's paradise the past two months?"

"I do care for you," she whispered, in a voice so low that only a lover could have heard it.

"Ah!" he cried impetuously; "then I will never let you go!"

"Ah, Will, I wonder if it is right for me to love you, or to allow you to love me?"

"Most decidedly it is right. Why do you doubt?"

"You have known me such a short time," she protested.

"I know that you are the dearest girl in all the world to me," he replied, holding her hand still more tightly clasped. "You are mine now, and nothing shall part us. I shall always remember this day as the happiest of my life. You do not know how dearly I love you."

"I shall know if you persist in telling me so often," she said, smiling at his impetuosity.

"Heaven bless you, Sappho, my dearest. I shall never tire of ringing the changes on love."

"Why should you care so much for me?" she asked wistfully. "I have no family, no friends, no money"—

"I have family enough for both of us," he returned quickly. "My mother loves you, my sister adores you; what more is there to be desired?"

"But there are things which you ought to know—things connected with the past"—

"I do not care for the past," he broke in; "all I ask is that you love me above all other men, as I adore you above all other women."

She was carried away by the vehemence of his wooing. All obstacles seemed, indeed, but trifles before this all-absorbing, passionate, eager warmth of youth's first love. Poor soul! Poor starved and storm-beaten heart! Something of life that was dead leaped again into existence and loosened the icy hand that had for years locked up the fountain of youthful joy. She felt drawn out of herself as she looked into the eyes of love and met the luminous light which transfigured the face of her lover.

Ask me no more; thy fate and mine are sealed. I strove against the stream and all in vain. Let the great river take me in the main. No more, dear love, for at a touch I yield. Ask me no more.

Silently she turned to him and placed the other hand within his clasp, and burst into a tempest of weeping.

"Sappho!" he cried, in a transport of delight, as he tried to dry her tears; "my darling, my wife!"

O happy Easter Day!

They sat there a long time in heart communion, reviewing the history of their short acquaintance, and the wonderful thing that had happened to them. They planned that Sappho should stay with Will's mother while he went abroad, and then when his course was finished they would be married immediately upon his return. They would keep their sweet secret a little while. They could not share this hallowed day with others. It was consecrated and holy to them because of its dear association with the hidden stream of their united lives.

John Langley was returning from an errand downtown, and attracted by the beauty of the morning, determined to cross the Garden on his way to the South End. Suddenly, beneath the trees he espied the lovers. He paused a moment. They were so much absorbed in each other that they had not seen him. He turned aside into a path which ran very near to them on one side, and paused beneath the shadow of some friendly trees where he was secure from observation and could watch their movements unseen.

The happy light on Will's expressive countenance did not escape him; he noted, too, the shy happiness and deep, tender love which shone in Sappho's eyes. His heart was on fire with hot, jealous rage, and he resolved that their marriage should never take place. He was not sure of Sappho's past, but he would try a bold manoeuvre and trust to luck. He would accuse her as though certain of the facts. If that did not work, he would try some other game. He who had laughed at love without money, found himself even contemplating the sacrifice of one for the other, if dishonest means should not succeed in winning her. He watched them for a time, and then, judging by their movements that they were about to leave the spot, turned reluctantly away, planning ways and means of bringing his schemes to a successful issue.

Sappho had been taking her meals with the family lately, but tonight she excused herself from dinner on the plea of a headache. Will had gone back to the hotel.

"Headache must be a great cosmetic," said Dora slowly. She had seen that Will and Sappho returned from morning church together and from certain signs had drawn her own conclusions about how matters stood between them. "I never remember seeing you look better or more beautiful than you do tonight." Sappho laughed joyously as she ran lightly up the stairs to her room. Tomorrow they would know her secret.

She glanced at her mirror as she passed it. Where was the usually pale, sad face that it reflected? They called her cold and proud. What would the world say if it could see that brilliant, vivid, flashing beauty that the mirror gave back to her astonished gaze? Truly love was a wonderful cosmetic. She sank into the inviting willow rocker, and for a while gave herself up to the happiness which was so intense as to be almost painful. There was no thought of evil mingled with the joy that wrapped her round about. No forebodings assailed her; the intoxication of the moment was complete. She was lost in dream as she sat there thinking of her lover. Will had said to her: "I am not a man to hold love lightly, it is no jest with me. My love is the one woman in the whole world to me above all others. I shall love you living and dying, and be true to you in life and death." The words rang in her ears like sweetest music.

There were extra services at all the colored churches that night, because owing to the fact that most of the worshippers were employed as domestic servants, evening was the only time convenient for their employers to spare their services. She heard the outer door close upon one after another until the house settled down to the perfect quiet of solitude.

She then arose from her seat and proceeded to change her street attire for a pale blue cashmere house dress with delicate ecru lace at the throat and wrists. She hummed strains of the Gloria heard that morning in church as she stood before the glass and took the pins from her hair. The shining coil of burnished gold fell almost to her feet. So she stood with the brushes poised in air as the door opened softly and John Langley came quickly into her room. Thus they stood for a brief second of time: she colourless with amazement and fear; he overwhelmed with the exquisiteness of the picture before him. The brushes falling from her hands broke the silence. Anger flamed in her eyes.

"I did not hear you knock, Mr Langley. What can I do for you?"

His face was pale, his eyes wavering and bloodshot; his whole expression indicated a terrible determination. The almost insulting coldness of her tone exasperated him.

"I did not knock," he replied, as he stepped into the room. "You do not offer me a seat," he sneered, as he sat down on the couch.

"This is hardly the time or place for parlor civilities," she replied significantly. "Do you not know that the house is empty?"

"I do; and as I wish to speak with you privately, and as this is my only chance, I will not let it slip me," said John.

"Really! I cannot understand what private business you can have with me," returned Sappho haughtily, "but if it be so, pray state the nature of it as quickly as possible."

"I will," he replied. He paused a moment, as if collecting his thoughts. "You and Will seem to have come to an understanding, judging by what I saw on the Public Garden this morning," he said finally.

Sappho flushed warmly as she replied: "And in what way does that concern you?"

The girl looked so beautiful and spirited that he longed to crush her with the weight of his surmises.

"Will Smith is a very proud man as well as a very just man. His pride of family is his one sin. Do you think that it will be for his best interest to marry you?"

"And why should it not be?"

"You can best answer that question," was the guarded reply.

"Mr Langley, your intrusion into my private apartment is unpardonable. Your innuendoes are still more so. If you have anything to say, please say it. If not, let us close this remarkable interview." She moved toward the door as if to open it. In an instant he seized her arm and stopped her.

"Do not be rash. It is better for you to listen to me and not arouse my enmity. I have seen Luke Sawyer, and I know your secret—Mabelle Beaubean!"

The attack was so sudden she did not think of defending herself. He had never in his life seen emotion so terrible depicted upon the human countenance as her face presented at that moment. She shrank from him with shivering dread, beating the air with both hands, as though in her agony she warded off the approach of some gruesome apparition.

"Not that name—not that name!" she gasped, as she turned her beautiful, ghastly face from side to side, as though seeking air. She seemed about to faint. Then she sank upon the floor and literally grovelled there, her face hidden by the long hair which enveloped her like a veil.

John was nonplussed at the perfect success of his plot; he was exultant. The terror of the girl was awful to behold. Surely he had her now. She must turn to him for help.

"Sappho," he said in feigned pity, "I feel for you. God knows I am sorry for this, and that I should have been the one to bring it upon you. But think of your story, and its effect upon Will if he should learn it after marriage!"

"I was a victim, an innocent child!" moaned the figure on the floor.

"I know," said John, "but girls of fourteen are frequently wives in our Southern climes, where women mature early. A man as supercilious as Will in his pride of Northern birth would take no excuse, and would never forgive."

"Ah, what can I do?!" cried the unhappy woman, as she rose to her feet and began to pace the floor. "Have I not suffered enough?" Now was the time for which he had waited and planned.

"Sappho, do not think that I forget how abominable I must appear to you. I know what you will say that I betray my friend, and worse than that, the girl who holds my promise; but my excuse is that my passion is stronger than honor, stronger than reason. There are men in the world who would not forsake you, and who would always befriend you. Give up will, and trust yourself to me. I am making money in my profession. I can and will do well by you. Your story need never be known."

"Doubtless you mean it in kindness," replied the girl wearily, "and I thank you, but I can never marry anyone but Will."

"Marriage!" exclaimed John, "who spoke of marriage? Ambitious men do not marry women with stories like yours!"

At last the murder was out—his meaning clear. For one moment Sappho was speechless with disgust.

"Infamous villain!" she said at length, "you abuse my forlorn condition. Leave me! Never till this moment have I realised the depths of my degradation!"

"I go at your command," said John. "I give you one week to think over what I have said. At the end of that time—"

"Go. Go! Will you go?" interrupted Sappho, pointing to the door with queenly dignity.

With a low bow John Langley passed out and closed the door behind him.

Sappho turned the key in the lock and sank upon the couch overcome with the horror of her situation. Nervous spasms shook her frame as she mentally measured the abyss of social ostracism and disgrace which confronted her. A thunderbolt from a clear sky had shattered her hopes and dashed the cup of happiness from her lips. Heart-rending sobs of anguish mingled with passionate appeals to heaven for mercy, tore her frame as she contemplated this sudden overthrow of her dreams of a bright future. The quiet which had attended her life since she had settled in Boston was rudely interrupted, and the ruin which threatened her was the more stupendous because unlooked for in the direction from which it came.

She got up at length, and going to the dressing table, began mechanically to collect her jewellry. She caught sight of her face in the glass. What a change from the glowing beauty of one short hour ago! She looked at the pale, drawn countenance with scorn. "Men call me beautiful," she murmured bitterly; "what has beauty been to me but a curse?"

She heard the closing of doors and the voices of the returned churchgoers. Could it be possible that she was the same happy girl whose smiling face had been given back from the mirror so radiantly a short hour ago? She heard the front door close again. It was Will's step upon the stair. He paused at her door a moment, and then passed on to the floor above. How often she had listened for that familiar tread. Her heart kept repeating: "Never again, never again."

Two hours later deep silence had fallen upon the house. A form attired in black, closely veiled, and carrying a travelling bag, passed from 500 D Street into the night, boarded an electric car, and was swallowed up in the heart of the metropolis.

Will in his room had fallen into his first sleep when he thought he heard the sound of noiseless footsteps in the hall. He listened a moment, and then concluded that he was mistaken. Who could be moving through the house at that hour? No, he was mistaken. His thoughts were all with Sappho. He lived over again the words and scenes of the morning. He heard the clocks strike twelve, one, two; then he fell into a deep, dreamless sleep.

CHAPTER 19

The next morning found the household early astir. It is a rule in hotels that a late watch, as it is called, exempts the employee from an early appearance for duty the next morning. On these mornings Will breakfasted with his mother and sister. Since Sappho had boarded with them this humble meal had become a feast to him.

He arose very early on this eventful Monday morning and hurried down the stairs, bursting to impart his good news to the sympathetic ears of his loved ones. He entered the kitchen just as Dora was laying the cloth for breakfast.

"What in the world brings you down so early?" she asked in a surprised tone as he entered the room.

"Oh, I couldn't stay in bed this morning of all others," he said, as he kissed her lightly on the cheek. "I am too happy."

"What under the sun is the cause of so much joy, that it brings so lazy a boy out of bed an hour before his time?"

"How did you feel when you were first engaged to John? Weren't you light-headed and silly?"

"Oh, I dare say I was silly enough," replied Dora with a sigh. At the mention of John a cloud seemed to settle down upon the brightness of her usually sunny face. "But what has that to do with your early rising? I don't see the analogy between the two."

"Congratulate me, Dora. Sappho has promised to marry me."

"Oh, Will! Why did I not think of that? I declare I suspected something of the sort yesterday, but other things put it out of my mind. I am so glad!" cried Dora. "Where—when—how did it occur?"

"Yesterday on the Public Garden. I met her coming from church," he replied proudly. "Do you see the analogy now between your engagement and my early rising?" he added, laughing.

"I should say so! How selfish of you to keep it to yourself all this time; you might have told us. Mother! Mother! Come quickly, I have something to tell you!" she called, moving toward the next room.

"Yes, Dora, dear," replied the voice of Ma Smith, "just a minute!"

"Oh, hurry, hurry, mummies; it won't keep."

"Yes, yes, you excitable child. What is it?" Nothing wrong with your brother"—she stopped as she caught sight of his smiling face. He went up to her and took her in his strong young arms—he was an affectionate son.

"Nothing wrong, mummies dear, but your boy is very happy. Will you take Sappho for a second daughter?"

"Gladly, my son," replied his mother; and then she sank upon a chair, overcome as she comprehended the full meaning of his words.

"Why do you cry, mother dear, if the idea is not unpleasant to you?" asked Will, somewhat alarmed by her tears.

"Oh, Will, my boy, you will not let this new love cause you to forget the love of your old mother?"

"Never!" cried Will,as he pressed his lips to the sweet old face. "I would not be worthy of happiness could I be so ungrateful."

"Don't mind mother, Will. She cries on principle, because it is the proper thing for weddings and funerals. Isn't that so, mummies mine?" laughed Dora, as she wiped a suspicious moisture from her own eyes.

"But what keeps Sappho so late? She's generally down by this time," she continued, with a glance at the little Swiss clock on the mantel.

"I'm going upstairs after the laggard, and have it out with her for keeping such news to herself. I know she's bashful."

Dora sprang up the stairs with a bound, and paused outside the door to rap. Receiving no answer she rapped again, and then tried the handle of the door. It yielded to her touch, and then she noticed that the key was on the outside. She threw the door open with a vague sense of something unusual in such a proceeding. The room was empty. She paused a moment in bewilderment as she glanced about her, and then saw the bed undisturbed in its snowy smoothness. Thoroughly alarmed now, she ran to the head of the stairs and called her brother.

Wondering what could be the trouble, Will hurried from the kitchen, closely followed by his mother. Upstairs they found Dora standing in the middle of the room with a frightened face.

"I found the key on the outside, the door unlocked. She is not here; and see, the bed has not been slept in; the closet door is open; some of her clothing is gone, and all her jewellry."

Will stood beside her, gazing about the cozy nest with troubled eyes. "When did you see her last?" he asked finally.

"At dinner yesterday; she complained of a headache, and went to her room to lie down."

"She was here at half-past eleven, when I came in, for I saw a light in her window as I came down the street."

"Well, children, there is nothing to worry about," said Mrs Smith. "She has probably gone out and will return shortly. There can't be any great mystery about her absence."

Just then the door bell rang.

"There she is now," said Will, as he bounded down the stairs in answer to the summons. The two women stood expectant, waiting for the sound of her voice. They heard nothing but the closing of the door and Will's steps returning. Presently he stood before them with a letter in his hand.

"It is for me," he said, in answer to their looks of inquiry. "I think it is from Sappho."

His face was ashen; his hands trembled. He turned the square package over once—again—then mechanically, as in a dream, he tore the envelope open. The anxious women watched him as he ran his eyes rapidly over the written page, and then with a groan sank into a chair.

"What is it, Will? What has happened?" cried his mother and sister with one voice. Great drops of perspiration stood upon his forehead.

"O my God!" was his reply to the agonised entreaties of the two women. He threw his arms upon the desk beside him and dropped his head upon them. The letter fell upon the floor.

Mrs Smith was a great sufferer from nervous weakness. Seeing her son's unhappiness, she began to tremble and sob hysterically. Dora was badly frightened; but knowing that she must be calm for all their sakes, said:

"Mother, calm yourself. Do you not see that Will needs help?" She closed the open door to keep out curious intruders who might possibly be about, and then she picked up the letter.

"Read it!" groaned Will. "I can never tell you."

Dora read it aloud:

Will,

When you receive this I shall be far away. What I am writing to you I ought to have told your family long ago. It must forever stand between us and marriage.

You remember the story told the night of the public meeting of the League by Luke Sawyer—the night I fainted? I am the unfortunate Mabella Benubean! I did not die. The good Sisters gave out that story in order to destroy my identity. Madam Frances is my grandaunt. The boy Alphonse is my child...O my God! How can I live and write these words?

John Langley came to my room tonight, after everyone was at church. He has found out my story, and has offered me the greatest insult that a man can give a woman. He has made me realise how much such a marriage with me would injure you. Disgrace shall never touch you or yours through me.

Forgive me for deceiving you—for loving you; it is all the wrong that I have done you.

O love—my love—how can I give you up? You will never know the bitterness of the step I am taking.

Sappho.

141

Mrs Smith shuddered as she listened to the words being read. Could it be possible that this strange, unexpected confession had come from the beautiful girl they knew so well?

Dora was weeping bitterly when she finished; so was her mother. They sat there stunned into silence. Every pulse beat at fever-pitch in Will's body. His nerves were strained almost beyond endurance; they were a thousand needle points of pain. How could he bear this terrible news that had come to him? Luke Sawyer's story was written before his eyes in letters of fire. He saw with acute clairvoyant sight the beautiful child—the brutal captor—the horrid surroundings of the vile den to which he had consigned her—her struggles within the brutal grasp—all the sickening details of that horrible violation of chastity were mirrored within his brain. Time could never eradicate them. God of heaven! how could he bear to think that his beautiful Sappho—his pure girl-love, had been subjected to such brutality! And then the child! Agony of agonies! He could not suffer more and live.

There was something awe-inspiring in his great affliction to the women who loved him. Dismal silence had seized upon them all. Then a sob, dreadful to hear, broke from Will. He staggered across the room and fell on his knees by his mother's side and buried his face in the folds of her dress It was a way he had in early childhood when anything distressed him. Then his mother comforted him as in childhood days, his head upon her tender breast, her dear wrinkled hands, as if in blessing, resting upon his grief-stricken brow.

At length Dora broke the silence.

"Oh, that poor, miserable girl! Think of her sufferings—of the weight of the secret she carried with her. What a crucifixion for a proud spirit like hers. This terrible curse of slavery! Shall we never lose the sting of degradation? Think of John too, how did he find it out? What a heartless scamp he must be! I confess the whole thing is an enigma to me.'

"To think she should believe us capable of feeling anything for her but sympathy! You must find her, Will, and bring her back home," said Ma Smith.

"Yes, mother; but any girl would act as she has. Think of her humiliation to be obliged to own such a story to her lover! I do not wonder that she turned a coward and fled. But Will will find her, never fear."

Will had regained something of self-control. But what a change had come to that debonair countenance! Dora's heart ached as she looked at him. He arose from his knees by his mother's side and stood a moment as if bewildered.

"I am going to hire the best detective in the city to find her. But first I will settle with John Langley," he said at last.

"Give him this!" cried Dora, snatching her engagement ring from her finger. "Tell him I hope never to see his face again."

"Poor little sister. Must you suffer, too?"

"Don't pity me, Will!" she exclaimed with flashing eyes. "I am well rid of such a man."

Will kissed them both solemnly and went out.

The two women, left alone, went softly about the pretty room folding away the scattered articles of wearing apparel, which they watered with many bitter tears, and finally closing the blinds and drawing down the curtains. She will return, they told each other, hoping against hope. We will leave things as they are. And then went out and locked the door.

Such incidents as we have pictured above are not uncommon in any community where slavery has cast its baleful shadow. Emancipation has done much, but time and moral training among the white men of the South are the only cures for concubinage.

We may right a wrong, but we cannot restore our victim to his primeval state of happiness. Something is lost that can never be regained. The wages of sin is death. Innocent or guilty, the laws of nature are immutable. So with shoulders bent and misshapen with heavy burdens, the Negro plods along bearing his cross—carrying the sins of others.

Fortunately it happened that it was an hour when the inmates of 500 D Street were busy attending to their various vocations. No one need know more of Sappho's disappearance than the family felt to tell. They made one exception to this resolve. It was about ten o'clock when Dr Lewis called. The mother and daughter were just sitting down to the meal so sadly interrupted. In answer to questions asked in friendly solicitude because of their troubled looks, the whole miserable story came out.

"It is fortunate that I happened in," he said, when he had heard all they could tell him.

"I will go right down to Langley's office. It is useless to allow more trouble to grow out of this unhappy affair. Those men must not meet alone."

Amazed, startled, dumbfounded at this romance in real life, he hurried away toward the business portion of the city. But under his anxiety to serve his friends, who could blame him if thoughts of the broken engagement and all that it meant to him would intrude upon him? His heart kept singing: Free to be won—free to be won.

John had risen early and left the house before any one was astir. He could not sleep. Up and down the deserted streets he paced, gazing at the silent stars and baring his head to the cold, refreshing breeze of the

143

April morning. Haunted—tormented—conscience not yet sufficiently seared to commit so mean an act without regret, would be heard. What if the girl should defy him—expose him! He cursed his own folly, her beauty, his own infatuation. Turn as he would, he could not shut out the beautiful, despairing face.

There is something magical in the mystery of night and the shadows of early dawn. Then the mystery of creation and our own hidden nature seem to be revealed faintly to our dull sensibilities. The soul beholds itself all unadorned as it must stand before Almighty God. He raised his eyes to heaven and there beheld the beauty of myriad stars and undiscovered worlds bespangling the firmament. Never before had he noticed their sublimity. By the tremulous half-light of the early dawn his deed of the night before appeared despicable—devilish. For a time his head dropped in shame before the accusations of his soul. There came dimly to his beclouded faculties a realisation of the possibilities of a life which might have been his under opposite conditions from those in which he was born. Events of his childhood in the South came to him through the mist of years. He saw himself a half-starved beggar in the city streets, a deserted child claiming kindred with none, allowed a shelter in a poor Negro cabin for charity's sake, begging his bread from the generous passerby. Somehow he had learned his letters. Then he became ambitious to learn more. He heard talk of a country to the north which seemed to his childish imagination a fairyland. He determined to go there; so he started on his wearisome journey at an age when the loving mother trembles to have her darling exposed to the perils of the busy streets without a strong hand to guide him through its dangers. All his capital was in his nimble baby feet. He charmed coin from the people wherever he went by his expert dancing. He could do the breakdown and many intricate shuffles in a way that delighted his audiences. When he reached the North he managed to buy a bootblack's outfit; then he worked his way into a hotel kitchen. He went on from one thing to another, always keeping the one end in view—to acquire an education.

He had prospered. He had accomplished the acquisition of knowledge at the expense of the non-development of every moral faculty.

He did not realise that he was a responsible being, or that morality was obligatory upon him. With him, might was right. This man was what he was through the faults of others. If there be truth in the assertion that we create ourselves in the life we live on earth, the sphere that makes our heaven or hell within the illimitable realms of futurity, then it may be that the pitying eye of Heaven sees the struggles of these irresponsible ones of earth who are monuments of man's inhumanity to man, and sends a warning, pleading voice along the dim, resounding aisles of self-communion. It is a law of the All-wise that Nemesis shall walk beside us in every wrong that we commit. For joy we pay, for sorrow, too, and also for the ill we do. We call the recoil which comes from evil-doing, retribution, which being the fruit of evil, is coexistent with it. John had given no thought to the needs of his soul in his pursuit of wealth and position. Tonight he had the feeling that he had given all for nothing; that in his blind, egotistical seeking for his own gratification he had overstepped the bounds, and that retribution would put a check upon his desires.

That night his better angel triumphed, and he resolved that he would apologise to Sappho, make up with Dora, and tell Will all his surmises about Mr Withington. But when day light flooded the city he had resolved to let matters remain as they were. Love, honours and a competency were his for the taking, but he had risked all—for what? He would soon know.

Ten o'clock found him sitting listlessly before his desk. It happened that he had no cases in court that morning. He pushed his work one side; he could not think; ever before his eyes was a vision in pale blue, with floating golden hair and appealing eyes. His hand shook as if with the palsy as he raised his pen to dip it in the ink well. With an oath he dashed it from him. He did not indulge in liquor as a rule, but he made up his mind to have a glass of whisky when he went to lunch. Presently he heard the door open. He looked up at the sound, and met the eyes of the friend he had betrayed—Will Smith stood before him! John sprang to his feet. His eyes dropped before the steady regard of the other. Thus they stood a moment. At last Will broke the painful silence.

"What have I ever done to you, John, that you should treat me as you have?"

"What do you mean?" stammered John.

"Do you ask me that?"

"I do," came faintly from John's lips.

"I will reply by asking you another question. Has your love for Dora turned to hate, that you can deliberately humiliate the girl you have wished to make your wife, as you have her?"

John's courage seemed to have deserted him. He stood before Smith like the culprit that he was.

"Of what do you accuse me?!" he cried at length, in desperation.

"Does not your conscience answer? If not, read that." Will handed him Sappho's letter.

John took it, and even as his hand grasped the sheet of paper he began to turn over in his mind a way out of this dilemma. As he finished reading it his mind was made up. He returned it to Will with a shrug of his shoulders and a smile more significant than words. The ashen face of his friend should have warned him.

"I did not intend to humiliate Dora, for men do many like things which never come to the ears of the woman they call wife. Accidentally I learned Miss Clark's story. I also learned by observation that there were other stories just as piquant. You will thank me when you know all. She is beautiful. Am I different from other men who have made like proposals to a beautiful woman?"

Scarcely had the words passed his lips when Will was upon him.

"You miserable, lying hound!" he shouted, beside himself with rage and grief. He grasped John by the throat. Again the door opened, and Dr Lewis ran toward the struggling figures.

"Will! John! Are you both mad? Do you want to create a public scandal?" He succeeded in separating them, and then threw himself between them. So they stood panting and glaring at each other like angry beasts.

"Take me out of this, then!" cried Will, "or I won't answer for myself! Here is your ring!" He took the ring Dora had given him, and threw it at Langley. "I will give you until tonight to get your luggage out of my house. If you are there tomorrow morning, I will shoot you."

Dr Lewis drew him from the room. The door closed. Thus they who had been friends for years parted.

John stood there alone in his silent office, looking out on the dreary vista of brick walls and the network of wires, in awful solitude with his thoughts of the past and his blank future. The sun of prosperity had set on him forever—he felt it—knew it. His own hand had wrought this ruin to himself, said his heart and conscience.

CHAPTER 20

Meantime Sappho had descended from the car at the corner of Arlington and Boylston Streets on that eventful Easter night. She entered the Garden, and impelled by an uncontrollable impulse, walked again through the paths where a few hours before she had known so much happiness. She knew no fear; the darkness concealed her. Again she sat upon the seat where she had passed the brightest moments of her life. A neighboring clock struck one. It was then the first hour of a new day—the dawn for her of fresh misery. A cold, sharp wind struck her with chilling force; she shivered, but still sat there buried in hopeless despair.

Fearful indeed is the plan of existence which rules our mortality. Innocent or guilty, our deeds done in the flesh pursue us with relentless vigour unto the end of life. Sometimes the rough winds of adversity are tempered to the shorn lamb who is not responsible for acts which are forced upon him. God in infinite wisdom and justice remits the severity of our sufferings; but the tracings still remain upon the sands of life—we bind up the wounds—they heal, but the scars remain.

Sappho possessed a brilliant mind and resolute character. If she had been a religious devotee she would have been as devout and as fervid as a disciple of old. If a sinner, the queen of them all. She had strength of will enough for a dozen women, which, if ever started on the wrong road, would be difficult to redirect into the paths of right. She had suffered much in meekness, but now dumb rage awoke her passions. For a time the spirit of revenge held full sway in the outraged heart. Revenge was all she craved. She shivered at the dark thoughts which came to her. 'Revenge', whispered the swaying branches of the trees above her head—'revenge' seemed whispered in the chilling winds about her—revenge upon her seducer and upon the man who had dashed the cup of happiness from her lips and most wantonly insulted her in her weakness. Then came the blessed relief of tears—like a flood—they relieved the over charged brain and saved her reason. She fancied, as she sat there trying to account for the evil that pursued her, that Conscience spoke in condemnation of her neglect of her child. She had felt nothing for the poor waif but repugnance. Her delicate nervous organisation was naturally tinged with superstition, and she felt that God had sat in judgment on her willingness to forget her child. "Dost thou question the providences of God? Know that my ways are not the ways of men. A tender soul will be demanded at thy hands in the vast eternity. Who art thou, to question the ways of Infinity? Jesus Christ came into the world under the law. Who art thou, to question the wisdom of the Most High? Low, there is the field—the life of a child—work for a bounteous harvest." At length she rose from that seat resolved that come what would she would claim the child and do her duty as his mother in love and training. She would devote her life to him. They would never more be separated.

She met no one in her lonely walk through the now deserted city streets. She was so be numbed by the shock she had received that she would hardly have noticed any insult that might have been directed to her. At length she reached the door of Madam Frances' house. All was dark. No light, no welcome. So was her life made dark and desolate by the curse of slavery. She rang the bell twice with a strong hand. Presently she saw the faint gleam from a lamp through the sidelights, and then her aunt's familiar voice asked: "Who is there?"

"It is I, Sappho. Open the door, Aunt Sally."

She heard the click of the key as it turned in the lock, and in another moment she stood within the entry facing her aunt's curious, frightened face. In another moment she dropped her weary frame in a chair in the reception room. Sappho told her aunt the whole story. The elder woman was nonplussed and startled; she had not counted that any one would be able to identify her niece with poor, unfortunate Mabelle Beaubean. They sat there for a long time going over the situation, and consulting about what was best to be done. Sappho told her aunt that she was determined to take the boy with her in future. Madam Frances said nothing, for she saw that her niece was determined.

"I must leave Boston; that is clear," said Sappho.

"Certainly, that will be best for a while," replied her aunt. "But you must remember that it is always darkest just before the dawn."

"I shall return to New Orleans and lose myself in that city. I shall get work there, and my case will not be noticed, because it is not uncommon. In time I shall forget."

"As soon as you are settled there I will join you with the boy. I will continue to tell fortunes, and we shall live very happily, no doubt. I shall not be here long; my sands are almost run, but I should like to see you safe and happy before I go. But remember what I say to you now, Sappho child: in doing your duty, happiness will come to you, the greater and more abiding for the trouble which has preceded it."

"Perhaps so," replied Sappho, "but, Aunt Sally, I shall take the boy with me tomorrow when I leave for the South. I will never part with him again on earth."

"Well, my dear child, I see no necessity for you to become a martyr in order to do your duty. However, do as you think best. Now go and try to get a little rest."

"Here is one of my mother's diamond rings; take it, Aunt Sally, and sell it for me. I have no money."

The old woman took the ring, and Sappho went into the small side room where Alphonse slept. She undressed and lay down beside the boy, but not to sleep. She gazed on the innocent face with mingled feelings of sorrow and regret as she thought of the lonely, loveless life of the child. She had been so wicked to put him from her. It was her duty to guide and care for him. She would do her duty without shrinking. Her head ached and her eyes burned and were hot and dry; they refused to close. So the moments flew by as she tormented herself with fancies of Will's horror of her when he should learn her story on the morrow, and remembrances of John Langley's coarse insults, which even now made her cheeks burn with shame. She wept bitter tears over her cherished love dream. But under it all there was a feeling of relief now that she had made up her mind to a future which the child should share. Her shipwrecked life seemed about to find peace. There was a new light in her eyes as she gazed on the sleeping child. Impulsively she folded him in her arms, and Alphonse awoke. The awakening of childhood is beautiful. She gazed with new-found ecstasy at the rosy face, the dimpled limbs, and thought that he was hers. Her feeling of degradation had made her ashamed of the joys of motherhood, of pride of possession in her child. But all that feeling was swept away. Alphonse looked at her first in wonder and then in alarm. Again she kissed him passionately, the frail little child whose delicate frame seemed cut from alabaster. She had only this tender creature to cling to in all the world; the only plank between her and desperation.

"I am your mother, Alphonse," she said in answer to his looks of inquiry.

"My mamma is gone away to heaven," replied the child solemnly, as he watched her earnestly with great dark eyes of wonder.

"No, dear, I am your mamma, come back to keep you with me always. Won't you love your poor unhappy mamma?"

The child put up one slender hand and smoothed her cheek.

"You're the pretty lady I saw at the fair. I didn't know you were my mamma."

"Mamma couldn't claim you then, darling, but now she's going to take you away, and you will always live with her. Won't you like that?"

The boy nodded his sleepy little head, put up his dewy red mouth and pressed a sweet, wet kiss on her face, then he nestled confidently in her arms and fell fast asleep again. She held him closely folded against her throbbing heart, and something holy passed from the sweet contact of the soft, warm body into the cold chilliness of her broken heart. The

149

mother-love chased out all the anguish that she had felt over his birth. She wondered how she had lived without him—how she could have remained separated from him. In this new and holy love that had taken possession of her soul was the compensation for all she had suffered. She could not see it then, but in the long intervals of time it would be revealed to her understanding. Now she felt that her losses could not be paid. But in the years which followed she learned to value the strong, chastening influence of her present sorrow, and the force of character it developed, fitting her perfectly for the place she was to occupy in carrying comfort and hope to the women of her race.

The next evening Sappho left Boston. As the train rolled out from the station on its southward journey her heart sank; tears were in her eyes; she felt that now, indeed, all links were severed between her and Will. She had borne up bravely, and now she told herself that she must not give way. She clasped the tender fingers of the boy closer still. He was her anchor. The lady passengers on the train regarded her curiously, she was too beautiful for pity; the men with equal curiosity, but compassion for her youth and beauty mingled with it. When she reached Washington fatigue began to tell upon her—fatigue and hopeless misery. She longed for the journey's end. Mentally and physically she was overtaxed, and but for the child she would have broken down. She did not mind anything now. As she moved farther south the brutality of the conductor who ordered her out of the comfortable day-coach into the dirt and discomfort of the 'Jim crow' car, with the remark that "white niggers" couldn't impose on him.

The Sisters of the Holy Family always have representatives at the various railroad stations in New Orleans. These Sisters not only solicit alms, but look out for friendless or unfortunate colored women. As Sappho stepped from the train, holding the child by one hand and her baggage check in the other, a Sister, impelled by something in the white, worn face, stepped up to her and spoke a kindly word of interest. Sappho looked at her and tried to answer, as she placed the check and her purse in the Sister's hand. The nun put out her arms just in time to receive Sappho's form as she was sinking insensible upon the platform, her strength at last succumbing to the terrible strain upon mind and body. The nun obtained a carriage and took the two travellers to the convent— the child to the orphanage, the mother to the hospital. So once again Sappho found a refuge in the convent in her time of dire necessity. No one recognised her, for a complete change had been made in the Sisterhood.

A long spell of low fever ensued, but to Sappho in her weakness the rest and comfort that came to her harassed mind was like sun and shackle in a grassy glade of perfect peace. The nuns were greatly interested in her, and concluded that she was as good as pretty.

"She is like the angels in the picture of the Crucifixion, so sweet and sad. She has more tears in her heart than in her eyes."

"She is not of our faith," said another, "but we will do our best for her, as the Mother says: le bon Dieu knows best."

It was evening in New Orleans. The streets, the great arteries of a crowded metropolis, were lighted by the glare of myriad gas lamps, thus dispelling the darkness like artificial suns. The roll of vehicles blended with the other sounds, the hum of millions rising in a confused roar above the house tops and mingling with the clouds of evening.

In a small, bare room Sappho lay, at the end of a long corridor. The rays from a lamp outside the room came faintly in, dispelling the semi-darkness. The light from the soft Southern moon gleamed faintly through the windows, making the room like the cloisters of heavenly mansions. To that quiet haven of rest the turmoil and bustle of life did not reach. There the dying, the sick, the convalescent lay undisturbed by the hurrying march of humanity. She had just sent Alphonse away. Every day he had been allowed to go to her since she had been getting better. It was a rare sight to see the two together—the lovely girl who held the child in such a passionate embrace, and the delight of the child in his "beautiful mamma."

No questions had been asked her concerning her life or history, but she felt it her duty to make a confidante of the Mother Superior. Tonight she had sent for her, and presently the Mother glided in, with her noise-less step and gentle, assuring manner. The holy woman sat there a long time in silence after listening to Sappho's story. Such confidences were not new to her. At length she placed a toil-worn brown hand upon the girl's head with a murmured "Benedicite."

"What shall I do, Mother?" asked the girl, as she reverently kissed the gentle hand.

"Ah, we must think and pray. You do not wish to become a Sister?"

"No; I must accept the desire of God in the child. I will take a mother's place and do my duty."

"It is hard for one so young and beautiful to resist the world and its temptations," replied the Mother regretfully; "but we will help you, and the convent will be a home for you always."

Sappho thanked her tearfully.

"My child, I will think over all you have said. I will pray to be shown what it is best to do. Now, go to sleep, rest, and pray to the Holy Mother of Sorrow, and Christ will comfort you."

She glided noiselessly from the room. Sappho, already comforted by her benign influence, fell asleep.

A month later Sappho had very nearly recovered from the effects of her illness. She moved—a quiet and subdued figure—about the convent corridors, helping in every way. She had written to her aunt, and received an answer saying that she would soon be in the city. The old fortune teller returned to her home only in time, however, to die at the convent. So Sappho found herself doubly alone in the world.

One day soon after the death of her aunt the Mother Superior sent for her to come to her in her private room—the parlor of the convent.

"My child," she said, "I have been thinking much about you, and I have tried to benefit you. Are you still determined to pass as the boy's mother?"

"Yes, Mother, I am."

"Well, then, you must be Madame Clark."

"No," replied Sappho hastily; "no more deception."

"I am glad to see that you are ready to bear all things in meekness for His sake. But you are not called upon to make too many sacrifices. God sees your heart and will reward you in his own good time. I have a place for you that I think will just suit you. Monsieur Louis of Opelousas is in want of a governess for his two granddaughters. He is a man of color, and has lost all of his family but these two children. He is an old man with a competency, and he will pay you well for your services. Alphonse can stay with us; you can pay a stipulated sum for his board and be able to see him every week. What do you think of it, my daughter?"

"I will do as you advise, Mother. You are only too kind. When shall I go?"

"Monsieur Louis will be here tomorrow to see you. If everything is satisfactory, you can go next week."

The morrow came, and with it Monsieur Louis. He was a tall, aristocratic-looking man of dignified bearing, though one soon perceived that age had bent his once firm shoulders. His hair, now entirely white, added to his venerable appearance. His face was gentle and kindly, and immediately won Sappho's heart. He, in his turn, was much impressed by her youth and beauty. He thought of the days of his own youth, when such a face as hers would have robbed him of his sleep. He thought, too, of the wife and daughter who had been taken from him, leaving his life but a succession of lonely days. "Let the past die," he murmured impatiently to himself. "I feel this beautiful girl-widow will bring peace and joy to my poor motherless girls."

In another week Sappho had accepted the liberal terms Monsieur Louis offered her, had taken a tearful farewell of Alphonse and the Sisters, and was ensconced in her new home.

The house was pleasant. It stood in its own grounds, an old fashioned, typical Southern residence, with wide gardens and a carriage drive winding around a smoothly cut lawn. The interior was well furnished, comfortable, and every want abundantly supplied. She combined the duties of housekeeping with those of teaching, and soon became the moving spirit of the home, warmly loved by her little charges, and enthusiastically admired by the servants. It was a happy, restful life; it suited her. Its retirement, its quiet interior, recalled her childhood's happy home. Monsieur Louis, although much older, reminded her of her father, and attracted her by his gentleness. Travelling in a desert, as it were, she had come suddenly and unexpectedly upon an oasis of grass, cool shadows and running streams. Here, indeed, was peace. Had her lot been always cast in these pleasant, peaceful shades, how different her life might have been. But the iron of suffering had seared her heart. Her life now bade fair to be tranquil and monotonous enough. Why could she not be happy? She asked herself. She tried not to allow herself to think upon the past; but when night came she lay awake hungering for the sight of a face, the touch of a hand, the glance of an eye. Sometimes the craving grew almost too powerful to be resisted, and once she started to dress, resolved to return to Boston, find Will, and trust all to his love. But she remembered. "His scorn I could not bear. I should die at his feet." She told herself that life was done and nothing remained but patience. So she sat dumb and submissive beneath her martyrdom.

Monsieur Louis was puzzled by the beautiful girl-widow, but he asked no inconvenient questions. He was content to accept the goods which the gods had provided him in the person of his governess, deeming himself very fortunate to have a woman of her refinement to take charge of the education of his granddaughters. He did not believe her to be a widow. He had strange thoughts when he looked at the pretty child Alphonse, who came so frequently to the house to visit his mother. The child was always made welcome for his own sake as well as for his mother's. He shook his head and sighed as he watched the two together. Such cases were only too common in the South. Like a wise man he accepted the inevitable, and tried to do the best with it that he could. "Let me bring as much good as possible out of evil," was his thought in self-communion. So he smiled on the two forlorn ones; encouraged the mother and respected her secret. One year glided slowly by; another followed. Sappho had grown accustomed to her new duties and resigned to her life.

Monsieur Louis's great hobby was his rose garden. There he worked, assisted by the children. Alphonse spent a great part of his time with his mother, sharing the instruction of the two girls. No one would have recognised in the gay lad the quiet, melancholy child of three years

153

before. Sappho would often sit on a garden seat watching the three children. For a time she would forget her troubles in the joy of gazing upon the animated, happy face of her child. Yes, there lay consolation for all her sufferings. Alphonse was expanding like a flower beneath the influence of his mother's love and devotion. He was her consolation.

Late one afternoon she sat on the terrace, a book in her lap, her thoughts far away. Alphonse brought her a bunch of roses. The child looked at her earnestly a moment, and then said:

"Mamma, why are you always so sad when you sit on the terrace alone?"

"I am not sad, Alphonse," she replied, kissing him on his forehead.

"Oh, yes, you are. When I am a big man I shall find the tall, handsome gentleman who gave you flowers at the fair."

"Why, Alphonse!"

"Have I said anything wrong, mamma?" he asked anxiously.

"Not wrong, my child, but mamma prefers that you never speak of the past to anyone."

"I will do just as you say, Mamma Sappho!" he cried, impetuously throwing his arms about her neck in a bear-like hug.

Somewhat startled by the child's precociousness, she sat there after he left her, watching the red sun slowly dropping out of sight in the west. The peaceful stillness of approaching darkness rested on the landscape. She heard a step and turned to perceive Monsieur Louis, who seated himself beside her on the rustic settee.

"We shall have a thunder shower before morning; see how heavy the clouds are hanging."

"I have been watching them," replied Sappho.

"Miss Clark, how long have you been with us?"

"A few months more than two years. Why, Monsieur Louis?"

"You have been happy?" he asked, ignoring her question.

"Happier than I can say."

"Do not let what I am about to say distress you; but I want you to make me your confidant and tell me all your sad story, not from idle curiosity, but because I have grown to love you and the boy."

"Oh, monsieur!" was all Sappho could say.

Then he spoke again. She had only a confused idea of his words, but his meaning was clearly written in her heart.

"My child," he said gravely, taking her hand. "I am an old man, experienced in the ways of the world. I have seen and understood more of your story than I have seemed to. My heart yearns for you and the child. I am old and selfish, perhaps, but I offer you a home for yourself and the boy, an honourable name, and ample means to protect you when I am gone. In short, will you consent to marry an old man and make his few remaining years peaceful? Take time to reflect," he said, as she started to interrupt him; "and my child, while you reflect, think of me. You have grown about my heart strings. I could not rest in my grave if I left you alone and friendless."

About Sappho's heart there was a strange feeling of suffocation, a feeling such as a martyr might have experienced at the stake.

"I cannot answer now," she said at length. "This is a strange idea to me."

"Take time," he replied; "but weigh my proposition well. There is plenty here; there is no one in the wide world to mar your peace, only an old man and two little girls. You shall be happy and honored."

"I will give you my answer in a week," she said, as she arose trembling from her seat.

"It is two weeks to Easter. Let me know your answer then." And turning, he left her as abruptly as he had come.

155

CHAPTER 21

The days dragged their weary length along. May passed; June and its roses faded into the languid heat of July. Still no trace was found of Sappho. Madam Frances had gone from the little house on J. Street, and she, together with the child, had vanished and left no trace. There had been a nine-days' wonder over the departure of Miss Clark, but outside of the few who were in the secret, no one knew the facts.

Will had received his degree from Harvard and was now looking forward to going abroad. But the eager zest and joy of pursuit and accomplishment were gone; duty alone remained.

It was rumoured that John Langley had attached himself to the family of a well-to-do colored man of prominence in the city, and that he was very busily engaged in ingratiating himself into the good graces of the daughter of the house. People gossiped and speculated as to the cause of the broken engagement between him and Dora Smith, but from lack of information this sensation died out also. Three months after Dora had broken with Langley the situation between her and Dr Lewis was unchanged. The intimacy of early childhood was resumed, but she was shy and reserved beyond a certain point. Finally Dr Lewis had been obliged to return to his charge in the South, but before he went he had obtained a promise from Dora to enter into correspondence with him. He had not dared to express the real interest and meaning which lay behind his request. The poor girl felt humiliated; her womanhood shamed; although to her surprise the happiness of life which had seemed quenched behind this flood of sorrow that had overtaken her was beginning to shine upon her again as buoyant youth regained its wanted sway. She respected Dr Lewis, and appreciated the value of the position he had made for himself, but she did not intend to enter into another engagement immediately; she had almost determined to remain single for life until she heard of Langley's conduct. After that came the fear that he might think that she regretted the past. No; she could not remain single; she would marry one whose manliness she could respect, if she did not love him. Love was another thing, with which, she told herself, she was done.

Dora possessed the rare talent of being an interesting correspondent. Indeed, her literary talents would have been valuable if cultivated. Dr Lewis soon found this out. She gave him fascinating glimpses of the possibilities of an inner nature which perfect love and trust might develop. These short views thrilled his being with the hope of winning so rare a prize for his life companion. He pursued her unceasingly. Flowers of rare beauty and fragrance, fruit and books, found their way to her home each week. John had been rather an indifferent lover; but who could resist the impetuous onslaught of a generous nature that truly loved?

Now, when the heat of July had brought with it his annual vacation, he had returned to the North. Upon their first meeting he said to her:

"Dora, I will take no denial. No, do not speak. I know what you would say. I am willing to wait for love, because I feel sure that it will come in time."

And she, nothing loth, yielded to the stronger nature with a feeling of peace and contentment to which she had long been a stranger. So October was set for the wedding, and as the days passed, Dora felt that this time she had made no mistake.

It was toward the end of July. Ma Smith sat in her pretty parlor talking with Mrs Ophelia Davis. Mrs Davis had just heard the news of Dora's prospective marriage to Dr Lewis.

"I'm just as glad as I can be. Dear, dear, it don't seem possible that so many things have happened to change the prospectus since last winter when we sat in this very room having such a good time, and Miss Clark had just been introduced, and was so handsome, and such a way with her and so forth. You know, I thought your Will was going to get completely smashed on her. It's funny how mistook a body can get about fellas and gals. You think they're going crazy over each other when all of a sudden—Lordy! They've up and married some poor plain critter that you never thought they'd give a second look to. They'd have made a handsome couple, too. Just made for each other. Then there's the smash-up 'twixt Dora and Langley. Mercy knows, I don't blame her. I always thought he had a downish sort of look. Draft them sickly, peeky lookin' men! Me, no ma'am! I wouldn't look at one of them. No ma'am. Dear, dear, it do seem strange. But that wasn't what I wanted to say tickler to you."

She smoothed down her long white apron as she murmured to herself: " 'Phelia, where is you?" She was evidently embarrassed. After thinking a moment she continued:

"Now, about this house. What are you going to do with it?"

"We haven't concluded yet what we will do with it. I'm going South with Dora until Will finishes at Heidelberg; then, after he has settled upon his future field of work, I am to live with him."

"Exactly so. Then I suppose you'll be willing to rent the house if you get a good tenant?"

"Yes, I suppose so."

"Now, Sis Smith, I want to ask you if you've any objections to my taking it?"

"Certainly no objections; but isn't it a great responsibility for a woman alone in the world?" asked Mrs Smith, greatly surprised.

Mrs Davis smoothed the folds of her ample white apron nervously coughed, stammered, blushed.

"Well, truth is, Sis Smith, you know people make changes in this life. Fact truth, indeed, ma'am, we's always changing, and I'm thinking of changing to double harness for a while."

"I want to know!" exclaimed Ma Smith, now properly astonished and interested. "And who is the happy man?"

Mrs Davis wiped the perspiration from her face with the back of her hand as she replied with a nervous laugh:

"Oh, you know him well! It's Mr Jeemes."

"What! Mr James! Why, he's nothing but a boy!" exclaimed Ma Smith.

"Course I know he's young, but I'm not so old myself."

"Why, how old are you, Sister Davis?"

"I don't know that I mind telling you, 'cause you're safe. I'm all of thirty-five. Generally speaking, I never tell nobody my exact age, 'cause it's none of their business."

"Thirty-five years! Impossible! Why, it's thirty-five years since the war. You were a widow at that time, weren't you?"

"That's my age, anyhow," was the sullen answer.

"But, Sister Davis, you must be fifty years old at the very least," said Ma Smith, persisting that she was right in her calculations.

"Fifty nothing!" replied Mrs Davis, somewhat offended at Mrs Smith's pertinacity. "I'm thirty-five years old, and I reckon that I'm the one what knows best when I was born."

"I'm sure I hope you will be happy with Mr James," Ma Smith hastened to reply, seeing that Mrs Davis was really offended.

"Is he going to leave college?" she continued, retiring with graceful discretion from the contest.

"No. He's going to graduate. The society he's been preaching for Sundays is going to give him their church, and I'll keep the laundry a-going and rent rooms."

"I'm sure I'll be very glad to let you have the house. I don't know anyone else I'd rather let it to."

"Then that's settled," said Mrs Davis, with a sigh of relief. "I thought you'd say that. Now, you see, all your old lodgers can keep their rooms, and it will seem just like home to them. Mr Jeemes is that fond of me tell Sarah Ann calls me an old fool, and says all he wants is my money, and a right smart woman to work for him. I told Sarah Ann, 'go get a man for yourself and quit being jealous.' She says to me, 'I will, and it won't be a boy just turned twenty one.' Sarah Ann and me will have to part after I'm married, she's that jealous."

Mrs Davis had regained all her good humor, and was very complacent over Ma Smith's evident interest in her story.

"Now that would be a pity, after you've been together so long," remarked the latter.

"She's got to drop saying ticklish things to me. A woman's got a right to get married, ain't she?" Mrs Davis was now fairly started on a congenial subject, and her words flowed in a torrent.

"Mr Jeemes says he knows the Lord sent me for to be a help meet to him, and I the say he's right. Sarah Ann says my money's the 'help meet' he's after, and somebody to cook good vitals to suit his pallet. But I know better; he's a godly man if he ain't much to look at."

"How did you happen to take a fancy to each other?"

"Lord, he's such a good critter. The first I noticed was the night you had that party here last winter. Some of the men got to talking 'bout woman being the weaker vessel, and subjugating theirself to be led by men and not go perspiring after work and such likes which belongs to men. Mr Jeemes he held to it that woman's all right to educate herself even to be a minister, for no man could be superior to woman, 'cause she was his rib. And ever since that I kind of thought what a shame it was for a man to be minus one of his ribs, until I made up my mind that if Jeemes wanted me he could have back his lost rib. All this spring he's been a-riding me on his bike down in the kitchen every day after we got through washing and had cleaned up, so I could go riding with him out of town this summer. After I'd leant, one day he came in with a beautiful bike and saddle. The next day we was to ride to the park. I held on my new pale blue bicycle suit with a pink shirt and a white sailor hat and tan colored shoes and gloves. I tell you I looked some...Mr Jeemes had on a black suit with a grey linen duster, and he did look extinguished in his beaver hat and that white choker and tie of his which I must say I do admire. We got along pretty well. Everybody was looking and gasping at us. Sarah Ann says it was 'cause we looked like a couple of jay birds stuffed.

"We got along all right until we was coming down a hill. Mr Jeemes was coasting, and the tail of that linen duster of his was sailing out behind like a flag flopping in an east wind. The first thing I knowed he was a-sticking fast head first into a pile of sand where they was making mortar to build a cellar, and me on top of him! Wasn't it a mercy that we wasn't stuck in the mortar? Jeemes is pretty black, but he was a white man when he got out of that sand heap. As for me, I tore my gloves, lost my hat, and busted a new pair of corsets right off me. Besides that, I nearly swallowed my upper teeth, an' I lost my bangs. They picked me up and carried me into a house they was a-building, and give me a chance to fix myself up a bit. But I declare to you them corsets was no good never after that; and it cost me ten dollars to fix that upper set of teeth so I could wear them again. I never have seen them bangs since.

"We was that done up that Jeemes sent for a carriage to bring us home; and fifty dollars won't excuse the damages to them bikes. Coming home and sitting so close together, beside the trouble we'd had making us feel kind of tender of each other, Jeemes put his arm around me—and I don't see how ever in time he did it, being the corsets weren't no good, and me about as small as a bag of tatters. He put his arm around me, he did, and says he: 'Lets get married, 'Phelia!' I was that astonished and set back you could have knocked me down with a feather, and was that weak from being overcome by my feeling that all I remember was that I fell on his neck like the patrihawks did in the Bible where they tell 'bout Abraham, Isaac and Jacob, Shem, Ham, Meshack and 'Bednego—you remember how the minister told us all about that in the Scripture lesson last Sunday night, don't you? I ain't got no ability for reading, but I'se got a memory, thank God. As I was saying, I just fell onto his neck, and I says to him: 'Mr Jeemes, if you want your rib, I'm her.' That's the way it came about, and we's going to be married pretty soon, 'though Sarah Ann says I'm a insane maniac, and Jeemes knows what he's a-fishing for. She's insulting, most insulting."

Mrs Smith sympathised with her, and after more talk about the rent of the building and other matters dear to the heart of the housewife, they separated.

For a long time Ma Smith sat there in the quiet, shaded room, buried in deep thought. She made a charming picture. White was her favorite color for summer wear, with a tiny crimson cashmere shawl thrown about her shoulders to keep off the chill which comes so naturally to old age. She had been a handsome woman, and still retained traces of former beauty. Thick bands of snowy hair, falling in natural waves, were coiled closely at the back of a well-shaped head. Her clear olive complexion contrasted pleasantly with eyes large, soft, and black, heavy black eyebrows and long curling lashes. An aquiline nose, thin lips and delicately shaped ears gave her a very pleasing countenance.

As she sat there her whole life passed in review. She thought of her children, and how much she had to be thankful for in them. But more than all, the story told her so often by her father of his early life and that of his father and mother, was fresh within her mind as she sat there dreaming. Months afterwards she looked back upon that day, and remembered with wonder her own tranquillity.

She heard the door bell ring, but it did not disturb her reverie. There was a knock at the door of the room where she was sitting. Then the door opened, and Mrs Davis ushered in a tall, elegant white man of distinguished address, and about her own age. Mrs Davis closed the door behind him and vanished.

"Mrs Smith, I presume?" he said in a pleasant voice as he advanced toward her. It was a voice of rare carrying power—deep, rich, musical, and had moved the House of Commons to enthusiasm on more than one memorable occasion in the politics of Great Britain.

"Yes," she replied, rising from her seat.

"I called to see Mr William Smith, and I dislike to be disappointed. Will he be at home soon?" He handed her his card as he finished speaking, and she read the inscription:

Charles Montfort-Withington, MP.
Berkshire,
England.

"Pray be seated, Mr Withington," she said, as she placed a chair for her visitor. "I am William's mother. He will be in very soon."

Mr Withington thanked her, and having seated himself, glided easily into conversation. At the same time his keen eye noted his surroundings. Nothing in the quiet, unpretentious, shaded room escaped him. The large glass bowl of flowers—sweet peas and nasturtium predominating—filled the room with fragrance. There were three or four water-color paintings set in simple frames—pictures of rural scenes. The few choice pieces of china and bric-a-brac which adorned the mantel, the open piano, the general good taste, even elegance of the apartment, appealed strongly to the artistic sense of the cultured gentleman who had been reared in the luxury of ample wealth. Mrs Smith herself was a revelation to him. By what art of necromancy had such a distinguished woman been evolved from among the brutalised aftermath of slavery?

"I had the pleasure of meeting your son and conversing with him at the annual dinner of the Canterbury Club in February last. I was much impressed with his views on the condition of the Negroes in this country. Being interested in every phase of racial development which bears upon the science of political economy, I felt that after my Canadian business was settled I would try and meet him again. I intended to write and ask him to meet me at the Vendome, but on second thoughts I concluded to try and see him in his own home."

"He will feel greatly flattered at your kind remembrance," Mrs Smith replied.

"Are you aware, madam, that your son possesses rare intellectual gifts?" he continued, after a slight pause. "I must confess to a feeling of curiosity to learn how such characters are nourished among a people like

161

yours."

Mrs Smith looked at him thoughtfully a moment, and then said:

"Sir, it would afford me great pleasure to give you a sketch of his life so far, if you would care to listen."

"It is what I desire most to hear."

The great man listened to her humble story with marked attention, as she related the history of early struggles which her husband and she had braved for the maintenance and education of their children. It was a story common enough among Negroes ambitious to avail themselves of the privileges which were now open to them—a story of faithful fathers bearing insult and injury to keep the meanly paid employment of mothers "spending weary days and nights over the washtub and ironing board in order to get money to educate their children". It seemed marvellous to the listener. As she closed, he said impressively:

"Your story is a revelation to me, madam. Are there many histories like yours among your people? In what a different light you would appear as a race, if the statements made by your detractor could be stripped of calumny and deception. Believe me, you have my heartfelt sympathy, and I shall do all that I can to promote kindly feelings in England for our unfortunate black brother in America. And it is against such spirits of nobility and self-sacrifice that many would close the entrance door to the higher education of the century! Blind and foolish prejudice! Monstrous injustice!" He paused a moment to collect himself and overcome his indignation.

"Madam, how is it that you maintain so excellent an address and manner? And from whom, may I ask, without being considered impertinent, did you inherit your superior intelligence?"

"Ah sir, that is a sad story connected with the lives of those long since passed away."

"But you seem perfectly happy."

"Yes. But it is the happiness chastened by wrongs endured and grief subdued." She paused as though forgetful of her visitor, and then resumed in a low tone:

"Yes; there are strangely tangled threads in the lives of many colored families—I use the word 'colored' because these stories occur mostly among those of mixed blood. But few have a stranger or more romantic history than my father's—Will's grandfather. I never speak of it for fear of ridicule. I was attracted by the name of Montfort on your card. It is uncommon. I was a Montfort before marriage."

Mr Withington uttered an exclamation which was unheeded by the woman before him, who was lost in the clouds of the past. His face wore an expression of intense interest. Presently she continued:

"It is a homely subject to introduce to one familiar with the sorrows

162

of the wealthy and prosperous alone, but it teaches that misfortune is the common lot of all mankind."

"I await your story with anxiety." And truly it seemed so, for Mr Withington had left his seat and was pacing slowly up and down the room. Mrs Smith began her tale like one who describes a vision passing before her eyes. She told it in almost the exact words of the story which we have given as the first part of this narrative. In the midst of the recital Will entered the room from another door, and paused in astonishment at the scene before him. Mr Withington shook hands with him noiselessly, and signed him to keep silence and not disturb the speaker. His own emotion was intense; tears trembled in his eyes; his bosom heaved; his countenance was pale and distressed. When she had finished he said:

"And have you no proofs of this story—no letters?"

"Alas, nothing! Poor father destroyed all in a fit of despondency when his brother's letters ceased to come. Then he lost his little property, and after that he removed to Boston. I believe my father died of a broken heart. God did not intend that his wrongs should be righted." As she finished, the tears were streaming from her eyes.

Mr Withington ceased his nervous promenade, and taking both her hands in his, replied solemnly:

"Not so, dear cousin, for such I believe you to be; never doubt God's goodness or justice. I believe that I hold the key to solve this riddle! I believe that I am your relative, descended directly from your father's brother; your grandfather's brother," he said, turning to Will, who stood an amazed spectator of this extraordinary scene.

"Impossible!" exclaimed mother and son with one breath.

"Nothing is impossible with God. How often have I heard my father tell very much the same tale I have just listened to. Let me assure you that the letters of Jesse Montfort to his brother Charles are still in existence! They are preserved as a sacred legacy, together with a sworn statement of the main facts as we know them in this remarkable case. Your uncle Charles married his rescuers daughter, and as is the custom among old English families where the name would become extinct upon the marriage of the only child—a daughter—he assumed the name of Withington in conjunction with his own. The United States Government was sued by Withington, Sr., and he recovered one hundred thousand dollars damages for Charles, but no trace of Jesse could be found. The money is held for him or his heirs by the Government. I can furnish you the necessary proof upon my return to England. Tell me not that the time of miracles has departed! Is not this a direct intervention of the hand of Providence that we, so widely separated, should at last become known to each other?"

He paused, overcome by emotion. Mrs Smith wept quietly. Broken words of praise to God, of joy, of sorrow for the dead, of hope for the future, passed her lips from time to time. Ah! who can paint such a scene? Finally Mr Withington embraced them both—his kinswoman and Will, his kinsman.

"Be assured that I shall bend every effort to prove this story, and spare no money to establish you in your rights."

Then, unable to control his feelings any longer, telling Will to join him in an hour at his hotel, he hastily left them.

Alone together the mother and son fell upon their knees to give thanks to God for his unspeakable goodness.

When Mr Withington had thought over the story which had come to him so strangely, he was profoundly impressed with the inscrutable ways of God. How wonderful was the knowledge that he had been led by devious paths to find these humble relatives. By accident alone had it been accomplished. "No, not by accident," he told himself, "but by the direct intervention of All-wise Justice." So noble was the nature of this man that he never once thought of the possible ridicule that might come to him through his new relatives. He thought only of the tie of blood. When it was placed before him in this light by Will, his reply was characteristic of the man:

"At home it will not be noticed; the opinion of narrow-minded, prejudiced people here does not matter."

Mr Withington now spent long days with the Smiths. There was much to learn of the past history of each family. These were days of happiness to the newly found relatives—days fraught with wise lessons to himself. He was the best of friends with Dora. Indeed, he was a man who inspired confidence and love. Very soon he was the recipient of the story of all her recent trials with John, and poor Will's unhappy love episode. He approved Dora's choice in Dr Lewis, and had the latter's promise to take her across to Europe at the earliest opportunity. For Will he had a strong man's sympathy, and encouraged him to hope that all might yet be well. So potent was his hopefulness that Will brightened perceptibly and became more like his old ambitious self, to the great delight of his mother and sister.

He in his turn told them the story of Charles Montfort, how his benefactor had returned to America in the hope of finding and rescuing Jesse, after establishing the boys' claim to the estate of their murdered father. He found that the child had disappeared, leaving no trace behind him. How Charles had rejoiced over the later discovery of his brother, and how he had grieved over the final estrangement. Then on the eve of his departure for America to personally search Jesse out, he was stricken with paralysis, and remained a helpless invalid until his death. Meantime the business of establishing the identity of the Smiths was going forward as swiftly as possible.

Mr Withington communicated with his family lawyer, who came from England, bringing with him certain valuable papers bearing upon the case, engaged a leading firm of American lawyers to act in conjunction with the English lawyer, interviewed the authorities at Washington, and secured the services of one of the best detectives in the country to ferret out evidence to prove Jesse's identity. Money flowed from his lavish hand, and all the legal machinery that was essential to prompt action was soon set in motion. One day, Mr Withington received a letter from the detective asking him to go to Bermuda and see an important witness. He started immediately upon receiving it, accompanied by Will Smith and his lawyer. A letter from Will to his mother after they had reached the island was filled with fresh surprises. What follows is an extract:

We have come across a wonderful coincidence. In hunting for evidence in Bermuda, the detective heard of an old woman—a centenarian—who was formerly a slave in North Carolina. We found her living with her daughter and granddaughter (both old women; the granddaughter is sixty); all of them were once slaves. The old woman's mind is clouded on all subjects but one—the Montfort murder! She was an eye-witness of the atrocious crime. She lived for years as the mistress of Anson Pollock, and knew that he tracked Jesse to Boston, where he lost all trace of him. The day we visited her it was pathetic to hear her grieve over the children, one would have thought them still helpless little ones. My dear mother, this woman is but another evidence of the all-powerful hand of the Almighty—this poor, decrepid, half-blind centenarian is Lucy, Grace Montfort's foster sister and maid!

The granddaughter is married, and her husband and children are here. When the Civil War ended they determined to settle in Bermuda, and here they have lived ever since in a cottage which is almost a hut, supporting themselves by selling sugar cane in small sticks—the same as our candy shops sell sticks of candy to the children—and other products of their garden, in the market place. Prepare yourself for another surprise.

The youngest woman had a child while in slavery, by Anson Pollock, Jr., a grandnephew of old Anson Pollock, whom we all have so much reason to remember. The poor woman seems much distressed over this boy, who, it appears, was taken from her when he was but six months old, and sold with many others to a man who farmed Negro babies for the market. She asked me if I had ever in my distant home met a young man called John Pollock Langley. He is her son! I gave her an evasive answer, and told her I would inquire about such a person, and let her know the result. I shall write John these facts. He can use his own pleasure then about claiming his relatives. How fortunate the estrangement which resulted in breaking the engagement between John and Dora. I never could have tol-

erated the idea of a descendant of the Montforts being united in the close relation of marriage with one of the villainous and unscrupulous Pollocks. Let us thank God for another mercy. Mr Withington feels as I do. He has invested some money in a small annuity for our humble friends—enough to keep them from want. The nobility of this man is something remarkable. We sail from here for home by the next steamer, so we shall be in time for the wedding. Your loving son,
Will.

P. S.—I reopen this letter to tell you of the death of Lucy; old age the cause. After she learned that I was Jesse's grandson, and heard the story of his life, with the renewed intelligence often vouchsafed to those just upon the border of the happy land, her prayer was: "Now let Thy servant depart in peace." How soon her prayer was answered.
Will.

In the last beautiful days of October Dora became the wife of Dr Lewis, and went with him to his far-off Southern home to assist him in the upbuilding of their race.

And what a wedding it was! The skies were fair and bright. The romantic story of the Smith family had become noised about, and as it was a church wedding the sacred edifice was crowded to suffocation. Dr Lewis was well and favourably known, and that was of additional interest to the spectators. The small girls who formed Dora's class in Sunday school, dressed in white, preceded the pretty bride, strewing flowers in her path. Then the bride followed on the arm of her brother, Dr Lewis meeting them at the altar, where he had been accompanied by the ushers. Dora would have no bridesmaids. Gowned in the simplest white muslin frock she stood and solemnly plighted her vows to the man of her choice.

They were a striking couple: she serious, he so grave and steadfast. So it should be, taking up a new life, with its endless need of forbearance, trust, and mutual affection. Each knew that with one all was not yet given with the abandonment of perfect love. Each felt, too, the deep waters that surrounded Will—the shadow of a tragedy that lay about his life. What wonder that an unusual solemnity enfolded this couple as they took their vows upon them. But it was a solemnity that quiets, soothes and strengthens.

As the bride came down the aisle on her husband's arm at the conclusion of the ceremony, she caught for one instant the full gaze of John Langley. She never forgot that look; so full of despair and unhappiness. She said nothing about it to husband or brother, but it haunted her for many an hour.

Well, well, it was over, and they passed out to the carriage, and thence to the house.

There was a great reception after the ceremony; but just before Dora left her room to take her place with the receiving party, a package was placed in her hand. She opened it, and found it a jewel box containing a heavy gold bracelet set with pearls, which outlined a delicate vine of pansies traced about the golden band. No note or card was attached— nothing but her name and the date of the marriage. Dora locked it away with her many gifts, amid painful thoughts; she knew instinctively that John was the giver. A week later the happy couple left Boston, accompanied by Mrs Smith, followed by the heartfelt good wishes of all who knew them, for their future prosperity. So with fair skies and favorable winds they entered upon the untried sea of matrimony.

The case of Smith vs the United States did not come to a public trial. It was heard privately before a court composed of the judges of the Supreme Court of the United States. The English heirs had received their portion years before; the Government only awaited the production of the necessary proofs to establish the identity of Mrs Smith beyond a peradventure. Detectives went over the ground carefully. The records of real estate transfers, chattels, etc., were all found intact among the files of the courthouse at Newberne, North Carolina. Jesse was traced from the time he fled from Anson Pollock until he settled in Exeter, New Hampshire, and married Elizabeth Whitfield.

By this woman he raised a family of twelve children, five of whom, including Mrs Smith, were born in Exeter. Up to the time of her birth he had prospered, and had accumulated a good property, but in an evil hour he went upon the bond of his employer, who, failing to meet his liabilities, involved Montfort in his ruin. Unmanned by recurring misfortunes, Jesse Montfort removed to Boston, and never again seemed to have the ambition to try to retrieve his losses. Born in an evil hour, under an unlucky planet, this man's life was but a path of sorrow to the grave, which he welcomed as a refuge from all vicissitudes.

As Mr Withington had said, the letters in his possession from Jesse to Charles Montfort, yellow and time-stained, completed a perfect chain of evidence. The sum of one hundred and fifty thousand dollars was awarded to Mrs Smith as the last representative of the heirs of Jesse Montfort. Justice was appeased.

The case was a nine-days wonder, startled society and all the world— a life drama whose power touched the deep wells of human feeling.

CHAPTER 22

Three years rolled slowly away and were numbered with the past. Will Smith had finished his course at Heidelberg, and for nine months had travelled in foreign capitals. He was much changed. Honours were thick upon him. His bearing was that of a man accustomed to the respectful attention of his equals, sure of himself, his position, his attainments—a wealthy cosmopolitan. He had been a handsome young fellow, he added now to mere good looks, grace, ease, elegance, and an imposing, well-developed intellectuality which marked him as a thinker and an originator. His eyes alone were unchanged, and had the same kindly expression, although there lurked within their hazel depths a sadness which in repose became absolute mournfulness.

The ambition of his life was the establishment of a school which should embrace every known department of science, where the Negro youth of ability and genius could enter without money and without price. This was his pet scheme for the future. No wife or child would ever be his, he told himself; but he would be a father to the youth of his race. Thus he mused and planned until one day there came a letter from his sister saying that his mother's health was very much broken, and that she longed for the presence of her boy. Will packed up, and April found him in the United States once more, at the home of his sister in New Orleans.

Thoughts of Sappho were seldom far from him; he thought of her as one gone to the land of delight—purified by her sufferings here. The first night that he passed on board ship he had dreamed of her. He dreamed that he stood in a grand cathedral, and listened to strains of delicious melody chanted by an invisible choir. Presently upon the altar before him appeared a vision of the Virgin and Child, but the face of the mother was Sappho's, the child by her side was the little Alphonse. He tried to reach her in vain. She smiled and beckoned him on as she receded at his approach; then he awoke. His dream haunted him. He interpreted it as a promise that they should be united in heaven. The meeting with his mother and sister and the renewal of old ties somewhat deadened painful memories, until reawakened when he heard them call his sister's beautiful child "Sappho."

The home to which Dr Lewis had taken his bride was very beautiful. One passed from the highway down a long avenue framed by majestic palms, and so upon the college campus which was surrounded by dormitories built of substantial brick. Dr Lewis's house was a fine brick cottage, plentifully supplied with porches and piazzas. Its framework was a succession of terraces planted with gorgeous beds of flowers indigenous to the Southern clime. The long French windows stood open to catch the soft breezes of April. This house and the numerous dormitories, museums, the chapel, and buildings which held lecture rooms and classrooms, were all built by the pupils of the school. The students made the brick which entered into the composition of the various buildings; the carpenter shop, carriage and blacksmith shops afforded fine facilities for imparting practical knowledge of these useful industries.

Beyond the college grounds, to the right, extended the market gardens, which not only supplied the school with vegetables, but also added a goodly sum to the college fund. There, too, were the grazing pastures for horses and cows. The dairy was a long, low, shed-like brick building, beautifully clean and sweet; its brick floors were spotless, the walls adorned with shining utensils for setting milk for cream, and for churning this same cream into butter. Hundreds of hens and chickens roved in small family bands about the immense poultry yards, from all of which came some revenue to help defray the expenses of this human hive of industry.

Many institutions do not spend one cent for domestic labour during the whole school term. The time usually given to football and other games in white colleges is utilised by the colored student in useful toil. Dr Lewis's school was of this class. The tuition, board, lodging, laundry work and incidentals were not over twelve dollars per month.

Will threw himself into the work of visiting Dr Lewis's pupils and the neighboring schools with eagerness. He acquainted himself thoroughly for future reference, with the curriculum of academical life as conducted along the lines pertaining to Negro education. After gaining a clear insight into it all, he said to Dr Lewis:

"I hold that a man to gain true self-respect and independence must not be hampered in any way by prejudice. I would remove my school far from such influences."

"Where would your choice fall for the establishment of such a paradise?" asked Dr Lewis with a smile.

"There are places enough in the world. One could easily find such an environment abroad. There across the water, associated on equal terms with men of the highest culture, the Negro shall give physical utterance to the splendid possibilities which are within him."

"Commercial and quixotic," returned Dr Lewis with a shake of the head. "It can't be done."

"I shall try it, nevertheless, and leave the results I hope for to the levelling hand of Time."

If ever a doubt of Dora's happiness had troubled Will's thoughts, it was dispelled now that he saw her a contented young matron, her own individuality swallowed up in love for her husband and child. She had apparently forgotten that any other love had ever disturbed the peaceful current of her life. She was pained, however, to find, in their first private interview, that Will still clung to a hopeless memory, as it seemed to her.

"You say that you never expect to see her again, that you think her dead. Why not, then, seek to solace yourself for her loss by marrying some good girl who will make you happy?"

"Sappho is the kind of woman to occupy a man's thoughts. Beside her all others are uninteresting and tame."

"I know it, Will; but it would please me, and mother would die happy if she knew that you were at peace in your mind."

"Do not talk of it!" he cried impatiently; "I cannot please you in that way. I shall never marry."

After that Dora said no more, but tried to make his visit pleasant in every possible way. Will wished to establish a home with his mother in the North, but she was feeble, and he did not care to separate her from Dora. So he drifted with the tide, waiting for circumstances to direct his wandering feet.

"Have you visited the Sisters of the Holy Family yet?" asked Dora on Good Friday morning as they sat at breakfast.

"No," replied Will. "Arthur has promised to accompany me there, but something always intervenes."

"Don't miss it on Sunday morning. The Easter service is divine."

The convent of the Holy Family was founded in 1842 by three good women, in the very heart of the stronghold of slavery, and under the most depressing influences. There is but one other mother-house and novitiate for colored women in the United States, and that is in the city of Baltimore. The service held in the chapel by the Sisterhood of the Holy Family on Easter morning is famous throughout the South. Easter is Easter the world over, and the earth seems to take on an added beauty in honor of the day. But Easter in New Orleans is something to dream of, and defies description.

Will's thoughts were solemn ones, and mingled with pain, for was not this the anniversary of his greatest joy and his most bitter sorrow. He walked toward the chapel through silent streets filled with earnest worshippers on the way to early Mass. It was a familiar sight to Will, who had passed so many months in Catholic countries. Morn was breaking in the east; the air was filled with the faint sounds of returning life; the sweet odour of the magnolia, mingled with a thousand other subtle perfumes, intoxicated the senses. The sun had not yet risen as he glided quietly into the church and took a seat in a secluded corner, to watch the entry of the congregation.

Until Easter morning the pictures of Christ, Mary and Joseph were veiled, but now the statues had emerged from their concealment in indication of the spiritual change in us which was wrought by the coming forth of Christ from the tomb. Tapers glowed and flowers bloomed everywhere. The Sisters stood with their dark faces uplifted in the full light which fell from the stained glass windows, making a picture long to be remembered. The stillness, the coolness, the swiftly moving, silent figures, the slanting rays of sunlight growing higher and higher, seemed to calm the troubled spirit of the man, and to impress his very soul with the greatness and glory of pure religious devotion. Involuntarily his thoughts were wafted upward in solemn supplication to the Father of all good.

He saw the entrance of the convent boarders, the orphan girls, the orphan boys and the novices, still in an exalted state of religious enthusiasm. All in the crowded edifice were on their knees now, listening to the intonations of the gold-robed priest. The sun burst forth in full glory and poured its rays in dazzling hues through the rose-stained windows. Simultaneously, the choir of female voices filled the air with the heavenly strains of the Kyrie Eleison gliding swiftly into the grandeur of the Gloria in Excelsis. It filled every corner of the building, stole into the heart and overflowed into space. Then the whole congregation, led by the Sisters, moved toward the Holy Communion—backward and then toward the right. As the children passed him Will started to his feet and almost cried out, for there before his eyes was the figure of little Alphonse, clad in the regulation garb of the orphanage! He restrained himself by a mighty effort, and fell back in his seat overcome. Tumultuous thoughts overwhelmed him. The mother must be near! Could it be possible that she lived? And if she lived, was she indeed dead to him in her refuge behind convent walls? He heard no more of the service, but waited impatiently for the end. It came at last.

It was some time before he could reach the street on account of the dense crowd, but finally he found himself upon the sidewalk, and asked a passerby to direct him to the orphanage. The stranger politely piloted him to the door of the house on St. Peter Street. He rang the bell, and sent his card to the Mother Superior by a novice in the regulation black dress and white bonnet. She bade him enter, and left him in a bare room overlooking a paved court, where groups of children could be seen at play. He stood there with his back to the door, buried in deep thought and filled with misgivings. Suddenly a door opened behind him and a voice said: "I will bring him back tomorrow, Sister."

Surely he knew that voice! He turned, and there before his blinded vision stood the realisation of his dream, holding the boy by the hand! One swift glance showed him that she was in street attire; that she was not a member of the Order. She saw and recognised him at the same instant. With a mighty cry of joy and thanksgiving he clasped her in his arms.

Sappho was welcomed affectionately by Dr Lewis, Dora and her mother, as one risen from the dead; tears, smiles, kisses greeted her. It seemed that they would never be able to control their emotion. Then she told them of her flight to New Orleans with the child, of the death of the old fortune teller, and her own employment as a governess in the family of the wealthy colored planter in Opelausus, and the placing of the boy with the Sisters. She in her turn listened with wonder to the fairylike tale of the wealth that had come to her lover's family.

Late that afternoon she sat once again in close heart communion with her lover. Each had much to tell.

Seated beside her on the sofa, Will folded her closely to his heart again with one deep, heavy sob which attested the man's suppressed anguish.

"Oh," he said, at last, "it has been like a hideous nightmare since I read that letter which you sent me. I can scarcely believe in the blessed reality that I hold you safe in my arms once more."

She put back the clustering curls from his brow, noting with pain the many white hairs which threaded those raven locks. She laid her cheek against his as she said:

"I know only too well all you have gone through."

"Why did you leave me, Sappho? Had you no confidence in my love for you? How meanly you must have judged me if you thought me capable of holding you responsible for the monstrous wrong committed against you."

"Ah, Will; I had suffered so much at the hands of selfish men! Can you wonder that I mistrusted you, and felt that you would only despise me when you knew all?"

Then he told her of his interview with John Langley, holding back nothing but the insulting insinuations.

"But, dearest, the detectives were at the convent; they even interviewed Luke Sawyer, poor fellow, he was completely overcome when he found that you were alive, and he dropped his work and devoted months to tracing your whereabouts in this very city. How you have managed to hide yourself, and Dora living right here in New Orleans with you, is the mystery."

"Yes; but it is an easy matter to become lost in a great city like this. You must remember that I kept away from every familiar spot; even the

Sisters in the convent had been changed, so that there was no one to remember me, the former Mother Superior having died. When I was strong enough to go about, you had ceased searching for me."

"And all this secrecy was for what?" asked Will reproachfully

"I thought it was for the best."

"I loved you, Sappho; could you not trust that love?"

"Ah, Will, forgive me for all the suffering I have caused you."

Will laid his cheek to hers. "What is there I would not forgive, if anything there were to forgive, for the sweet comfort of holding you once again to my desolate heart."

Then she wept a few delicious tears within the shelter of his arms, and he told her of his plans for her and the boy. They would go abroad; but first they would seek out Luke Sawyer and reward him for his faithfulness; every one who had ever been kind to her or the boy should be rewarded.

That evening Will accompanied Sappho home. Alphonse was left with Dora. Monsieur Louis was astonished to see a handsome stranger assisting Sappho from the carriage. Her joyous face told its own story, and the kind old man knew instinctively that she had found her lover and he had lost the joy of his old age. Will was delighted with all he saw and heard in the peaceful, happy home, the refuge of his love. In the soft twilight of the fragrant terrace Sappho told Monsieur Louis her story, her hand tightly clasped in Will's. "Ah!" cried Monsieur Louis, "I thought it, I thought it!" Then Will supplemented it with the romantic history of his family, and his life since Sappho's flight. The old gentleman listened entranced. "It is indeed a fairy tale of love and chivalry such as we read of only in books," he said at last with a long-drawn breath. Then he told them many interesting tales of slave life and its complications as he had known them. It was nearly midnight when Will left, promising to return the next day and complete arrangements for a wedding which was to take place immediately. Monsieur Louis insisted that he should furnish the wedding dress and breakfast, and be allowed to give the bride away. So a second Easter Day closed on happy love—a love sanctified and purified by suffering.

John Langley, soon after Dora's marriage and the acquisition of fortune to the Smith family, suddenly gave up his business, and started off with the first daring adventurers who were allured from home by the dazzling promise of immense fortunes to be dug out of the earth in the new Eldorado—the Klondike gold fields.

John was unhappy. He was willing to admit that he had viewed things in a false light, and consequently had made a mess of his own happiness. He still retained an ardent enthusiasm for his profession, but he needed a change. He would divert his mind from his recent disappointments by travel in strange lands, and after he had acquired a large fortune he would settle down to the practice of law and do good among his fellows as a sort of atonement for his early mistakes. He placed his business in the hands of his partner, first making a will, in which he bequeathed to his mother's family in Bermuda the savings he would leave in the bank, in case he did not return.

"I only make this will for form's sake," said he to his partner, as he gave it into the latter's keeping. "I'll be back here inside of two years and dazzle you with my wealth."

He joined a party made up of hardy Eastern men, and they started on their journey with bright anticipations of a golden future. After many adventures and much suffering they reached the goal, only to find gault famine awaiting them with gruesome countenance. Day by day the cold increased; day by day the stock of provisions dwindled. Each morning they counted up the dead. One morning it was five; the next, fifteen. Ten only remained alive out of a party of thirty, and these so weak as to be unable to remove the bodies from the common cabin. John learned to pray then: "May the Lord, in His infinite mercy, come to our rescue."

One morning seven more bodies lay close together in the bunks. It was plain then that a few hours would end the sufferings of the remainder. The last spark of fire had gone out. Two biscuits and a quart of water was all the sustenance left. Delirium seized upon all but John. He felt sick at heart. He prayed: "God's will be done!" All that night a heavy gale blew, and before morning two more poor souls went out into space. John was then alone, the last survivor of thirty gallant men. He dragged his body outside the door and away from the charnel house. "Let me die under the open sky, with the moon and stars for company." He told himself that the old fortune teller had been right in her prediction: the field of ice and snow which had been shown to him stretched before him in dreary, unbroken silence. Overhead unknown constellations looked down upon his misery. The moon, cold, large, and spectral, poured an intense yet dreary light upon the scene.

He recalled the deep wisdom of lessons he had recently learned—the philosophy of life and death, assurance of the soul's individuality, and the worthlessness of this earthly clay tenement. He thought of his newly-found mother, whom he had been ashamed to acknowledge. His sight failed, his limbs lost their feeling, his heart was nearly pulseless—it was death. "O God! receive my soul. Dear, dear mother"—The child of sunny climes folded himself more closely in his blankets for the last time, and slept to wake no more on earth. So the dawn of Easter Sunday found him. That undisciplined soul went forth to wander in celestial spheres, there to continue the salutary lessons begun on earth, under the guidance of God's angels, who minister to the needs of the immortal soul.

Not many months after a merry party might have been seen upon the deck of a Cunarder bound for Europe. It consisted of Dr Lewis, Dora, little Sappho, Ma Smith, Will, Sappho—now Will's wife—and little Alphonse. They were all going to make the long-promised visit to Mr Withington.

Sappho was happy in contemplating the life of promise which was before her. Will was the noblest of men. Alphonse was to him as his own child. United by love, chastened by sorrow and self-sacrifice, he and she planned to work together to bring joy to hearts crushed by despair.

They stood upon the deck that night long after the others had retired to their staterooms, watching the receding shores with hearts filled with emotion too deep for words.

My wife, my life. O, we will walk this world, yoked in all exercise of noble end, And so through those dark gates across the wild. That no man knows. Lay thy sweet hands in mine and trust to me.

NEW! Black Classics

NEW from The X Press— an exciting collection of the world's great forgotten black classic novels. Many brilliant works of writing lie in dusty corners of libraries across the globe. Now thanks to Britain's foremost publisher of black fiction, you can discover some of these fantastic novels. Over the coming months we will be publishing many more of these masterpieces which every lover of classic fiction will want to collect.

TRADITION by Charles W Chesnutt

In the years after the American Civil War, a small town in the Deep South struggles to come to terms with the new order. Ex-slaves are now respected doctors, lawyers and powerbrokers--And the white residents don't like it one bit! When a black man is wrongly accused of murdering a white woman, the black population, proud and determined, strike back.For a gifted black doctor, the events pose a huge dilemma. Should he take on the mantle of leading the black struggle, or does his first responsibility lie with his wife and children?

THE BLACKER THE BERRY by Wallace Thurman

Emma Lou was born black. Too black for her own comfort and that of her social-climbing wannabe family. Resented by those closest to her, she runs from her small hometown to Los Angeles and then to Harlem of the 1920's, seeking her identity and an escape from the pressures of the black community. She drifts from one loveless relationship to another in the search for herself and a place in society where prejudice towards her comes not only from whites, but from her own race!

IOLA by Frances E.W. Harper

The beautiful Iola Leroy is duped into slavery after the death of her father but manages to snatch her freedom back and start the long search for the mother whom she was separated from on the slave trader's block. She rejects the advances of a white man, who offers to relieve her from the "burden of blackness" by marrying her and eventually finds love and pride in her race.

THE CONJURE MAN DIES by Rudolph Fisher

Originally published in 1932, *The Conjure Man Dies* is the first known mystery novel written by an African-American. Rudolph Fisher, one of the principal writers of the Harlem Renaissance, weaves an intricate story of a native African king, who after receiving a degree from Harvard settles into Harlem of the 1930's. He becomes a fortune teller or 'Conjure Man' and quickly becomes a much talked about local figure. When the old man is found dead the rumours start spreading. Things are made even more confusing when he turns up very much alive!

THE AUTOBIOGRAPHY OF AN EX-COLORED MAN
by James Weldon Johnson

Until his school teacher points out to him in no uncertain terms that he's a "nigger", the anonymous narrator of *The Autobiography of an Ex-Colored Man*, believed that his fair skin granted him the privileges of his white class mates.

The realisation of what life holds for him is at first devastating, but as he grows into adulthood, he discovers a pride in his blackness and the noble race from which he is descended. However a disturbing family secret is soon to shake up his world.

THE HOUSE BEHIND THE CEDARS
by Charles W. Chesnutt

A few years after the American Civil War, two siblings, Rena and John Walden, 'pass' for white in the Deep South as their only means of obtaining a share of the American dream.

With a change of name and a fictitious biography, John starts a new life. But for Rena, the deception poses a bigger dilemma when she meets and falls in love with a wealthy young white man.

Can love transcend racial barriers, or will the dashing George Tryon reject her the moment he discovers her black roots?

MORE *Black Classics*

Three more forgotten greats of black writing will be available from November 10th 1995. Check out: *A Love Supreme* by **Pauline Hopkins**, *The Walls Of Jericho* by **Rudolph Fisher** and *The President's Daughter* by **William Wells Brown**. Ask for details in any good bookshop. Only from The X Press.

Books with
ATTITUDE

THE RAGGA & THE ROYAL by Monica Grant Streetwise Leroy Massop and The Princess of Wales get it together in this light-hearted romp. £5.99

JAMAICA INC. by Tony Sewell Jamaican Prime Minister, David Cooper, is shot down as he addresses the crowd at a reggae 'peace' concert. But who pulled the trigger and why? £5.99

LICK SHOT by Peter Kalu When neo-nazis plan to attack Manchester's black community they didn't reckon on one thing...A black cop who doesn't give a fuck about the rules! £5.99

SINGLE BLACK FEMALE by Yvette Richards Three career women end up sharing a house together and discover they all share the same problem-MEN! £5.99

MOSS SIDE MASSIVE by Karline Smith When the brother of a local gangster is shot dead on a busy Manchester street, the city is turned into a war zone as the drugs gangs battle it out. £5.99

OPP by Naomi King How deep does friendship go when you fancy your best friend's man? Find out in this hot bestseller! £5.99

COP KILLER by Donald Gorgon When his mother is shot dead by the police, taxi driver Lloyd Baker becomes a one man cop-killing machine. Hugely controversial but compulsive reading. £4.99

BABY FATHER/ BABY FATHER 2 by Patrick Augustus Four men come to terms with parenthood but it's a rough journey they travel before discovering the joys in this smash hit and its sequel. £5.99

WICKED IN BED by Sheri Campbell Michael Hughes believes in 'loving and leaving 'em' when it comes to women. But if you play with fire you're gonna get burnt! £5.99

FETISH by Victor Headley The acclaimed author of 'Yardie', 'Excess', and 'Yush!' serves another gripping thriller where appearances can be very deceiving! £5.99

PROFESSOR X by Peter Kalu When a black American radical visits the UK to expose a major corruption scandal, only a black cop can save him from the assasin's bullet. £5.99